EU Foreign Policy beyond the

Also by Neil Winn

EUROPEAN CRISIS MANAGEMENT IN THE 1980s

Also by Christopher Lord

ABSENT AT THE CREATION

BRITISH ENTRY TO THE EC UNDER THE HEATH GOVERNMENT, 1970–74

DEMOCRACY IN THE EU

LEGITIMACY IN THE EU (*with David Beetham*)

THE POLITICAL ECONOMY OF MONETARY UNION (*with Malcolm Levitt*)

POLITICAL PARTIES IN THE EU (*with Simon Hix*)

EU Foreign Policy beyond the Nation-State

Joint Actions and Institutional Analysis of the Common Foreign and Security Policy

Neil Winn
Senior Lecturer in European Studies
University of Leeds

and

Christopher Lord
Jean Monnet Professor of European Politics
University of Leeds

palgrave
macmillan

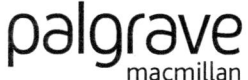

© Neil Winn and Christopher Lord 2001

All rights reserved. No reproduction, copy or transmission of this publication may be made without written permission.

No paragraph of this publication may be reproduced, copied or transmitted save with written permission or in accordance with the provisions of the Copyright, Designs and Patents Act 1988, or under the terms of any licence permitting limited copying issued by the Copyright Licensing Agency, 90 Tottenham Court Road, London W1T 4LP.

Any person who does any unauthorised act in relation to this publication may be liable to criminal prosecution and civil claims for damages.

The authors have asserted their rights to be identified as the authors of this work in accordance with the Copyright, Designs and Patents Act 1988.

Published by PALGRAVE MACMILLAN
Houndmills, Basingstoke, Hampshire RG21 6XS and
175 Fifth Avenue, New York, N. Y. 10010
Companies and representatives throughout the world

PALGRAVE MACMILLAN is the global academic imprint of the Palgrave Macmillan division of St. Martin's Press, LLC and of Palgrave Macmillan Ltd. Macmillan® is a registered trademark in the United States, United Kingdom and other countries. Palgrave is a registered trademark in the European Union and other countries.

ISBN 0–333–69980–7

This book is printed on paper suitable for recycling and made from fully managed and sustained forest sources.

A catalogue record for this book is available from the British Library.

Library of Congress Catalog Card Number: 2001021188

Transferred to digital printing 2002

Printed and bound in Great Britain by
Antony Rowe Ltd, Chippenham and Eastbourne

Contents

List of Tables	viii
List of Abbreviations	ix
Acknowledgements	xi

1   The Study of Pillarization 1

   Questions raised by pillarization 8
   What are the joint actions and why are they a good
   test of pillarization? 12
   Pillarization and the making of foreign policy
   beyond the nation-state 15

2   An Historical Analysis of Pillarization 20

   The development of foreign policy co-operation 1957–91 20
   EPC and the bureaucratic interpretation of national
   foreign policy-making 23
   EPC as a rule-based system of co-operation 26
   The blurring of EPC and the EC 29
   Appraising EPC 34
   EPC to CFSP: transformation or incremental development? 39
   Conclusion: path dependence and the emergence of
   pillarization 42
   A note on changes introduced by the Treaty of Amsterdam 45

3   An Institutional Analysis of Pillarization 47

   Introduction 47
   Why conduct an institutional analysis of CFSP under
   pillarization? 48
   Designing an institutional analysis of pillarization? 53
   A rational model of CFSP under pillarization 54
   A policy network of CFSP under pillarization 58
   A 'garbage can' analysis of CFSP under pillarization 61
   Using joint actions as case studies of pillarization 64
   Case study methodology 68
   Approach to hypothesis testing 72

4 The Mostar Joint Action, 1994: Agenda-Setting, Decision-Making and Implementation — 74

STAGE 1: CHRONOLOGY
Introduction — 74
Background — 75
Political assumptions — 76
STAGE 2: MAPPING AGENDA-SETTING, DECISION-MAKING AND IMPLEMENTATION
Mapping the contribution of the different actors — 80
Mapping agenda-setting: the EUAM mandate in Mostar — 82
Mapping decision-making — 85
Mapping implementation: bottom-up and top-down perspectives — 89
STAGE 3: EVALUATION
General conclusion — 93
Notes — 103

5 Implementing the Dayton Agreements, 1995–98: Agenda-Setting, Decision-Making and Implementation — 106

STAGE 1: CHRONOLOGY
Introduction — 106
The Dayton Agreements: objective and contents — 107
Key European Union 'Joint Actions' and Dayton — 108
Towards an assessment of Dayton — 109
STAGE 2: MAPPING AGENDA-SETTING, DECISION-MAKING AND IMPLEMENTATION
Mapping the contributions of the different actors — 112
Mapping agenda-setting — 116
Mapping the decision-making stage — 126
Mapping the implementation stage — 127
STAGE 3: EVALUATION
Conclusion — 129
Notes — 138

6 The European Union's Policy towards the Caucasus, 1996–99 — 140

STAGE 1: CHRONOLOGY
Introduction — 140

STAGE 2: MAPPING AGENDA-SETTING,
DECISION-MAKING AND IMPLEMENTATION
Mapping the contributions of the different actors 143
Mapping agenda-setting 145
Mapping decision-making 147
Mapping implementation: the social exchange of
power from the 'bottom up' 157
STAGE 3: EVALUATION
Conclusions 159
Notes 165

7 **Conclusion** **167**

Conclusions of the case studies 167
Pillarization, theoretical and conceptual implications
of the study 173
Broader implications of the study 178

Bibliography 180

Index 188

List of Tables

1.1	Pillarization under the Treaty on European Union 1993–99	6
1.2	Tonra's classification of contributions to the literature on foreign policy analysis	17
3.1	Frequency with which joint actions used in comparison with other instruments available to CFSP, 1994–97	66
3.2	Areas of the world towards which joint actions directed, 1995–97	66
7.1	The relationship between the key stages of the policy process and policy outcomes	168

List of Abbreviations

AFCENT	Allied Land Forces Central Europe
BSA	Bosnian Serb Army
CFSP	Common Foreign and Security Policy
CIS	Commonwealth of Independent States
COREPER	Committee of Permanent Representatives
COREU	European Correspondent System
CJTF	Consultative Joint Task Force
CSCE	Conference on Security and Co-operation in Europe
CTF	Consultative Task Force
DG	Directorate General
DG1	Directorate General for External Economic Relations
DG1A	Directorate General for External Political Relations
DM	Deutsche Mark
ECHO	European Community Humanitarian Office
EPC	European Political Co-operation
EC	European Communities
ECJ	European Court of Justice
ECU	European Currency Unit
EDC	European Defence Community
EEC	European Economic Community
EP	European Parliament
EU	European Union
EUAM	European Union Administration of Mostar
FPA	Foreign Policy Analysis
FYROM	Former Yugoslavian Republic of Macedonia
G8	Group of Eight Leading Industrialized Nations
GAC	General Affairs Council
HDZ	Bosnian Croat Nationalist Party
IFOR	United Nations International Bosnian Protection Force
IMF	International Monetary Fund
INGO	International Non-Governmental Organization
IWU	International Police Force Document Mostar
JA	Joint Action
MoU	Memorandum of Understanding
NATO	North Atlantic Treaty Organization
NGO	Non-Governmental Organization

OSCE	Organization for Security and Co-operation in Europe
PIC	Peace Implementation Council
QMV	Qualified Majority Voting
SACEUR	Supreme Allied Commander Europe
SDA	Bosnian Muslim Nationalist Party
SDS	Bosnian Serb Nationalist Party
SEA	Single European Act
SFOR	United Nations Bosnian Stabilization Force
TACIS	European Union Technical and Assistance Programme for the Commonwealth of Independent States
TEU	Treaty on the European Union
TOR	Treaty of Rome
UPFM	Unified Police Force of Mostar
UK	United Kingdom of Great Britain and Northern Ireland
UN	United Nations
UNPROFOR	United Nations Bosnia Protection Force
US	United States
USA	United States of America
WEU	Western European Union
WTO	World Trade Organization

Acknowledgements

The authors would like to thank 60 anonymous interviewees working in the European Commission, European Parliament, Foreign and Commonwealth Office and the Quai d'Orsay for giving up their time to be interviewed for this book. The authors would also like to thank the University of Leeds for making a grant available under the Academic Development Fund to the interviews for this study.

1
The Study of Pillarization

The study of pillarization is nothing less than an enquiry into the central organizing principle that lies behind the contemporary European Union (EU). Although the Treaty on European Union (TEU) agreed at the Maastricht European Council of December 1991 and brought into force in 1993 states that 'the Union shall be served by a single institutional framework' (European Commission, 1992, Article C), that framework is, in fact, sub-divided into three pillars. The first consists of a wide portfolio of economic, social and environmental policies, more or less related to the European Single Market; the second of the EU's Common Foreign and Security Policy (CFSP); and the third of Justice and Home Affairs (JHA), covering collaboration on matters of internal security. The 'single institutional framework that is equally competent across all pillars' (European Council, 1995) does not endow all the Union's institutions with the same powers and competencies across all policies. Rather, it is an arrangement whereby just one of those institutions – the Council of Ministers – approximates to parity of role and influence across the range of the Union's responsibilities.

This triple-pillared arrangement distinguishes the post-1993 European Union from the European Community of 1957–1993, which, on the whole, only provided Treaty authority for the one institutional formula, informally known as the 'Community method'. Under that method, the European Commission, acting in its role as a supranational and independent executive, has a monopoly right of initiative; a Council of Ministers, consisting of one representative per member state, has the final decision on whether Commission decisions are adopted; the European Court of Justice (ECJ) rules on points of law; and the European Parliament (EP), directly elected by the public since 1979, enjoys various forms of legislative partnership with Commission and Council, stretching from mere consultation to full co-determination (Quermonne, 1994). Since the introduction of pillarization in 1993, the Community method has only applied to the first pillar, and, for the first time, alternative inter-institutional configurations have been specified and authorized in the Treaties, to service what are now the second and third pillars.

As this discussion is already beginning to suggest, pillarization is best understood by contrasting it with its two logical alternatives. The first of these is that certain responsibilities – such as foreign policy, internal and external security, and justice and home affairs – should have no place in the Treaties. They should, therefore, be off-limits to any institution set up under the Treaties. That, in fact, was more or less the position before 1993, with the exception of a brief chapter under the Single European Act (SEA) of 1987. Although foreign policy co-operation had existed from as early as 1970 (European Political Co-operation, abbreviated as EPC) and collaboration in security and policing since the mid- 1980s (Trevi Group) (Bieber and Monar, 1995), both of these processes were initially established outside the Treaties and with an aspiration to avoid common institutions by delivering collaboration through direct contacts between counterpart ministries in national governments. In contrast, the TEU allows the 'Council to deliberate CFSP or JHA questions under the same conditions as Community ones' (European Council, 1995), and, to a lesser extent, it authorizes the participation of the Commission, EP and ECJ.

If, then, the first alternative to pillarization is 'off-Treaty' collaboration in selected policy areas, the second alternative is not only that all forms of collaboration should be mandated by Treaty and authorized by national publics or parliaments, but also that uniformity of institutional process should apply to the full range of institutions established under the Treaties. It should not, in other words, only be the Council that enjoys comprehensiveness of policy reach with more or less the same powers in all issue areas. According to this perspective, the same bodies – the European Commission, the European Council, the Council of Ministers, the European Parliament, and the European Court of Justice (ECJ) – should have broadly the same powers, follow roughly the same decision- making procedures, and fit together into the same political system of inter-institutional relationships, whether they are regulating the internal market, formulating a common foreign and security policy or collaborating in matters of justice and home affairs. As Youri Devuyst describes this point of view it is that the only division of competencies between institutions should be a functional one – pertaining to their different roles in the policy process (agenda-setting, decision-taking, representation and adjudication) – and not a thematic one that is geared to substantive differences in issue areas (Single Market, CFSP, JHA and so on) (Devuyst, 1999, pp. 113–14). Such an approach was, indeed, the principal alternative to pillarization considered by the Intergovernmental Conference (IGC) on Political Union in the lead-up to the Maastricht European Council in December 1991. During the IGC, those who advocated the management of all policies by more or less the same institutional framework adopted the image of a tree whose various policy branches would grow out of a common institutional trunk, in order to distinguish themselves from those who preferred to 'pillarize' the Union into multiple institutional formats (Laursen and van Hoonacker, 1992).

Why during the course of European integration have actors been prepared to argue so fiercely for various of the structural alternatives mapped out above? Attempts to define areas of 'off-Treaty' and 'institution-free' collaboration often reflected a notion that foreign and security policies, whether of an internal or external kind, were *domaines réservées* of states: a form of 'high politics', where, in contrast to the 'low politics' of economic and social decision-making, responsibility could not be alienated, or even temporarily delegated, without national governments abandoning those roles in relationship to their citizenry that defined states as states (Hoffmann, 1966).

The following are amongst contrasting arguments that have been made for applying a more or less uniform approach to all institutions across all policies. One is the claim that shared institutions can only operate as a European government in embryo where policies and initiatives accumulate within a single framework. However, even those of less explicitly federalist disposition have often argued that the standard Community needs to be reproduced in all policy areas if there is to be a balance between the supranational and intergovernmental components of European integration. The rule that the Council can only take a decision where it has received a proposal from the Commission protects both small states, and functional interests that cross-cut national boundaries, from outcomes that would otherwise be mainly determined by the distribution of inter-state bargaining power (Devuyst, 1999, p. 115). On the other hand, the need for all Commission proposals to gain the support of the Council provides indirect legitimation by elected national governments.

At the end of the day, however, the TEU adopted the temple of many pillars, and not the tree with a single institutional trunk. Given that the British and French Governments both preferred pillarization to communitarization – and the active collaboration of those governments held the key to development of an effective Common Foreign and Security Policy – it was unlikely that any other outcome would ever have emerged from the IGC (Forster, 1999, p. 114). Yet, pillarization was introduced in a tentative and experimental spirit none the less. Before it had even started operation, the TEU, provided for a further Intergovernmental Conference (IGC) to open in 1996, inter alia, to review the performance of the new structures (European Commission, 1992). On the one hand, the need to keep pillarization under review reflected uncertainty as to whether the EU could operate three different institutional processes in parallel, and still deliver the objectives of the Single Market, CFSP and JHA (not to mention Monetary Union, which effectively creates a fourth institutional framework). On the other hand, the CFSP was introduced into an international system in flux, and designed at a time when the principal contours of the post-Cold War order were still under-determined. A mere 25 months separated the fall of the Berlin Wall (November 1989) from the Maastricht European Council (December 1991). While the 'twelve' could make a contribution to resolving such uncertainties by using the construction of a new CFSP to reconfigure their own potential for collective action, the final test of the adequacy of their institutional provision for external influence would depend on the as yet unknowable moves of other international actors, including moves taken in response to the early stirrings of the CFSP itself.

By the time, however, that the review IGC opened in 1996 the member states of the EU, recently enlarged to 15, were too constrained by considerations external to the conduct of foreign policy itself to consider abandoning pillarization altogether. The Maastricht ratification crisis of 1992–93 had transformed the politics of Treaty change by dividing publics, splitting parties and straining governing majorities in several member states. The still unhealed political scar tissue of that episode – and its demonstration of the ease with which powerful counter-coalitions to European integration could be mobilized – meant that the need to anticipate all possible sources of domestic controversy now became the critical constraint in shaping Treaty amendments. An added motive for the 'safety-first' approach was that any political crisis provoked by the need to ratify a new Treaty would coincide with a round of decisions that had to be taken during the course of 1997–98 if member states were to convince financial markets that they were able to meet the final deadline for Stage Three of Monetary Union (1 January 1999). The result was that the Amsterdam

The Study of Pillarization 5

Treaty – agreed in 1997 and enacted in 1999 – changed the detail but not the principle of pillarization. Part of the policy competence of JHA was moved into pillar one, and further attempts were made to clarify the operation of CFSP (see chapters 2 and 3 below), but there was no change in the management of those policy areas by a different set of inter-institutional relationships to those used to decide EC business.

The concern of this book is to use one of the policy instruments established under TEU provisions for CFSP – joint actions – to analyse the operation of pillarization over the period between the entry into force of the TEU (1993) and its replacement by the Amsterdam Treaty (1999). Before justifying and elucidating that research strategy it is, however, necessary to specify the TEU version of pillarization in full. Table 1.1 provides a summary of the principal institutional arrangements. Amongst features designed to ensure that pillars two and three would be more intergovernmental than pillar one were the following.

- Individual member states, as well as the Commission, have rights to propose new initiatives for CFSP and JHA (European Commission, 1992, J8 and K3). This contrasts with pillar one where the Commission normally has an exclusive right of initiative, and the Council is unable to act until it has received a proposal from the Commission.
- To all intents and purposes, unanimity is the dominant decision-rule under CFSP and JHA. Although the Council can at any stage identify those aspects of a joint action on which it is prepared to proceed by Qualified Majority (QMV), that change of voting rule must itself be decided by unanimity (European Commission, 1992, Article J3).
- Under CFSP and JHA, the European Parliament has the right to be consulted (European Commission, 1992, Articles J7 and K6), and, therefore, to warn and criticise; but concrete powers of parliamentary control, such as the denial of finance and legislation, are not explicitly mandated and can, at best, only be secured by roundabout methods outside pillar two.

It is, however, important to note how the foregoing translate into inter-pillar variations in the distribution of power between institutions.

- The reduced agenda-setting powers associated with only allowing the Commission a shared right of initiative in relation to pillars two and three has a 'knock-on' effect to final policy outcomes, over which the

Table 1.1 Pillarization under the Treaty on European Union 1993–99

	Pillar Two	Pillar Three	Comparisons with Pillar One
Commission	Member states and Commission share right of initiative.	Member states and Commission share right of initiative in relation to six out of nine objectives. Commission has no right of initiative in relation to the remaining three.	Commission has exclusive right of initiative in relation to most policy instruments.
European Council	European Council has Treaty authority to define guidelines for CFSP.		
Council of Ministers	Majority voting may be used for implementation, but only if a prior decision has been taken by unanimity to proceed in such a way. A Committee of Political Directors prepares Council meetings on CFSP questions.	Majority voting may be used for implementation, but only if a prior decision has been by unanimity to proceed in such a way. A Co-ordinating committee prepares JHA Councils.	Majority voting the most frequently used decision-rule. The Committee of Permanent Representatives (COREPER) prepares meetings of Council.
European Parliament (EP)	The EP is consulted and informed.	The EP is consulted and informed.	In relation to most policy areas, the EP either has the power to amend or co-determine the policies or legislation of the other institutions.
European Court of Justice	Not mentioned.	Member States can draw up conventions between themselves that give ECJ jurisdiction on a case by case basis.	

Council can expect to maintain a tighter hold that it does in pillar one. Under pillar one the institutional formalities confer powers on the Commission to 'gate-keep' the policy process by limiting the Council's scope to consider options that do not correspond to the Commission's preferences. In contrast, the Commission is more exposed under pillars two and three to attempts by the Council to 'instruct' it to take actions about which it has reservations.

- The norm that the Council operates by consensus – or unanimity – in second- and third-pillar matters means that the Commission does not only have to share its right of initiative in CFSP and JHA, it also has to use it in more circumspect fashion than in pillar one. Not only does the Commission have to share agenda-setting powers with member states under pillars two and three, the relevant lowest common denominator at which it has to target any proposals is made up of the preferences of all 15 governments, and not just those of a qualified majority (11 or 12). It is, however, worth noting that this may change under Amsterdam, which allows for a process of constructive abstention under pillar two. In such cases, the Commission may not need to anticipate every possible objection from all member governments.
- Absence of direct parliamentary powers to change policy outcomes under CFSP and JHA means that the question of whether EP preferences are closer to those of the Commission or Council – or to particular member states in the Council – are largely irrelevant to the operation of the second and third pillars. The exception is where the Parliament can link the delivery of a CFSP or JHA policy objective to a budget line or legislative proposal in pillar one.
- As seen, it is the Council more than any other body that provides the join between the three pillars. The Council's own analysis of such singularity of framework as is provided by pillarization is that it consists of its own management of all three areas of policy, as 'made possible by synthesising functions of COREPER and the unity of organisation to be found in the new General Secretariat of the Council' (European Council, 1995).

Although of less importance to the analysis of this book than the foregoing points, the TEU also contained some interesting differences between pillars two and three. These, briefly, are as follows:

- The TEU makes it clear that it is for the European Council (heads of government) to define the 'principles and general guidelines for the

common foreign and security policy (European Commission, 1992, Article J8). The provisions on JHA do not even mention the European Council, though they do refer to the importance of direct communication between the interior ministries of member states (European Commission, 1992, Article K3).
- Unlike pillar two, pillar three excludes some areas of policy competence from Commission initiative altogether (ibid.).
- The CFSP title in the Treaty makes no reference to the European Court of Justice (ECJ). That for JHA allows the Council to make provision for the ECJ to interpret conventions established under the third pillar, and 'to rule on their application' (ibid.)

Questions raised by pillarization

The foregoing account of pillarization begs a series of questions, some of which are spelled out as follows, using the example of CFSP and its relationship with pillar one.

How institutionalized is pillarization? It would be a mistake to assume that pillarization should only be defined negatively as a means of restricting the role of supranational institutions and minimizing the application of majoritarian decision-rules. There is a danger in such an approach of failing to understand the extent to which pillarization constitutes a significant measure of institutionalization in its own right.

To be sure, the first pillar comes far closer than the others to meeting the following Eastonian (1957) conditions that have been used by Simon Hix (1999, p. 2) to justify his claim that the EU needs to be analysed as a political system: stable and defined institutions for the making of collective rules and decisions; decisions that have a significant role in the allocation of values; regular attempts by citizens and groups to channel their demands into the institutions; and a continuous feedback loop between institutions, decisions and social actors. Yet, in relation to the first of these conditions, it will be seen in chapter 2 how CFSP is characterized by remarkable sophistication of procedure, and innovative patterns of role differentiation. In relation to the other conditions, CFSP does have a role in allocating political values, and it frequently engages in issues relevant to citizen attempts to influence public policy. This is most obvious where economic and social policy overlaps with foreign policy. But it also occurs where lobbies, advocacy coalitions and new social movements form around international questions. It is, therefore, by no means fanciful to predict that future accounts of CFSP may not only require an institutional analysis of its more routinized procedures, but a fuller application of political systems analysis to identify occasions where policy outputs are conditioned by feedback loops between the policy process, citizen demands, and groups that aggregate and canalize the latter in to the political arena.

How does the pillarization structure deal with co-ordination problems? CFSP introduces a common foreign policy and not a single one. This means that national foreign policies continue to run alongside positions agreed in CFSP, creating a double co-ordination problem: the 'external' dimensions of pillar one policies have to be co-ordinated with the CFSP, and member state policies then have to be co-ordinated with the outputs of both pillars one and two.

The Treaty, accordingly, requires both Council and Commission to ensure the 'unity, consistency and effectiveness of action by the Union' (European Commission, 1992, Article J8). It also introduces a series of 'pasarelles' between the pillars. Foreign policy is handled by the General Affairs Council (GAC) of the European Union and not by the foreign ministers meeting in a separate Council as was the case under EPC. Although GAC meetings are prepared by Political Directors appointed from the foreign ministry of each member state, the Committee of Permanent Representatives (COREPER) now receives copies of proposals and opinions that the Political Directors give to the GAC (Duke, 2000, p. 105). The importance of this is that COREPER functions as a key nodal point in pillar one policy-making, co-ordinating all the specialist branches of the Council, and taking several decisions on its own initiative. In addition, to these institutionalized connections between the pillars, we will encounter two other means of co-ordination during the course of this work: ad hoc and flexible forms of policy delegation to working groups or even particular individuals; and informal networking between relatively small groups of individuals, all expert in the same area of foreign policy-making, but representative of different institutions.

Is pillarization effective? An important question to consider is whether the pillarization structure means that CFSP has inherited institutional shortcomings commonly attributed to the process of European Political Co-operation (1970–93) which preceded it. To anticipate chapter 2, such shortcomings are often held to have included the following: decisions that are emptied of substance by the absence of clear means of delivering policy objectives; a preoccupation with the bargaining of agreed postures to the exclusion of any action or output; disjointed decisions that fail to cumulate into purposive and sustained efforts to influence the external environment; frequent 'defections' from agreed positions; reactive, rather than proactive decision-making; and inability to deal with crises. Perhaps the key institutional question is this: the pillarization formula acknowledges political constraints on centralising and communitarizing foreign policy, but does it also satisfy the preconditions for effective collective action?

Are the pillars really so different? It should by now be clear that the pillars are not distinguished by the absence of the Commission and European Parliament from CFSP and JHA. To the contrary, the Council, Commission and EP have access to all three pillars, but on the basis of different power distributions between themselves. Even this difference may be of only limited significance from the perspective of those who discount the impact of formal definitions of inter-institutional power. It is, for example, possible to question how far the Commission's agenda-setting powers are ever exercised without careful anticipation of the political preferences of the Council and of individual member states, even where it has a formal monopoly of initiative under pillar one. Conversely, the Council's dependence on an active Commission may have little to do with the latter's Treaty powers and a lot to do with the scope for member states to save themselves bargaining, transactions and compliance costs by relying on some independent and permanent source of executive power (Garrett and Weingast, 1993; Pollack, 1997). Those features are, however, present in pillars two and three as well as in pillar one.

There is a further possibility: a lesser role for the Commission in CFSP may only signify that Commission-like functions, particularly those of agenda-setting, are performed by other bodies. At what point, for example, does it cease to be analytically plausible to treat a working party of national officials as a series of loyal delegates of their governments? At what point does such a body become indistinguishable from a supranational body? When it starts to take a lead in forming preferences? When it becomes costly for political principals to monitor every move taken by the working party? As these questions suggest, CFSP may have tendencies towards 'supranational intergovernmentalism' (Hoffmann and Keohane, 1991).

A third area where the practice of policy-making may differ less across the pillars than the formal rules suggests has to do with voting mechanisms on the Council. EU decision-making is often thought to be characterized by the widespread use of 'informal majority voting': the majority tolerates prolonged discussions and makes multiple concessions; in exchange, the minority nods an agreement through without a formal vote; and everyone gains by avoiding the emergence of explicit divisions in which it is easy to identify those who have 'won' and 'lost' from a decision (Hayes-Renshaw and Wallace, 1997). Foreign policy co-operation may even have been at the forefront of such practices: according to some accounts, constructive abstention, which would not be formalized until the Amsterdam Treaty of 1997 has been a feature EPC/CFSP since the SEA of 1987 (Hix, 1999, p. 342).

A similar exercise in qualifying the rhetoric of pillarization can be extended to the role of the European Parliament. Parliaments the world over are rarely afforded high levels of direct control over the foreign policy process. Short of threatening to remove a government, they can usually only assert control over foreign policy by linking demands for policy change to other requests that the executive power makes for resources or legislation. The latter, however, is not so far removed from the political opportunity structure faced by the EP on CFSP questions. On the one hand, it is the Council operating in the role of executive power that needs to be able to make linkages across the pillars if it is to achieve its objectives. On the other, it is the EP that may sometimes be in a position to deny such linkages, even if it can only do so by using pillar one powers. The obvious example is provided by EP control over pillar one budget lines that the Council may want to change to secure pillar two goals. We will, however, also discuss the as yet under-explored implications of a further connexion: CFSP policies may need to be reflected in legislative changes in pillar one, opening the way for parliamentary amendment or even veto. The possibility of parliamentary self-assertion in CFSP matters is increased by two further factors: first, the EP is not executive-dominated and, second, the manner of election gives it an oppositional party political complexion relative to the Council (Hix and Lord, 1997).

Will the relationship between the pillars be static or will it change over time?
The role of the pillarization formula may well have been one of securing agreement to the TEU on the basis of what Ernst Haas (1964) once called a convergent coalition: a consensus in which different actors support the same agreement on the basis of assumptions that cannot all be true. Whilst the British and French governments argued at the time of the TEU negotiations that the pillarization formula gave inter-

governmental structures unprecedented recognition in EC Treaties, reversing the notion that the Union was committed to the progressive integration of all policy sectors to the Community method, an alternative view was that incremental communitarization was as relevant as ever. According to this perspective the role of the pillarization was from the outset more 'dignified' than 'efficient': it provided cover for member states that had domestic difficulties in conceding further institutionalization of foreign policy co-operation at the Union level; and it disguised the degree to which foreign policy co-operation was already being blurred with the work of what was to become pillar one of the EU, even before the TEU went through the largely phoney motions of appearing to separate the two processes.

What are joint actions and why are they a good test of pillarization?

The TEU endowed the new CFSP with two foreign policy instruments that had not been available to EPC. The first authorized the Council to establish common positions, which member states would then be obliged to follow in their own foreign policies, as well as in their contributions to other 'international organizations and international conferences', including those where only some EU countries participate, such as meetings of the G8 or the security Council of the UN (European Commission, 1992, Article J2). By adopting common positions it was thought that member states would improve the consistency of their dealings with third parties and limit the scope for others to play divide and rule.

It is, however, the second instrument of the new CFSP that is of more direct concern to this book. In addition to common positions, the TEU allowed the Council to design joint actions in areas where member states had important interests in common. The European Council would decide the types of problem where joint action would be appropriate; the Council of Ministers would then define the scope and objectives of each joint action; and stipulate, if necessary, details of its duration, resourcing and implementation (European Commission, 1992, Article J2).

Member states are bound to keep to agreements on joint actions in 'the positions they adopt and in the conduct of their activity'. In the absence, though, of a role for the European Court of Justice (ECJ) it is unclear who is to decide where there has been a breach of that obligation; nor is there any provision for sanctioning a transgressor (European

Commission, 1992, Articles J3 and J8). If joint actions are enforceable it is through peer- group pressure, and a need for any member state to keep to the informal rules of CFSP if it is to ensure the reciprocation of partners and the overall survival of the collaborative effort.

A further clause stipulates that joint actions will be 'gradually implemented'. One possibility is that this was intended to signify that joint actions would normally follow on from declarations and common positions and a failure of those lesser measures to solve the problem in question. Another interpretation of the clause is that it was intended to signify that joint actions would grow in frequency over time, as CFSP matured and member states converged in their foreign policy interests. A third possibility is that the clause signalled that each joint action should be introduced incrementally and from modest beginnings.

Case studies of joint actions are not the only means of testing the questions about pillarization raised in the last section. But they are amongst the most interesting. One reason for this is that joint actions test more than the ability of political actors to adopt consistent statements of position across the pillars. They also test their capacity to act purposefully and coherently across the pillars A second reason why joint actions are useful tests of the viability of pillarization is that of all the instruments and practices to be found within CFSP they are likely to be the most dependent on the first pillar for the concrete substance of external influence: the EU's budgetary or legislative powers will often be needed if the Union is to cross the critical threshold between the mere declaration of shared foreign policy preferences and action in common. For example Article 228a of the Treaty allows the Council to 'interrupt or reduce' economic relations with third countries, in order to achieve CFSP objectives. But two things are necessary if this is to happen: a common position or a joint action has to have been agreed in pillar two and the Commission then has to be persuaded to use its powers of initiative under pillar one to support what has been agreed in pillar two (European Commission, 1992, Article 228a).

What standards of performance should joint actions be expected to satisfy if pillarization is to be judged a success? The most obvious benchmarks of performance are the objectives that the TEU lays down for the new CFSP. These are defined as follows:

> to safeguard the common values, fundamental interests and independence of the Union; to strengthen the security of the Union and of its member states in all ways; to preserve peace and strengthen

international security, in accordance with the principles of the United Nations Charter as well as the principles of the Helsinki Final Act and the Paris Charter; to provide international co-operation; to develop and consolidate democracy and the rule of law and respect for human rights and fundamental freedoms. (European Commission, 1992, Article J1)

Although the foregoing Treaty definition of CFSP objectives places a heavy emphasis on the external promotion of what are taken to be the shared internal values of the Union – democratization, human rights and the binding of states into relationships of peaceful co-operation – it would be a mistake to read it as confirming the notion that the EU is developing as an international actor strictly confined to the exercise of 'civilian power' (Duchêne, 1971). To the contrary, the Treaty objectives suggest a comprehensive foreign policy mandate, in which 'fundamental interests' and the 'strengthening of security' take their place alongside aspirations to externalize visions of the good life. The reference to the Helsinki final act is also significant, since this includes provisions on the inviolability of boundaries throughout the European continent. Josef Janning (1996) remarks that, if anything, CFSP has engaged the EU with questions of security before it has completed its evolution as a civilian power. The examples of joint action since 1993 that are set out in chapter 3 confirm this ambiguity. Although directly concerned with civilian tasks of a pedestrian kind, they have often been developed within the context of a security problem.

The Treaty objectives do not, however, provide the sole benchmark against which joint actions should be judged. Criteria of appraisal can also be inferred from the public justifications that were given for the new CFSP. These were far from singular or consistent. Chapter 2 will, however, demonstrate that they included the following: the need to adjust the EC to changes in the international system brought about by the end of a bipolar world of superpower competition; anxiety that a reunited Germany would have the power to pursue a *Sonderweg* or independent course in its foreign policy unless it was encouraged to multilateralize its external dealings in a setting which institutionalized consultation with neighbouring countries; strains created by the EC's uneven development as an economic giant and a political dwarf; pressure on the EC to play a greater role in international public goods provision, including the policing of stability; and a wish to address defects in the predecessor system of European Political Co-operation (see, for example, de Schoutheete, 1997; Kohl, 1991).

Pillarization and the making of foreign policy beyond the nation-state

A further reason for wanting to study pillarization and joint actions is that they provide what is probably the most ambitious experiment to date in the making of foreign policy 'beyond the state' by a collective of governments. While pillarization constitutes the institutional setting for such an enterprise, joint actions provide evidence of process and attempted operationalization. Later in the book, we argue that the best way to develop testable theories about pillarization and joint actions is to adapt the field of study known as foreign policy analysis (FPA) to the ontological conditions of foreign policy beyond the state. FPA seeks to treat aspects of the 'internal' policy process – agenda-setting, decision-rules, patterns of actor participation, methods of implementation – as independent variables in the shaping of outcomes. This contrasts with the belief that it is sufficient to concentrate on the structural incentives and constraints of the 'external' international environment, in order to explain the main outlines of foreign policy behaviour. A difficulty, however, is that the existing body of theory associated with FPA cannot just be taken as it is and plundered for testable hypotheses about the impact of pillarization and joint actions on the performance of CFSP. This is for the simple reason that FPA has developed through case studies of foreign policy 'within the state'. Our own proposals for adapting FPA to conditions typical of foreign policy 'beyond the state' are set out in chapter 3.

How does our approach fit with other methodological reflections on how the making of the EU's foreign policy should best be studied? One issue concerns the *scope* of what needs to be included in any study of the EU's foreign policy. Ben Tonra (2000, pp. 163–9) contends that the study of the EU's foreign policy is moving away from policy studies towards a more holistic approach in which the study of process is set in its political and economic contexts. Roy Ginsberg (1999, pp. 429–54) has commented on the transformation of EU foreign policy towards studies of process *and* outcome, together with studies of economics and politics. Michael Smith (1996) has likewise pointed to the need for analysing EU foreign policy so as to incorporate a broader appreciation of the role of trade and economics in the Union's international capacity. Brian White (2001) argues that European foreign policy is not just the sum total of the individual foreign policies of the individual foreign policies of the EU's member states. It is also includes the foreign policy of the Union and the foreign external 'economic' relations of the EU (White, 1999, pp. 37–66; White, 2001). A range of recent studies have characterized the EU's foreign policy as being broader than CFSP, even if that process is necessarily a centre piece of the Union's attempts to mediate its relationships with its external environment (Bretherton and Vogler, 1999; Eliassen, 1998; Peterson and Sjursen, 1998; K.E. Smith, 1998; Jorgensen, 1997; Piening, 1997; Zielonka, 1998a, 1998b).

A second question concerns the specificity of the EU's foreign policy. This, in turn, sub- divides into two methodological issues. On the one hand, there is the issue of whether the EU's foreign policy is unique or whether it opens itself to comparative analysis through the application of 'middle-range theory' (Jorgensen, 1997; Piening, 1997; Eliassen, 1998; Peterson and Sjursen, 1998; K.E. Smith, 1998; Bretherton and Vogler, 1999; Peterson and Bomberg, 1999). On the other hand, there is the issue of how far the EU's foreign policy should be understood as something that is endogenously constructed through the 'will to policy' and the 'role of values', both of which are likely to be shaped by the practice of the policy itself (Wendt, 1999; Christiansen et al., 1999). The constructivist turn adds a further dimension of specificity, since it implies that the EU's foreign policy may be qualitatively different over time, as well as more or less sui generis in relation to other (predominantly state-based) forms of foreign policy. In other words, inter- temporal comparisons between two instances of foreign policy-making by the EU may need to be handled with as much care as spatial comparisons between foreign policy-making at the European and national levels of government.

Our own position on these questions is as follows. First, a wide conception of the EU's foreign policy is implicit in our focus on pillarization to the extent that the latter is supposed to institutionalize links between the external economic policy and the diplomatic démarches of CFSP. Second, we are sympathetic to the need to build a time-line, or temporal dimension, into the study of CFSP. But our preference is to use path-dependence theory, rather than constructivism, to do this (see chapter 2). This is not to question the value of the latter. Rather, it is motivated by a wish to avoid merely repeating insights developed by others. Third, we believe that specificity need be no barrier to either inter-systemic or inter- temporal comparisons. On the assumption that comparison is something we do in relation to different members of the same class of object, what matters is not that the EU's efforts should be identical with the external activities of other political systems – or that they should be invariant over time – but that they should satisfy a minimum definition of 'foreign policy', such as the following: purposive and sustained efforts to influence the international environment undertaken by a body that acts on behalf of a public, as opposed to purely private, interest.

As a final point, we take the view that, in common with much else in the study of the EU (Peterson and Begg, 1998), it is important to avoid a condition in which theoretical advance in the understanding of the EU's foreign policy outstrips empirical testing. This study is, accordingly, much more than an attempt to theorise pillarization as an institutional setting for the EU's foreign policy. Its central claim to originality lies in its three case study chapters of joint actions, none of which has been fully researched in previous contributions to the literature. A sympathy for a wide definition of the EU's foreign policy, and an aspiration to develop theoretical alternatives and methods of empirical testing that should consolidate its links with comparative foreign policy analysis, allows us to place ourselves as shown in Table 1.2.

To summarize, joint actions were supposed to be a primary means of achieving the objectives of the new Common Foreign and Security Policy introduced by the Treaty of European Union. However, the TEU also provided that the CFSP and joint actions should be mediated through a distinctive institutional structure known as pillarization. Not only is the viability of the pillarization structure and its impact on policy outcomes a legitimate question of academic enquiry; it also provides the ontological starting point for attempts to theorize joint actions as instances of foreign policy-making beyond the state. That is to say, all plausible alternatives will have to assume the basic institutional characteristics of pillarization in the same way as 'within-state'

Table 1.2 Tonra's classification of contributions to the literature on foreign policy analysis

	CFSP	EU foreign policy
Sui generis		Bretherton and Vogler
		Piening
		Smith
		Zielonka
Comparative	Eliassen	Peterson and Sjursen
		Jorgensen
		White
		The present authors' approach

Source: Tonra (2000, p. 164).

18 *EU Foreign Policy beyond the Nation-State*

foreign policy analysis has to assume essential institutional characteristics of the state.

Chapter 2 provides an historical analysis of pillarization. Its aim is to give a clearer idea of where joint actions and pillarization came from: of why they were thought to be needed, and of why they emerged as outcomes of the TEU negotiations. Its central argument is that the wider pillarization structure needs to be understood as a path-dependent development of the EPC process that preceded the CFSP. Along the way it introduces the reader to some of the institutional forms that have dominated the drama since earlier stages in the evolution of the EU's foreign policy: transgovernmental practices of policy-making; rule-based systems of foreign policy co-operation; and instances of blurring between supranationalism and intergovernmentalism.

Chapter 3 is an institutional analysis of how CFSP functions under pillarization. After justifying the application of institutional perspectives to CFSP, it argues that three such approaches are compatible with the characteristics of pillarization: rational actor, policy network and garbage can theories. The chapter concludes with a methodological section which proposes a strategy for testing joint actions against each of the three theories.

Chapter 4 then goes on to trace the evolution of the European Union Administration of Mostar (EUAM) in the period 1994–96, testing which of the models of foreign policy-making prevailed and why, and, finally, what consequences the EUAM had for the nature and performance of pillarization. The chapter also considers issues of process, actor behaviour, and policy outcomes.

Chapter 5 analyses the implementation of the Dayton Agreements between 1995 and 1998. Again, the chapter tests which of the models of foreign policy-making prevailed and why, and, finally, what consequences the policy-making style of the Union had for the nature and performance of pillarization. As in chapter 4, the chapter also considers issues of process, actor behaviour, and policy outcomes.

Chapter 6 examines EU policies towards the Caucasus in between 1996 and 1999. As in the previous two chapters, the analysis tests which of the models of foreign policy-making prevailed and why, and what consequences the Union's policy-making style had for the nature and performance of pillarization in the EU. The chapter also considers issues of process, actor behaviour, and policy outcomes.

Finally, the conclusion (chapter 7) considers which of the models of foreign policy-making emerged to best explain each of the cases under scrutiny. The conclusion will also focus on general and case-related observations derived from the analysis on the nature and performance of pillarization in EU Joint Actions. It argues that an understanding of process, of relationships between joint actions as an unusual policy-making method, actor behaviour and policy outcomes will allow us to better understand the relationship between pillarization and EU foreign policy joint actions in institutional and behavioural terms.

2
An Historical Analysis of Pillarization

With a view to arguing that the politics of pillarization in the 1990s were critically shaped by patterns of path dependence, this chapter moves through the following stages. The first section considers the development of the external dimension of European integration before 1991, focussing mainly on European Political Co-operation (EPC). The second section attempts an appraisal of EPC in an attempt to establish the institutional challenges that CFSP and pillarization could be expected to meet if they were to constitute an improvement on EPC. The third section reconstructs the bargaining process by which the Intergovernmental Conference (IGC) on political union (1991) fashioned CFSP and the wider decision to 'pillarize' the Union. The fourth section then concludes by specifying the form of path dependence that seems to have governed the evolution of CFSP and pillarization, and by justifying the contention that it offers a better understanding than the likely alternatives of the structures and processes studied by this book over the period 1993–99.

The development of foreign policy co-operation 1957–91

Far from being created *ab novo* by the Treaty of European Union, CFSP was a modification of the older process of European Political Co-operation (EPC), first established in 1970. Indeed, the ambition of creating a European foreign and security policy runs parallel to the entire history of European integration process. Salient themes, conflicts and choices that would later become the staple of EPC/CFSP were foreshadowed in the failed European Defence Community (EDC) of 1950–54 and in the Fouchet Plan of 1961–63 (Fursdon, 1980; Timmermans, 1996; Duke, 2000).

Although the Treaty of Rome of 1957 (TOR) has been regarded as mainly concerned with the internal construction of the European Community, it also shaped its future as an international actor by creating a distinction between forms of international action that would be 'in' and 'out' of bounds to the EC. Anticipating that the economic integration of selected West European countries into a Customs Union would have consequences for the international system and vice versa, the TOR broadly followed the principle that the EC should be allowed to form external relationships in matters where it had internal competence. It, accordingly, authorized the Commission 'to negotiate' and 'conclude accords' with 'a third state, a union of states, or an international organisation (Articles 228 and 238). It also empowered the 'Commission to recommend to the Council when accords with third states are needed' (Article 113) and 'called upon' ... 'member states to consult to prevent the functioning of the Common Market being disrupted from serious ... international disturbances' (Article 224).

While, however, the TOR mandated EC involvement in a series of international economic questions ('external policy'), it did not authorize it to develop a role in diplomatic and security issues (foreign policy). A series of factors lay behind the exclusion of the EC from the latter. First was a calculation that it was best not to discuss security questions outside the North Atlantic Treaty Organization (NATO) if the US was to remain fully engaged in the defence of Western Europe and the Soviets denied any opportunity to sow division between the NATO countries. Second was a belief that there was a distinction between the 'low politics' of socio-economic policy-making where states and their publics would often be prepared to accept sovereignty transfers in order to realize collective welfare gains and the 'high politics' of foreign policy-making where sovereignty transfers would be seen as existentially threatening to nation-states (Hoffmann, 1966) . Third was a related belief amongst the original policy entrepreneurs of European unification that integration would be best promoted through an incremental process beginning with small-scale acts of economic co-operation. Areas of co-operation perceived as 'core activities' of states, such as foreign policy, would be best postponed until elites had socialized themselves into the integration process, and economic spill-over had locked member countries into well-functioning Community institutions. The distinction between foreign and external policy has never been abolished. Instead, it has moved through a series of institutional manifestations, of which pillarization, a principal focus of this work, is only the most recent. A recurrent question, therefore, is whether the attempted demarcation represents a stable separation of powers and a viable division of labours.

When foreign policy co-operation was introduced in the form of EPC from 1970 it only reinforced the doctrinal and organizational distinction between foreign and external policy. At the Hague Conference of December 1969 the heads of government of the original European Communities committed themselves to the ambitious goal of paving 'the way for a united Europe capable of assuming its international responsibilities (EC Bulletin, 1970, no. 1, p. 11). The foreign ministers of the six were then delegated to 'study the best way of achieving progress in the matter of political unification ... [and to make proposals] before the end of July 1970' (EC Bulletin 1970, no. 1, pp. 3 and 5). In other words, national foreign ministries were invited to construct the form of foreign policy co-operation that most suited them. The result was a series of recommendations to the heads of government that included no role for common institutions, let alone the supranational bodies established under the TOR. Instead, national foreign ministries of EC member states would manage their own system of co-operation unaided by any external agency. They would do this through:

- regular exchanges of information and consultation [to ensure] a better mutual understanding of the great international problems;
- promoting the harmonization of their views, the co-ordination of their positions, and, where it appears possible, or desirable, common actions (EC Bulletin, 1971, no. 6, p. 21)

As will be explained more fully below, the shape and evolution of EPC require a careful understanding of the institutional interests and bureaucratic politics that lay behind the decision to construct EPC as a system of collaboration between foreign ministries unmediated by common institutions. By taking up the challenge of foreign policy co-operation for themselves, national foreign ministries were able to retain control and pre-empt any transfer of competence to the formal Communities, either through Treaty change or creeping shifts in the boundary between foreign and external policy. On the other hand, EPC also gave foreign ministries more autonomy within their own national governments. The growth of Community business since 1957 had seen the first appearance of transgovernmental patterns of policy-making based on direct contacts between domestic government departments of EC member states. This eroded the gate-keeping role of national diplomatic services by which most relationships with outside governments and international organizations had previously been routed through foreign ministries. The erosion of this co-ordinating function threatened the equality of policy leadership between foreign and finance departments around which many national governments had traditionally been structured.

It was, however, impossible for foreign ministries to discipline the transgovernmental activities of other departments without weakening a principal means by which EC member governments maintained their effectiveness relative to the Commission. EPC offered foreign ministries the alternative of at least consolidating control of their own policy domain by entering the transgovernmental game on better terms than other government departments. Not only did ready-made diplomatic infrastructures and expertise ensure they were uniquely well-resourced for co-ordination based on direct contacts between counterpart ministries in national bureaucracies. EPC also allowed them to 'Europeanize' policy discussions without conceding formal roles to Community institutions.

Given that it appeared to be 'institution-free', EPC seemed to be a pure gain to foreign ministries in terms of policy control: the locus of policy consultation shifted to discussions with other foreign ministries, and away from co-ordination with domestic government departments. Monopoly access to EPC conferred informational advantages, allowing foreign ministries to function in their national administrations as unique interpreters of what was an elite negotiation in the process of foreign policy collaboration. In game-theoretic terms, EPC discussions may not have been binding, but a decision by foreign ministries to move discussions into the EPC arena at any stage during the policy cycle would have the effect of increasing their agenda-setting power relative to all other actors in the domestic political system: it would restrict the capacity of the latter to intervene in the foreign policy-making process and put a constraint on their scope to overturn common policy positions that had been painstakingly negotiated with others and invested with their own government's credibility as a partner.

EPC and the bureaucratic interpenetration of national foreign policy-making

At first, there were few clues that EPC would develop into an elaborate structure of foreign policy collaboration. Early designs were for an occasional, even leisurely, process that would scarcely scratch the surface of the contributing foreign policy bureaucracies. The Luxembourg Report of 1971 envisaged that foreign ministers would meet every six months, and that they would be advised on EPC by a Political Committee of high-ranking national officials which would meet every four months. Almost from the outset, the Political Committee had to meet monthly, often only to remit the bulk of its work to a sprawling complex of working groups. Although the exact list of working groups is fluid, the more permanent have covered relations with other countries (United States, Soviet Union/Russia and so on), other regions (Central America, Eastern Europe, Middle East), other international organizations (UN) and horizontal issues (disarmament, non-proliferation and terrorism). There would seem to have been around 25 such groups at the beginning of the 1990s (Kirchner, 1992, p. 77) and estimates are of 'hundreds of meetings ... each year' (M.E. Smith, 1998, p. 314). The effect of establishing these working groups was that national foreign ministries were not drawn, as originally intended, into EPC at a level of political or administrative principals, but at that of desk officers, who form the basic organizing units of national diplomatic machines.

In addition to face-to-face meetings, officials were soon tied together into a continuous exchange of information and assessments. The Copenhagen report of 1973 established the so-called Correspondence Européenne (COREU), a telex system between EPC member states designed to encourage almost instantaneous transmission of information from one capital to another (EC Bulletin, 1973, no. 9, p. 11). Anthony Forster and William Wallace (1989, p. 417) claim that 'traffic around this network grew from an estimated two to three thousand telegrams a year to some 9 000 in 1989'.

A further effect of EPC was to intensify contacts between the foreign ministries of EPC countries 'in the field' and not just in 'the office'. From as early as the Conference on Security Co-operation in Europe (CSCE) which opened in 1973, the EPC countries began the practice of trying to co-ordinate their positions for international conferences and other fora where more than one member state was involved. This produced a literature based on the one measurable indicator of diplomatic cohesion that provides a continuous flow of statistics over time: the frequency with which countries vote together in the United Nations (UN). Although there are difficulties in interpreting these figures (voting may only occur on atypical issues), the flaws in the data are presumably relatively constant, with the implication that they can be

A Historical Analysis of Pillarization 25

used to indicate trends. One such trend was that the formation of EPC coincided with an increase in the frequency with which its member states all voted the same way in the UN from 30–40 per cent in the early 1970s to 70–80 per cent in the 1980s, even though the odds on unanimity were significantly lengthened by EC enlargement (Hurwitz, 1976; Lindemann, 1982; Luif, 1993).

In parallel with intensified co-operation in international organizations, EC embassies in non-member states began to work together. Michael E. Smith has made a special study of this practice, which he describes as follows:

> EC ambassadors [in third countries] prepared joint reports, shared information and made policy recommendations to officials at home. They also conducted common démarches in third countries, held common debates with high representatives of third countries, and co-operated during crisis situations without much guidance from foreign capitals ... links between missions became a vital 'backdoor' channel to achieving political co-operation. This was occasionally even resented by Foreign Ministers and by the Po Co; the French even attempted to put an end to such activity in the 1980s. (M.E. Smith, 1998, pp. 314–15)

In 1981, the London report added a 'crisis procedure' to EPC. If at least three member states feel there is a crisis deserving the urgent attention of EPC, a meeting of either the Political Committee or of ministers can be convened within 48 hours. A like procedure can be invoked in third countries at the level of heads of mission. The London report also aimed to improve arrangements for the anticipation of crises and the preparation of contingency actions: 'working groups are encouraged to analyse areas of potential crisis and to provide a range of possible reactions by the Ten' (EC Bulletin, 1981, no. 12, p. 9; See also Keukeleire, 1994, pp. 137–79).

Given that persuasion was often the only source of influence available, it was all the more important that EPC should speak with one authoritative voice. As a result, the practice developed of delegating external representation to the rotating Presidency of the Council of Ministers. Yet the interlocutory function could have a dynamic of its own. Since dialogue with outsiders could not be conducted on the basis of continuous reference back to other member states, the Presidency often had to anticipate the consensus in EPC, rather than follow it.

To summarize, therefore, EPC touched foreign policies at almost every level of their making. Meetings of foreign ministers were only the tip of an elaborate substructure which included working parties of officials from different member states; continuous communications between desk officers working on similar parts of the world; collaboration in international organizations, including the development of common negotiating positions; and joint representations by EC embassies to third countries.

Yet although it was procedurally ambitious, there was no one body whose specific task it was to provide EPC with either institutional presence or continuity. In addition, EPC was doubly voluntaristic: not only did decisions require unanimity; they were also non-binding – even when they had been agreed. On the other hand, there were at least two ways in which EPC did develop an institutional dimension from an early stage: the first was that it was in some sense a rule-based system; the second was that it was affected by its relationship with the formal institutions of the European Communities. It is to these two themes that we now turn.

EPC as a rule-based system of co-operation

Where actors are unwilling to transfer authority and resources to central structures, they may, none the less, institutionalize their behaviour in less obvious fashion by developing a series of self-enforced rules. In addition to extensive bureaucratic interpenetration between the diplomatic services of member states, the literature has attributed a series of behavioural norms to the operation of EPC. Although there is room for disagreement as to the content and status of these norms, the following examples can be gleaned from a combination of official documents and the expert testimony of EPC practitioners:

Member states have an obligation to consult. This was first given Treaty form under the Single European Act, which committed members to 'inform and consult on any foreign policy matters of general interest'. It also stipulated that 'consultations shall take place before' member states 'decide on their final positions' (European Commission, 1986, Article 30). The TEU added security questions to the obligation and clarified that consultation would take place through the Council. The goal of consultation was, moreover, defined as one of ensuring 'that the combined influence' of CFSP 'is exerted as effectively as possible by means of concerted and convergent action' (European Commission, 1992,

Article J2). It is easy to dismiss this as a weak obligation on any one of the following grounds: it implies no commitment to act; member states only have to go through the motions of consultation; and, apart from some exposure to peer-group criticism, they are their own judges on when to consult and how. Yet, even assuming that no co-ordination results, consultation may increase the effectiveness of individual national foreign policy actions by improving the information each member state has about the intentions of the others. Moreover, the obligation to consult can be linked to an aspiration to create a 'co-ordination reflex' which has existed in EPC since the Copenhagen report of 1973. The idea here was that although EPC remains voluntaristic, member states at least committed themselves to explore the terms on which it co-operation be secured, before taking unilateral action (de Schoutheete, 1986; Fonseca-Wollheim, 1981; Hurd, 1981).

Obligation to take account of the positions of others. Once again, this is a norm that has textual foundation in the Treaties. In the Single European Act it appeared as an obligation to 'take full account of the position of the other partners' (European Commission, 1986, Article 30). The TEU further required that where only some member states had access to another international body they should take account of positions that had been agreed with their EPC partners. While it is difficult to assess the extent to which this obligation is followed, two forms of political behaviour suggest that the probability of mutual adjustment of policy positions is sufficiently high for participants in EPC to invest scarce resources in persuasiveness: rotating Presidencies devote a great deal of time to asking each member state to give a full and justified reaction on a point-by-point basis to positions submitted by others; and national foreign ministries exchange assessments and not just information, indicating that there are benefits in attempting to influence the conceptual frameworks by which others understand foreign policy problems.

Obligation to justify national positions. Unlike the former conventions, this norm has never been given textual recognition, yet, it is, in a sense, a corollary of the previous norm. Given temporal and resource constraints, member states cannot be expected to give carte blanche undertakings to give serious thought to any position advanced by an EPC partner. Only justified national preferences are likely to count. This may require governments to explain why a question is of vital importance to their country; and why their preferred means of attaining an objective

Attentiveness to precedent. A curiosity of EPC is the emphasis placed on aligning new decisions with previous ones. Variously described as the 'case-law' of EPC or the *acquis politique* (Ifestos, 1987; Lak, 1989; Dehousse and Weiler, 1991) attentiveness to precedent has been taken to the length of compiling a *coutumier*, which summarizes the content of previous decisions and procedures, and a *recueil*, which records all statements issued in the name of EPC (Hayes-Renshaw and Wallace, 1997, p. 144). But why have participants in EPC been prepared to allow themselves to be guided by precedent in this way? One possible explanation has to do with differences in patterns of policy cumulation between the internal policies of the EC and foreign policy co-ordination in EPC. John Peterson and Elizabeth Bomberg (1999) have argued that at least three of the factors that promote linkages between individual EC decisions are absent from EPC: the functional interrelatedness of socio-economic issues; clear incentives for societal actors to mobilize with a view to influencing policy in particular directions; and dedicated institutions in a position to give undivided attention to policy coherence in their sphere of activity (Peterson and Bomberg, 1999, pp. 232–3).

On the other hand, foreign-policy-makers come under pressure to satisfy at least two demands for policy coherence that can be more easily ignored by those responsible for the internal development of European integration: the need to avoid sending confusing signals to others in the international system; and the importance of ensuring that individual actions undertaken in the name of EPC blend together in the perception of outsiders to encourage role attributions that the EU countries can sustain (Hill, 1993). Attention to policy precedent is useful in promoting policy consistency. Convention-bound behaviour may, however, also be explained as another means by which actors arrange co-ordination in the formal absence of authorized institutions. Member states may internalize orientations laid down in EPC in order to save themselves two kinds of transaction cost: the 'discovery costs' involved in devoting scarce administrative resources to devising a policy response that may have to be constructed to a tight deadline; and bargaining costs involved in attempting to hammer out common European positions on each new foreign policy question.

Reciprocity. Of all the possible norms associated with EPC this is probably the least susceptible to precise specification. Interviews with practitioners suggest that EPC shares what is often considered a general feature of intergovernmental dealing in the EU: an awareness, on the one hand, that failure to spread the benefits of co-operation between members will diminish the quality of active co-operation with EPC procedures; and, on the other, that individual member states can gain by trading their preferences on matters of comparative indifference to themselves for those about which they feel strongly. Given its informality and apparent absence of a central institution capable of keeping a tally of vote and veto trading, it might be thought that EPC was, at best, only capable of diffuse reciprocation. On the other hand, research into 'elite circles' suggests that remarkably sophisticated systems of reciprocation can be sustained under just the conditions that prevail in EPC: regular face-to-face contacts between informed policy-makers meeting in stable groups; consensual decision-rules; high levels of discretion to enter commitments that are unlikely to be challenged by domestic constituencies; and considerable scope for issue linkage to be used for positive-sum or pareto improving decision-making (Sartori, 1987; Higley et al., 1993).

Nor was EPC devoid of mechanisms to facilitate reciprocation. By all accounts the Presidency assumed a role in identifying points at which strong weak preferences could be exchanged for strong ones, and in reminding governments where previous trades left them in 'debit' or 'credit' to others. This would, for example, explain why EPC quickly developed the practice of organizing Presidencies in to Troikas, providing a relay system in which the *acquis politique* was transmitted through co-ordination at any one time between the Presidency in Office, its predecessor and successor.

The blurring of EPC and the EC

In addition to occasioning a substantial interpenetration of national foreign ministries at every level of their activity, EPC had a second unintended consequence: it proved impossible to sustain a strict distinction between EPC and the formal European Communities. Even in relation to its earliest agenda items, participants in EPC soon found that it was difficult to pursue their discussions without knowing how these would impact on the policies of the Community. It also turned out that it was often the EC that had jurisdiction over policy instruments that the EPC partners would need to be able to access if they were to achieve their objectives (Nuttall, 1992, pp. 132–41).

In the case of 'normal' and non-conflictual relationships, where force had little utility, the most usable foreign policy instruments were precisely those powers over external economic relationships which had been transferred to the EC. Moreover, the identity of those instruments that had the best chance of securing foreign policy leverage was externally determined by the motives of those others. Only by accident would they correspond to any internally chosen demarcation of competence between EPC and the EC. Indeed, it may even have been systematically more likely that outsiders would be more interested in matters falling under the jurisdiction of the EC than EPC. Since West European countries were not self-sufficient security providers, the comparative advantage of cultivating their favours lay in access to their markets. Moreover, any rigid adherence to the distinction between EC and EPC would have reduced scope for concluding bargains by means of issue linkage. Mike Smith observes that this would have been peculiarly dysfunctional in a context in which many 'international problems were being made intractable precisely because of the ways in which economic, political and security elements were intertwined and interdependent (M. Smith, 1996, p. 249).

At first, the member states attempted to co-ordinate EPC and EC without involving the Commission in EPC discussions – for example, by inviting the Commission to comment on agenda items in writing (Nuttall, 1992). The Commission was, however, included in working groups from as early as the mid-1970s, a practice that was only innocuous to the extent that working groups were 'top-down' processes that worked to the guidelines of political or administrative principals in national capitals (ministers and political directors), rather than 'bottom-up' processes which shaped the preferences and constrained the options available to superiors.

Following the London Report of 1981 the Commission was included in COREU and its involvement in all EPC working groups was acknowledged. With the Single Act of 1987 it was formally associated with EPC and given joint responsibility with the Presidency of the Council for ensuring consistency between EC and EPC. The Commission could presumably have used this to justify comprehensive access to EPC and tested any refusal in the ECJ on the grounds that any withholding of information would have prevented it from meeting its Treaty obligation. In practice, the Commission had no need to take such an adversarial approach. Presidencies sympathetic to its participation extended the practice of its involvement in a manner their successors found hard to reverse. Moreover, the Presidency and the Commission were increasingly tethered in two kinds of working relationship: the SEA gave them joint responsibility for answering parliamentary questions; and effective external representation required them to agree joint démarches or conduct joint visits to third countries.

For its part, the Commission began to commit resources to following EPC and developing its capacity for external action more generally. It established its own network of diplomatic missions, which by the early 1990s had a more comprehensive coverage of world capitals than many member states. Wherever outside governments had an interest in lobbying on trade and aid questions, Commission delegations would be especially influential participants in the so-called micro-EPCs (M.E. Smith, 1998) that were established between the embassies of member states and Commission missions in third capitals. Within the Commission itself responsibility for EPC was assigned to the Secretariat-General which reported directly to the Presidency (Nuttall, 1992, p. 135). During the first two Delors Commissions this facilitated some notable examples of quick response policy entrepreneurship, such as a Commission initiative to arrange emergency funding to Eastern Europe in 1989. Far from member states being able to insulate EPC from all contact with the Commission, Nuttall (1992, p. 139) has even noted an opposite effect by which the Commission was able to lever up its own powers and resources in response to requests that it should help in the delivery of EPC objectives.

It is, however, useful to specify the exact institutional mechanisms by which EPC became dependent on the active co-operation of the Commission. The need to access EC budget lines in all cases where member states were unwilling to finance EPC out of their own resources gave the Commission the 'power of the cheque book' (Nuttall, 1992, p. 139). From the early 1990s the fashion for political conditionality – the linkage of aid to considerations of good governance and international behaviour – meant that it was often the Commission, and not EPC, which was required, in the first instance, to pass judgement on the political performance of outside countries (M.E. Smith, 1998, p. 327).

While the established literature documents these financial linkages between EPC and the EC, it gives rather less attention to the consequences of EPC reliance on the Commission's legislative resources, notably where member states sought to gain foreign policy leverage over outsiders by manipulating rights of market access. This had the effect of indirectly extending the effects of the Commission's monopoly of legislative initiative to EPC. Wherever EPC wanted change in the status quo but the Commission did not, the Commission would be able to get its way by keeping the legislative gates closed. Wherever the two bodies agreed on the direction of change but disagreed on its degree, the Commission would be able to shift the Council some way from the ideal preferences of member states towards its own. Wherever the Council was clear that it wanted some kind of initiative but hazy on the detail, the Commission would be able to exercise an element of political leadership by using its legislative powers to 'construct' conceptions of the policy options available (Peters, 1994). It may, moreover, only have been necessary for a matter of EC competence to be involved in just one item of a package deal or at one point in a long sequence of foreign policy moves, for policy outcomes in EPC to be affected by the decision-rules of the formal Communities.

A corollary was to remove the fire-break between EPC and the constitutional development of the Community. Any policy reassigned from national to the formal Communities was open to being coupled with EPC in a manner that was unlikely to have been anticipated at the moment that competence was transferred. Environment policy provides a good example. From the 1970s significant powers were transferred from national to European level. By the end of the 1980s, environmental policy featured increasingly prominently in both the means and ends of foreign policy. Not only, however, did this open up a new possibility for the intermeshing of foreign policy co-operation and the formal Communities, it also created a new form of 'spill-over' between changes to EC decision-rules and EPC/CFSP. Changes to the way in which environmental policy was made – as it moved from Unanimity to QMV on the Council and the Parliament first gained rights of amendment (Co-operation) and then powers of rejection (Co-decision) – would have the secondary consequence of reconfiguring who was likely to get what out of any attempt to link environmental policy to objectives established in EPC/CFSP.

It is, however, important to note three further aspects of blurring. The first is that the Commission did not show special eagerness to inject itself into EPC on the basis of the Community method. By carefully insinuating itself into EPC through proving its usefulness to the achievement of policy aims, rather than by asserting doctrinal claims to access, it avoided mobilizing the opposition of more sovereignty-conscious states. Such an approach also gave it a margin of autonomy which meant that the nature of its participation would have to be resolved to the mutual satisfaction of Commission and member states, and not unilaterally by the latter.

A second and neglected feature of 'blurring' is that it involved the Council of Ministers as much as the Commission. Indeed, there were some respects in which the Council was the weakest point along the EC–EPC frontier. Given that the rotating Presidency for both processes was held by the same member state, the task of co-ordinating EPC was in the hands of the same national foreign ministry as that responsible for handling the Council's work programme on EC questions. In some cases, this produced overload, creating an opportunity for the Commission to pick up tasks which could not be adequately serviced by a stressed-out Presidency. In other cases, the Presidency was itself eager to identify practical ways by which the Commission could extend its involvement in EPC, particularly where the office was held by governments uncomfortable with the theological divide between the two processes. While EPC was only fully merged with the General Affairs Council (GAC) under the TEU, the GAC was empowered to consider EPC questions from the time of the Single Act in 1987 (Kirchner, 1992, p. 50). In addition, EC and EPC developed strikingly similar patterns of policy delegation, with ministers and top officials coming to preside over elaborate substructures of working groups (see above). Although intended as a means of delivering effective intergovernmental decision-making within constraints of time and human expertise, observers of committee governance have often noted the ease with which it can slip into what Stanley Hoffmann and Robert Keohane (1991) have called a 'supranational intergovernmentalism'.

Another neglected aspect of blurring was that it went far wider than the relationship between EC and EPC. On the security side, EPC discussions shaded off into meetings of the CSCE, NATO, the UN and, increasingly, the WEU; and on international economic questions, they often duplicated deliberations in G7 summits, the IMF, the WTO, or, once again, the UN, particularly on the politics of aid. To a certain extent the porosity of institutional boundaries was made inevitable by overlaps of membership. It could, however, also be the product of political manipulation, as influential actors chose the arenas in which they were most likely to obtain results closest to their preferences. Either way, it created a tendency for policy problems to drift between fora, of which EPC was just one; or for EPC to find that it was just one of several processes dragged into the management of a problem, without the mix of responsibilities being clearly and stably defined. As Christopher Hill and William Wallace (1996, p. 4) put it in relation to the Bosnian crisis, 'the cycle of decision-making (and decision avoidance) went from the EPC/CFSP to NATO to the UN and back'.

Appraising EPC

EPC has received mixed reviews. It has been praised, first, for the flexibility and inventiveness with which it assembled co-ordinating procedures of significant problem-solving capacity without creating an integrated foreign policy bureaucracy; second, for seducing member states into a slow yet substantial convergence in their national foreign policies, where premature attempts to form a common foreign policy could have entrenched particular countries into fixed positions on either side of cleavages, defined either by attitudes to national sovereignty in foreign policy, or by differences about the kind of international actor the EC should aim to be, or by disagreements on priorities to be given to other parts of the world in the EC's external relationships. A third argument in favour of the approach adopted by EPC was that it concentrated on consensus methods that increased the probability that states would only commit themselves to those things they were prepared to deliver; a fourth is that it at least provided the EC countries with a 'regime of common aversion' (M.E. Smith, 1998, p. 322) capable of alerting member states to cases where their national foreign policies would duplicate, cancel each other out, or produce other mutually sub-optimal outcomes that could be improved by co-ordination. A fifth claim is that EPC went beyond the mere reduction of policy inconsistency between member states to provide some benefits of scale and collective action (Ginsberg, 1989); and a sixth is that by using reassuring civilian methods, limiting its pretensions, and evolving gradually, it allowed the EC countries to begin to develop a collective actorness without opposition from elsewhere in the international system.

Moreover, formalization of foreign policy collaboration tended to follow developments in policy practice, with the Treaties codifying EPC/CFSP, rather than inventing it. The result, its defenders might argue, is that it used pragmatic adaptation to develop working methods of greater sophistication than could have been dreamt up by a single designing intelligence. To critics who question its substantive achievements between 1970 and 1993, defenders of EPC might reply that it is hard to imagine how a fuller and speedier path to institutionalization could have been followed, given a combination of the contemporary international setting, and those characteristics of foreign policy-making that distinguish it from other responsibilities of government. States are only likely to collectivize their dealings with a risk-laden international system after they have built trust through a long track record of working together in voluntaristic forms of policy co-operation. Furthermore, reassignments of policy competence between the national and the European arena are more likely to achieve consent in a sovereignty-sensitive area where they are experimental, reversible, or, as seen, a formalization of already emerging practice.

Indeed, EPC has largely avoided mobilizing counter-coalitions anxious to defend national sovereignty. It has even enjoyed a certain following amongst those eager to hold it up as an exemplar of inter-governmentalism that, in their view, demonstrates that co-ordination problems can be solved with a lesser role for supranational institutions than that which they enjoy under the standard 'Community method' of decision-making. The result, defenders of this position might argue, was that when the time came for EPC to make the transition to CFSP it was able to do so without becoming hostage to the emergence of European integration as a new cleavage in the domestic politics of member states. (A possible exception is Denmark where the argument that citizens could be required to 'die for Europe' became an issue in the 1992 referendum.)

Yet, EPC has also been much criticized. A common starting point for most critiques is that it lacked definite foreign policy instruments, without which its diplomacy was largely 'declaratory'. It has been charged with treating procedure as a substitute for policy (Wallace, 1983), and the issuing of statements as a substitute for the taking of decisions. Because it lacked direct powers to mobilize economic or military resources, it often contented itself with statements of ideal positions unmatched by any action. Even the unambitious task of issuing statements of common positions could not always be distilled into clear and consistent signals, since they had to be pitched at a high level of generality, or punched through with exceptions and circumlocutions, given the consensus methods by which EPC was constrained to proceed.

Even where consensus was reached, a series of factors often combined to give EPC policies a fragile or ephemeral quality, in which it was continuously vulnerable to loss of commitment by key players, if not outright breach of agreements. Its shortcomings have been usefully summarized as an absence of 'three i's' – shared interests, institutions and identity – without which it lacked the essential prerequisites of international actorness. There were structural limits to how far any process of elite socialization could eliminate all conflicts of foreign policy interest between member states. Interest in collectivizing a particular area of foreign policy – and if so, on what terms – was bound to vary according to the geographical position of member states; their location in the international division of economic labour; their accumulated security resources and commitments; their rights of representation in other international organizations; their sunk investments in non-EU relationships; and the interface between foreign policy and systems of domestic political competition. Fraser Cameron (1996, p. 221) recalls Delors' exasperation at the difficulty of getting member states to answer three questions: 'What are our essential common interests? Are we prepared to act together to defend those interests? If so with what resources?'

Turning from interests to institutions, it is possible to identify three forms of criticism: failure even to make the most of what was supposed to be the easy part of EPC, a painless convergence of national positions; the dysfunctionality of consensus decision-making in relation to certain kinds of foreign policy problem; and the disjointed and unstable character of orientations agreed in EPC. On the first point, Cameron suggests that even CFSP (and a fortiori EPC) has failed to exhaust all possibilities for convergence in member state understanding of foreign policy problems. There has been no 'joint structure for the evaluation of information, policy analysis and the preparation of policy actions' (ibid., p. 225). On the second point about consensus diplomacy, EPC often seemed better suited to 'slow fuse' problems that could be analysed at a leisurely place than to the management of sudden crises.

It is, however, the third criticism that is probably the most serious indictment of EPC. Convergence, where it was achieved, was often unstable. As seen, there was never any obligation to follow EPC agreements, still less any institutional enforcement mechanism. In many cases, ease of exit may even have been a precondition for agreeing the policy in the first place. The literature on EPC is littered with examples of such defections. The exposure of EPC to the effects of a change of government in a member state was illustrated by a French statement of December 1981 which had the effect of unilaterally pulling Europe out of attempts to influence the Middle Eastern peace process (De La Serre, 1996, p. 24). The difficulty of sustaining common positions over periods of time long enough for domestic opposition to mobilize in particular member states or disagreements to develop between governments in the handling of subsequent developments was illustrated by the decision of the Italian and Irish governments to drop sanctions against Argentina a month into the Falklands crisis of 1982. The fragility of agreements that include the reluctant was underscored by the UK's prolonged opposition to the imposition of sanctions on South Africa in the 1980s, followed by its unilateral decision to lift them on the release of Nelson Mandela in February 1990, even though other EPC partners preferred to retain leverage over the further relaxation of apartheid for some while longer (Holland, 1995).

In contrast to the argument that consensus decision-rules made it more likely that member states would stick to agreements, there may have been one respect in which the effect was the other way round. The need for unanimity meant that small member states had the same procedural rights as the large in the shaping of EPC positions. This introduced a tension to the system: if equality between all member states was maintained, the consensus decision in EPC would often be one that left larger members in a position where they were more likely to achieve their preferences by breaking ranks; if, in contrast, EPC adapted to the reality that it might need its larger member states more than vice versa, the smaller members were liable to complain of a *directoire*.

Difficulties in achieving agreement and defections from what had been agreed meant that EPC often appeared to be capable of only selective and episodic policy-making, with policy only being made in fleeting moments of chance conjuncture between national preferences. According to this critique, it never amounted to a sustained and purposive effort to shape the external environment. It was too often proved reactive to agendas set by others. Nor did it ever last long enough to lock participants in to a pattern of compliance by changing their payoff structures. Nor, above all, was EPC ever sufficiently durable to fashion clear ideas of what Europe was about in international politics, so anchoring its activity in a sense of identity that was internally agreed and externally articulated.

Although these shortcomings might be dismissed as the product of innocent experimentation, or learning experiences in unprecedented collective diplomacy, Christopher Hill (1993) has argued that pretensions unmatched by capabilities were a source of profound political risk. Foremost amongst these was that other actors in the international system might press unrealistic roles on EPC, as conspicuously occurred when the US Administration supported a lead role for EPC in the early stages of the Yugoslavian crisis during 1991–92. It is, however, worth noting that a slightly different take on the capabilities–expectations gap identified by Hill is implicit in Josef Janning's critique that

EPC/CFSP has 'strengthened the national level' at a time when 'public goods of security and well-being are less and less produced at the level of national political systems' (Janning, 1996, pp. 231–2). In other words, EPC may have inflated expectations about the continued the capacity of the state to make effective foreign policy.

The institutional weaknesses of EPC were probably most evident at the time that the member states began to arrange for its transformation into CFSP. The fragility of the obligation to consult was demonstrated in January 1991 when the French Government tabled a Gulf crisis peace plan at the UN that had not been discussed in EPC (Janning, 1996, p. 35). The difficulty of sustaining a common line in the face of domestic contention and temptation to 'bounce' partners was reflected in the cause célèbre of unilateral German recognition of the breakaway republics from the former Yugoslavia in December 1991, a mere two weeks after the member states proclaimed their intention to form an effective CFSP in the Maastricht European Council and three before the issue was due to be discussed by an EPC meeting.

Yet the crisis in Yugoslavia, so often cited as the prime example of policy failure, may also explain why European efforts at foreign policy collaboration have so often been surrounded by both paean and despairing criticism. The failures of EPC/CFSP in the face of psychopathic forms of conflict in the former Yugoslavia were, arguably, matched by some limited successes in humanitarian roles and in moderating the behaviour of those still concerned to have a future in the European mainstream (von Jagow, 1993; Wiberg, 1996; Kintnis, 1997). What this may suggest is that appraisals of EPC/CFSP could benefit from the practice common to the study of the EU's internal political arena of distinguishing between levels of decision-making (Peterson and Bomberg, 1999, pp. 10–28). In the international sphere 'high-level' decisions would probably be those touching on fundamental questions of foreign policy identity: the values, communities and territorial units that foreign policies exist to defend; 'middle-level' decisions might cover those concerned with relationships, alignments, and the allocation of resources between foreign and domestic priorities; and 'low-level' decisions might include those concerned mainly with finding the optimal means of achieving goals defined at the other two levels. Cutting across these three types of decision there is a further distinction between high and low risk international policy.

As a matter of *analysis*, it may well be that EPC/CFSP is more likely to be effective towards the lower and middle levels of foreign policy-making, rather than the higher ones. As a matter of *evaluation*, it is by no means self-evident that any bias in its performance towards the lower and middle levels of foreign policy-making is an unsuitable arrangement for EPC/CFSP. European foreign policy collaboration can, and has been defended, precisely on the grounds that it has only limited potential to create a new (super-) actor in the international system or to engage with existential questions of foreign policy identity. From this perspective, performance is not the only test that should be applied to the various structures and instruments such as pillarization and joint actions that define the new CFSP. Internal and external acceptance is also a condition that needs to be satisfied, even if it requires the voluntary self-limitation of power through consensus decision-making and the foregoing of policy instruments common to national foreign policy-making.

EPC to CFSP: transformation or incremental development?

EPC was first given a Treaty base by the SEA (1987). Although there was little in the SEA that was not already established practice, and the relevant clauses were unenforceable by the ECJ, the effect of bringing into the Treaty was at least to give it some protection against attempts to neglect or abandon it on the grounds that it was a purely voluntary extra to EC membership (Ifestos, 1987, p. 358). The further step of transforming EPC into CFSP was negotiated against the background of radical change in the international system. The Single Act (1987) and the TEU (1992) were separated by the end of the Cold War, the reunification of Germany, the retreat of the Soviet bloc from Eastern Europe, the dissolution of the USSR itself and two major international crises in the Gulf and the former Yugoslavia. Such changes required the EC countries to rethink the entire architecture of their external relations. Although it seemed most likely that the United States would remain involved in the defence of Europe, the terms of its engagement were unlikely to remain unchanged, and any adjustments would almost certainly require Western European countries to assume expanded responsibilities in foreign and security policy.

There were at least two difficulties with leaving it to member states to respond individually to such changes: first, that would have meant foregoing benefits of collective action; and, second, German reunification upset the post-1949 equilibrium in the West European states system. Under such conditions, unilateralism threatened to create security dilemmas between the European states themselves: situations, in other words, in which one state could only make itself more secure by increasing the insecurity of others. This would have diverted resources available for Western European countries to assume greater international responsibilities. A further problem was that Eastern Europe became a zone of instability as it moved out of the Soviet bloc. On the assumption that some of its countries would soon be brought into the Community, the EC faced the prospect of having to find the foreign instruments needed to manage some troubled borderlands (Janning, 1996, p. 232).

Yet, a series of other factors may in any case have required some kind of overhaul of the multilateral frameworks available for foreign and security policy co-operation in Western Europe. One was a sense that the original model of EPC was reaching the limits of its capacity to produce effective collective action. On the one hand, it had taken ministry-to-ministry co-operation to lengths of sophistication that probably exhausted what could be achieved with the minimum of shared institutions. On the other hand, it was already beginning to develop, under the pressure of repeated improvization, into a mixed intergovernmental-supranational system, without that change being formally authorised or systematized. A second pressure for reform was that the success of the Single Market programme was taking the mismatch between the EC's status as economic giant and political dwarf to levels at which the Community needed to give more attention to its capacity to make effective foreign policy if it was to protect itself against all conceivable threats to its merged economic interests.

Common challenges associated with a changing external environment, and a patchy record in the foreign policy concertation, did not, however, prevent the emergence of cleavages on what should replace EPC. The IGC on political union which brought together representatives of member governments throughout the course of 1991 to negotiate the TEU divided along three lines: whether pillarization was an appropriate structure to manage a Common Foreign and Security Policy; the link between the CFSP and the provision of security; and rules for making decisions within the new CFSP. These points will now be examined in turn.

The institutional relationship between the new CFSP and the European Communities

Although bargaining on institutional questions often appeared to be polarized between those who wanted to integrate foreign policy into the standard institutions of the European Community and those who wanted separate yet connected pillars for the EC, CFSP and JHA, in

A Historical Analysis of Pillarization 41

practice the options considered for the TEU were not as binary as this suggests. On the one hand, proposals for communitarization anticipated the retention of substantial national veto rights. Since foreign policy only indirectly requires legislation, communitarization would not have institutionalized a monopoly of Commission initiative, nor would it have opened CFSP positions either to amendment or rejection by the EP or to enforcement by the ECJ.

Conversely, what was distinctive about the pillarization solution was not that it kept CFSP out of the standard Union institutions. To recapitulate from chapter 1, EPC meetings of foreign ministers would henceforth be formally moved to the General Affairs Council of the Council of Ministers. The EPC Secretariat was absorbed into the Council Secretariat, and the Political Directors were linked to COREPER, where an estimated 80 per cent of the Council's first-pillar powers are taken (Hayes-Renshaw and Wallace, 1997). The Presidency of the Council was given formal responsibility for the external representation of the Union and the Commission was to be associated with that task. The Commission was neither excluded from any right of initiative nor given a monopoly of it: together with individual member states, it had the right to 'submit proposals on any question relating to the common foreign policy'. It was also included in the crisis procedures allowing it to request the Presidency to convene an extraordinary meeting of the Council at 48 hours' notice. Delors considered these new powers to be sufficiently important to justify the appointment of a Commissioner with special responsibility for CFSP and to resource the creation of a new DG. Under the Treaty, the Presidency and Commission also have to report to the EP on CFSP questions, as well as answer parliamentary questions (European Commission, 1992, Articles J7 and J8). A subsequent development has been the holding of three-monthly meetings between the EP's Committee on Foreign Affairs and the chair of the Political Directors (Hix, 1999, p. 343).

The link between the new CFSP and security organizations

From as early as the Stuttgart declaration of 1983, those opposed to extensive EPC involvement in military issues retreated from defending a line between diplomatic and security policy (EC Bulletin, 1983, no. 6, pp. 24–9). By the time of the Maastricht treaty negotiations it was accepted practice that EPC could discuss security policy, provided it avoided operational questions, which several member governments saw as the preserve of NATO-related frameworks (Forster, 1999, p. 106). The principal cleavage in the 1991 IGC was provoked by a Franco-

German proposal that the European Council should be empowered to request the Western European Union (WEU) to study military options. This would have allowed heads of government to link CFSP discussions to possible deployments of military resources. This proposal was resisted by an 'Atlanticist' counter-coalition (comprising the UK, Italy and the Netherlands) which emphasized the importance of not appearing to contemplate alternatives to NATO, where planning could be coordinated with the United States (Forster, 1999). To the extent that the TEU was ambiguous on how WEU would be linked to CFSP, the Atlanticist view is generally thought to have prevailed.

The decision-rules of the new CFSP

The introduction of some measure of majority voting has featured in many diagnoses of what is needed for EPC/CFSP to make effective decisions. The Luxembourg Treaty draft of June 1991 envisaged a general provision for unanimous voting to apply to the agreement of policies under CFSP and majority voting to their implementation by joint action. This was eventually replaced by the provision that members would take each question on a case-by-case basis and decide by consensus whether they were prepared to use majority voting for subsequent measures of a kind they would specify in advance. On the assumption that consensus was unlikely on the first unless it could be firmly anticipated on the second, this is generally held to be a nugatory clause.

Conclusion: path dependence and the emergence of pillarization

Under path-dependent theories of institutional development decisions taken in an earlier period ($t - 1$) change the pay-offs that actors face in the present (t). This seemingly banal observation has powerful implications. Imagine a group of stakeholders in an existing policy who face a choice between two options. They all agree that option 1 would have been their preferred choice if they had never co-operated before. But they still end up by going for option 2. Why? Because option 2 includes a kind of 'bonus' made up of all the increasing returns or external benefits of previous collaborative efforts. The fact that only some choices deliver increasing returns from previous decisions powerfully shapes the politics of institutional selection. It creates 'lock-in' effects, or a 'conservative bias' towards replicating existing arrangements.

The selection of the pillarization structure as the institutional framework for CFSP is normally explained by bargaining theory: the two

A Historical Analysis of Pillarization 43

governments whose co-operation was most needed for CFSP to work – the British and the French – were both opposed to the communitarization of foreign policy, with the result that the other governments had little choice but to strike a deal that was close to the 'ideal points' of London and Paris. In other words, pillarization is to be explained by the distribution of power and preferences in the 1991 negotiations.

Although this is a compelling and parsimonious account, it neglects the degree to which the negotiation over pillarization was always something of a 'phoney war': proposals for communitarization and pillarization were remarkably similar in their detail; in the distribution of roles and powers they anticipated between the institutions of the new European Union. Both sets of proposals in effect anticipated the decanting of the old EPC into a system of foreign policy co-operation based on the Council of Ministers. Neither would have allowed the Commission an exclusive right of initiative, though both formalized a role for the Commission that was already becoming a matter of everyday practice under EPC.

That all parties to the TEU negotiations should have converged on a bargaining 'core' shaped by the existing practices of EPC is easily explained by path dependence. Although the events that formed the immediate backdrop to the TEU negotiations might have suggested the need for a radical overhaul, EPC was covered by just those conditions where path-dependence sets limits to any deviation from existing practice. Following Paul Pierson, we might characterize these as high start-up costs, positive externalities, prior convergence of actor expectations around solutions to co-ordination problems, and an opaque policy-making environment (Pierson, 2000, p. 254). To understand the relevance of all this to the decision to use the pillarization formula for the new CFSP (and JHA), consider two possible alternatives to the latter: the member states could either have agreed to establish an integrated foreign policy bureaucracy at European level or they could have decided to do nothing at all, effectively continuing with the SEA provisions for foreign policy collaboration.

From a point of view of high start-up costs, the transition to CFSP was negotiated against a background in which EPC already represented twenty years of investment in the steady development of a dense system of foreign policy co-operation. As seen, this involved transgovernmental links between national foreign services at every level of their operation. Whereas there was no guarantee that the knowledge and expertise associated with foreign policy co-ordination would be instantaneously or costlessly transferable to an integrated foreign service at European level, continued reliance on national foreign ministries for the operation of the new CFSP offered increasing returns on all the institutional learning that had already taken place within EPC. On the other hand, the problem of high start-up costs also cut the other way: if the twelve did not do enough to adapt their foreign policy co-ordination to a changing international environment and to mounting evidence of the shortcomings of EPC, there was a danger that stakeholders would lose interest and confidence, and that collaboration would migrate to other fora. Increasing returns on prior co-operation would then be lost and the set-up costs of European foreign policy co- ordination would have to be paid all over again in the event of interest being rekindled in the future.

Positive externalities occur where pay-off structures are shaped by the patterns in which actors combine, and not just by their individual actions. Pre-existing positive externalities had a clear influence on the choice of the pillarization structure. On the one hand, the new CFSP had to reproduce EPC's intimate connections with national foreign policy-making if it was to enjoy the positive externality of a clear link to existing patterns of security provision. On the other hand, it needed to be sufficiently integrated in to the European Union if it was to benefit from positive externalities associated with first-pillar policy instruments. Access to such instruments would require Treaty provision for those responsible for CFSP to meet and decide within Union frameworks, and for some kind of Council–Commission tandem. The latter, however, could not be centred on an exclusive power of Commission initiative if the CFSP was to continue to incentivize trans-governmental patterns of collaboration.

Adapted expectations are an important source of path dependence where there is strategic interdependence between actors: those who are unable to calculate the effects of their own moves without making reliable guesses about the reactions of others, are likely to stick to codes or procedures that stabilize expectations about the behaviours of others, or at least only to change them in the same way as a ship might be rebuilt at sea. Previously adapted expectations were important in two ways to the choice of pillarization as the institutional framework for the new CFSP. On the one hand, an arrangement that largely formalized existing practice minimized the risk of domestic opposition being mobilised around the formation of the new CFSP. On the other, it meant that the CFSP could evolve within existing understandings that non-EU powers had of the role of the twelve in the international system, and of the relationship between their national and collective foreign policies.

The final point – that the opacity of the external environment encouraged caution – might seem a less convincing argument than any of the others for regarding CFSP as a path-dependent development of EPC. Yet although international change loomed large in 1990–91, it was still too uncertain in its direction to translate into easy agreement on precise prescriptions for the further development of foreign policy co-ordination. The result was not only that much of the CFSP Title of the TEU concentrated on codifying existing practice. It also left options open, notably by anticipating that the new CFSP would be the centre piece for a review IGC in 1996 (see above). This hedging of bets conformed to the mantra at the time that foreign and security policy in the post-Cold War world would require multiple overlapping frameworks. In a world no longer disciplined by superpower competition, it would be difficult to predict the location and circumstances of foreign policy problems and correspondingly prudent to work through a variety of frameworks with different geographical reach. At the same time new concepts of security emphasized complex patterns of causation in which threats to stability were linked to economic, political and social breakdown, as well as the possession of means of violence. On the one hand, this reinforced the case for making the economic instruments of the EC more easily available to foreign policy co-operation. On the other, it pointed to the need for any successor to EPC to sustain its links with conventional security providers, rather than gravitate towards a system exclusively geared to civilian diplomacy.

A note on changes introduced by the Treaty of Amsterdam

Although the Treaty of Amsterdam is beyond the scope of a book about joint actions under the TEU, it is useful to conclude by noting the changes to CFSP that were agreed in 1997. Since Amsterdam was a review conference, there is one sense in which its amendments to CFSP are strongly relevant to this book: they were at least partly based on experience with shortcomings in TEU arrangements.

Amsterdam attempts a clearer definition of the instruments available to CFSP by making it clear that 'joint actions' are for operational purposes while 'common positions' are general stances towards geographical regions or foreign policy themes. The new Treaty would also seem to increase the probability that majority voting will be used for joint actions and common positions by removing the mysterious and little-used provision in the TEU which allowed member states to decide by consensus whether they would employ majority voting at a later stage in their formulation of a policy. The new arrangement is that the Council will now be empowered to adopt a joint action or a common position wherever the European Council has decided that member states have shared interests in a 'common strategy'. The European Council will define the common strategy, its objectives, and the means available to it, by consensus. Once it has acted in this way, the Council of Ministers will, however, be able to use majority voting to decide on any follow-up joint action or common position. A related change is 'constructive abstention'. So long as member states do nothing to impede initiatives adopted by the majority, they need not be bound by them.

Amsterdam also attempts to improve the capacity of CFSP to execute decisions. The Secretary-General of the Council is to assume the role of High Representative for the Common Foreign and Security Policy. A new planning and early warning unit was introduced, and a declaration to the Treaty calls on member states and the Commission to co-operate fully, including with the provision of confidential information. The Treaty also creates a 'new Troika' consisting of the Presidency of the Council, the Secretary-General of the Council and the Commissioner responsible for external affairs. It is possible to imagine this providing a significant new source of inter-pillar co-ordination, but only provided two conditions are met: absence of tension between the three personalities engaged in the Troika; and the ability of each to command the confidence of his or her institution.

3
An Institutional Analysis of Pillarization

Introduction

The previous two chapters explained the pillarization structure that lies behind foreign policy collaboration in the contemporary European Union, and traced the origins of both CFSP and the pillared framework to the old process of European Political Co-operation (EPC) as transformed by the TEU (1992). As seen, the remainder of the book aims to use examples of one of the policy instruments established under the new CFSP – joint actions – as test cases of pillarization in action. Before turning to the case studies it is, however, essential to clarify what they are intended to demonstrate. This should ideally involve the following: the identification of some central question of academic or practical significance raised by pillarization; the development of alternative theories capable of answering that question; and specification of indicators that would allow us to tell which of the theories is vindicated by the case studies

This chapter, accordingly, moves through the following stages. The first section argues that the main gap in current understanding of how CFSP operates within the pillarization framework would be best addressed by developing a full institutional analysis of the second pillar and its linkages to the first. In other words, it should be possible to expand understanding of how process is linked to policy output through further work in specifying the impact of the following as independent causal variables in their own right: arrangements for agenda-setting and the preparation of decisions; forms of role specialization in the decision-making process; the cognitive framing of decisions; the rules for the taking of decisions, whether formal or informal; and methods for implementing what has been decided. The second section argues that there are three approaches to the analysis of institutions that provide a good fit with the ontological characteristics of pillarization: rational choice perspectives; policy networks under bounded rationality; and garbage can models. These alternatives would, moreover, appear to be both exhaustive and mutually exclusive. The third and final section of the chapter moves on to set out the case studies. It begins with some aggregate information about the overall population of joint actions from which our sample is drawn. It goes on to discuss our selection of three of those joint actions for study in depth. It concludes with a detailed list of the indicators we intend to use in our evaluation of where the cases fit the theoretical alternatives.

Why conduct an institutional analysis of CFSP under pillarization?

The study of CFSP is one of those unusual areas of academic enquiry in which the 'what question' is analytically more demanding than the 'why question'. It often seems harder to determine the nature of CFSP, and give it secure classification within commonly-understood categories (Hill and Wallace, 1996, p. 1) than it is to offer explanations for why it has developed. Pillarization would seem to be the most obvious source of such ambiguities. As seen in the last two chapters, the development of CFSP within the TEU's pillarization framework has features of all of the following:

Intergovernmentalism, amounting to little more than an ever-changing matrix of member state preferences, unconstrained by the parameters of shared process. Under the Treaty specification of the second pillar, CFSP reproduces the 'doubly voluntaristic' character of EPC: agreements require unanimity and there is no mechanism to enforce them even where agreement is reached. The result is that member states still have a high level of discretion as to whether they will mediate a foreign policy problem through CFSP at all, or, indeed, whether they will continue to focus on CFSP, rather than redirecting the policy energies to an alternative framework.

Transgovernmentalism, formed through direct contacts between the foreign ministries of member states. What is striking about these contacts is, first, their intensity – the volume of 'traffic' that they are made to carry through the exchange of information and discussion of common positions – and, second, the way in which they link the foreign services of member states together at every level of their operation: foreign ministers, political directors, desk officers, delegations to other international bodies and embassies to non-EU countries. Some of these practices – co-ordination between national delegations to other international bodies and between member state embassies – are explicitly included in the Treaty specification of the second pillar. However, it is probably fair to say that the whole of Title V by which CFSP is defined in the Treaty needs to be understood against the backdrop of those transgovernmental practices that had already been developed under EPC (see above).

Supranationalism. This is most obviously present in the blurring of pillars one and two through resource dependencies that CFSP may develop from time to time on either the policy leverage of the formal Communities over the outside world (access of non-EU countries to the internal market, development aid, disbursements from the EU budget and so on) or on the administrative services of the Commission. More speculatively, processes that are formally intergovernmental or transgovernmental – such as working parties of national officials – may themselves be open to reclassification as supranational where a mixture of socialization and scope for discretionary action changes them from delegates of their national principals to policy entrepreneurs in their own right. The first of these supranational features is certainly reflected in formal arrangements for pillarization, inter alia, through provision for the Commission to have a shared right of initiative, its co-responsibility for inter-pillar co-ordination in matters requiring 'a rapid decision', arrangements to fund CFSP initiatives out of the EU's budget, and inclusion of Commission missions to third countries in the list of those agencies that are supposed to consult 'on the ground' in the implementation of CFSP.

Use of Institutional Theory to elucidate the operation of CFSP under pillarization is, however, open to two related objections. One is that it presupposes the very issue that is open to debate. According to this point of view, it is only if pillarization occupies a position towards the supranational-transgovernmental end of the spectrum, rather than the intergovernmental-transgovernmental one, will institutional analysis have any application to CFSP. A second – and not so very different – objection is that the most basic facts about CFSP are enough to warn us in advance that institutional theory is unlikely to have any purchase over the second pillar. The CFSP has almost no dedicated office holders; it has next to no bureaucracy of its own; it has no budget; and it has no means of legal enforcement.

Yet the core definition of an institution does not strictly require any of those things. Elinor Ostrom (1986) defines institutions as systems of rules that 'prescribe, proscribe and permit' and Oran Young (1989, p. 5) defines them as 'identifiable practices consisting of recognised roles linked by clusters of rules' The rules that comprise an institution must determine 'who and what are included in the decision situations, how information is structured, what actions should be taken and in what sequence, and how individual actions will be aggregated into collective decisions' (Kiser and Ostrom, 1982, p. 179). By unpacking these definitions it is possible demonstrate, first, that pillarization arrangements for the conduct of CFSP cover all the criteria for the application of institutional analysis; and, second, that the boundary between an institutionalized and non-institutionalized process is by no means equivalent to that between an intergovernmental or supranational one. Drawing on the definitions offered by Ostrom (1986), Young (1989) and Kiser and Ostrom (1982) the applicability of institutional analysis to pillarization arrangements for CFSP might be defended as follows:

1. Pillarization arrangements for CFSP have distinctive effects on 'who is included in decision situations' (cf. Kiser and Ostrom's 1982 defition of institutionalization). As seen, the question of who is included in foreign policy decisions had already been dramatically altered by EPC (1970–93), which supplemented more conventional self-contained forms of national foreign policy-making with multinational working parties, information exchange, micro-EPCs in third countries and so on. The pillarization structure established under the TEU changed patterns of inclusion by authorizing the Commission to propose initiatives, and mandating it to take certain responsibilities for inter-pillar co-ordination (see above). In other words, formal rights of Commission access to foreign policy co-operation replaced more ad hoc blurring of the two processes.

2. Pillarisation arrangements for CFSP establish forms of role differentiation that are governed by rules (cf. Young's (1989) definition of institutionalization). Institutions can either assign similar roles to actors or differentiate them according to specialized functions or forms of expertise (Shepsle and Bonchek, 1997, p. 299; McCubbins et al., 1987). The following are examples of where CFSP does the latter: assignment of responsibility for external representation to the rotating Presidency;

the practice of inviting individual member states to work up policy proposals; the importance of the Commission in delivering pillar one instruments to meet pillar two objectives; dependence on particular member states to advance CFSP positions in other international organizations; and delegation of agenda-setting tasks to working groups. At least the first and third of these role assignments are, moreover, specified in the TEU's pillarization formula.

3. *Pillarization arrangements for CFSP have distinctive effects on the processing and storing of information about foreign policy problems (cf. Kiser and Ostrom's (1982) definition of institutionalization)*. Studies of foreign-policy-making bureaucracies emphasise the importance of standard operating assumptions and the use of analogies drawn from past experience in the making of new decisions. As an extension of EPC practices, CFSP exposes national foreign policy thinking to a wider range of assessments through COREU, Council Party working parties, and links between EU embassies in third countries. The *acquis politique* and the *receuil* can also be taken as evidence of CFSP developing its own sources of institutional memory. Pillarization, however, makes its own distinctive contribution over above any inheritance from EPC: by authorizing the Commission's 'full association' (European Commission, 1992, Article J9) with CFSP, the Treaty provisions for pillarization made it possible for the Commission to justify the expenditure of public resources on establishing a separate Directorate-General (DG1A) to manage its contribution to CFSP. The creation of a permanent foreign policy bureaucracy inside the Commission adds a new institutional dimension to the accumulation of standard operating assumptions, the processing and storing of information, and the injection of these things into the CFSP process. These effects will be more important in proportion to the use CFSP as an arena for discovery and deliberation, rather than the mere bargaining of preferences.

4. *Pillarization arrangements for CFSP contain rules that 'prescribe, proscribe and permit' (cf. Ostrom's (1986) definition of institutionalization)*. The previous chapter cited examples of EPC as a rule-governed activity. The TEU provisions add their own raft of prescriptions, prohibitions and permissions. These range from the general – that member states should, for example, 'refrain from any action ... which is likely to impair its (the Union's) effectiveness as a cohesive force in international relations (European Commission, 1992, Article J1) – to the specific – that joint actions should, for instance, 'commit member

states in the positions they adopt and in the conduct of their activity' (European Commission, 1992, Article J3). Whether the focus is on the informal rule-accumulation inherited from EPC, or on obligations that the Treaty parcels out between the various actors in the pillarization process, there are, of course, grounds to be sceptical as to how far CFSP really is grounded in prescriptions and proscriptions. Lack of legal enforcability provides one obvious objection. Yet, rules may shape behaviour in the absence of enforcement, specifically, as deeply internalized norms of appropriateness (March and Olsen, 1984), or as prudential norms that actors follow through their self-interest in effective collective action and reciprocal favours from partners. Nor even do high-profile examples of defections from the rules of CFSP support the conclusion that they are of no importance. Defection will always involve a cost. Apart from loss of reputation as a trustworthy partner, defection from an agreement reached in CFSP mean abandoning a position that has status as part of the Union's foreign policy, without which no claim can be made on the administrative resources or policy instruments of pillar one.

5. *Pillarization arrangements for CFSP have distinctive effects on 'what considerations are included in decision situations' (Kiser and Ostrom's (1982) definition of institutionalism).* In comparison with national foreign-policy making, pillarization does not just change the identity of who is involved in decision-making: it also changes what is considered in fundamental ways. The first reason for this is that pillarization shifts the policy initiative into a less structured setting than is typical of national foreign policy-making, where, in several member states, it is still possible for a core executive of just a few individuals to maintain control of policy development. A second factor is that the obligation to consult, multiple practices of information exchange under CFSP and the role of the Presidency as a broker effectively allow each member government to place itsems on the national foreign policy agendas of its partners. A third is that the movement of an issue from a purely national setting to CFSP changes the manner in which foreign policy problems and solutions are framed: it institutionalizes reflection on how national foreign policy issues interact; on the likely 'external effects' of individual foreign policies on other member states; an on policy spill-overs between the pillars. A fourth and neglected factor is that pillarization may encourage member states to experiment with new patterns of delegation in policy framing. This may, for example, happen where the knowledge needed for effective policy-making is specific to those – the

Commission or groups of experts – with a permanent presence in the European arena.

Designing an institutional analysis of pillarization

A possible starting point for an institutional analysis of pillarization arrangements for CFSP is with the foreign policy analysis (FPA) literature. Since Grahame Allison's path-breaking work, the *Essence of Decision* (1971), FPA has invested three decades of intellectual effort in isolating different ways in which the nuts and bolts of policy-making can influence actions and outcomes. Bureaucratic struggles between agencies for influence and resources, administrative distributions of responsibility and constitutional separations of powers between institutions, the systematic impact of institutionalized beliefs such as standard operating systems on the manner in which foreign policy problems are selected for attention and understood, arrangements for crisis management, and interpersonal dynamics have all been used to explain critical foreign policy choices (Allison, 1971; Jervis, 1976; Janis, 1982). The difficulty, however, is that this substantial body of research cannot just be taken 'off the shelf' and transposed to the study of joint actions developed within the Union's pillarization structures. This is for the simple reason that most previous efforts at FPA have assumed that foreign policy is a peculiarly state-like activity. That is to say, it requires a monopoly of legitimate violence, and centralized and hierarchical decision-making, capable of speedy reactions and the mobilization of massive societal resources.

The implication is that we need to develop new approaches to FPA that are specifically adapted to what we have defined as the ontological conditions of pillarization arrangements for CFSP: non-hierarchical decision-making in a setting where transgovernmental and even supranational actor formations supplement more self-contained practices of national foreign policy-making. In the pages that follow we show how three models of policy-making – rational actor models, policy networks, and garbage can models of decision-making – are compatible with non-hierarchical decision-making based around variable actor formations. These models will be shown, however, to have two further features of use to a research project: first, they yield very different predictions about the behaviours and outcomes that are likely to be associated with CFSP; and, second, they span a spectrum, with one assuming high actor rationality (rational actor models), another that rationality is patchily developed amongst policy experts (policy networks), and a third that actors stumble around in a fog of imperfectly understood means-ends relationships (garbage cans). The implication of the first of these features is that it should be possible to test which of the models best captures the operation of the pillarization process, when and where. The implication of the second is that the alternatives are exhaustive and mutually exclusive. We now examine each of the models in turn.

A rational model of CFSP under pillarization

Rational models of decision-making assume that actors have complete and consistent preferences; thay they use information efficiently; and that we can, therefore, model and predict political behaviour as an attempt to maximise precise objectives within known constraints (Tsebelis, 1990). This does not mean that actors consciously enter into calculations of such a kind. They may achieve rationality without realizing it, first, through continuous adjustment to competitive pressures and, second, through the use of simplifying rules of thumb that are efficient on average.

In any complex decision-making setting such as CFSP it may, however, be difficult to determine who should be treated as the efficient maximizers for the purposes of analysis: the individuals who participate in the shaping of joint actions? The departments and agencies which pay their salaries? Or the governments or Union institutions they represent? Foreign policy analysis based on rational choice would usually incline towards the third possibility, first, because there are strong competitive pressures on governments to represent coherent and agreed views; second, because each democratically elected government has mechanisms for reaching final and authoritative views on what its foreign policy should be, even if particular individuals and agencies are occasionally inclined to pursue frolics of their own.

At first sight, rational models might seem to be institution-poor: efficient and rational actors ought in principle to be able to solve collective action problems simply by bargaining and communicating themselves. Andrew Moravcsik's application of rational models to the history-making deals in European integration thus attempts to demonstrate that explanations of outcomes can be reduced to the preferences of the principal member states and power distributions between them. Not only, in Moravcsik's view, is the institutional framework comparatively unimportant, he sees little need for specific theories of European integration, since bargaining behaviour is much the same as it would

An Institutional Analysis of Pillarization 55

be in any other international setting in which states operate to optimize their preferences (Moravcsik, 1991, 1993 and 1998; Moravcsik and Nikolaides, 1998).

Yet, there is an alternative strand of rational theory which does attribute considerable causal importance to the institutions through which decisions are mediated (Peters, 1999). To understand institution-rich rational theory it is best to begin by clarifying one thing it has in common with its institution-poor counterpart. Both predict that actors will choose to construct common institutions to save transaction costs involved in the negotiation, production or enforcement of 'club goods' (benefits that can only be produced by collective action). Institutions, therefore, exist to reduce incentives to cheat; to increase the credibility of agreements; to facilitate profitable bargains that would otherwise be discouraged by asymmetries of information and the difficulties in arranging simultaneous performance of obligations; to prevent efforts to 'create value' being consumed by arguments over the 'distribution of value' (Haas, 1992); to introduce procedural order to a multidimensional decision-making process that would otherwise have no unique point at which one majority of actors can conclusively beat all others (Arrow, 1951; McKelvey, 1976); to fill in the detail of agreements that are incomplete at the time of their signing (Williamson, 1985 and 1996); to allow actors to specialize and divide their labours in the confidence that there are incentives and enforcement mechanisms to ensure that others will deliver their contribution to the club good (Shepsle and Bonchek, 1997, p. 311). What, therefore, unites institution-rich and institution-poor versions of rational theory is a view of institutions as instruments of achieving pre-existing actor preferences. Observance of rules is calculative rather than moral (Peters, 1999, p. 46). Institutions are created and shaped according to what is the most efficient means of realizing preferences that would exist even if the organizations in question had never been established. They are places where actors go to get what they want, not where they go to find out what they want by learning or influencing one another.

Where 'institution-rich' approaches differ from 'institution-poor' approaches is in their prediction that once inside institutions individual actors will find them significantly constraining of political choices and behaviour. All rules for setting agendas and taking decisions drastically limit the range of possible outcomes once we assume that actors are optimizers and rules reduce indeterminacies (Shepsle, 1989). All conceivable divisions of labour and delegations of responsibility have substantive policy implications, since the costs of continuous supervision define an area where agents have discretion to introduce preferences of their own (McCubbins, Noll and Weingast, 1987) Almost all institutions have the effect of linking games into sequences across time and networks of arenas, with the result that rational actors are constrained to change their behaviour in order to maximize across a range of games, often choosing a suboptimal approach to some games in order to improve their pay-offs in others (Tsebelis, 1990, pp. 7–9).

Now that we have surveyed reasons why rational actors choose institutions, and why those arrangements go on to constrain rational actors, it is an easy step to use rational choice to construct an institutional analysis of pillarization arrangements for the conduct CFSP. A useful starting point is with the observation that policy delegation seems to be precisely what the Treaty text has in mind. Using the example of joint actions, the Council of Ministers decides whether a matter should be subject of joint action on the basis of guidelines from the European Council. It then lays down the specific scope of the joint action; the general and specific objectives in carrying it out; its duration; and the means, procedures and conditions of its implementation (European Commission, 1992, Article J2). At such a point it can specify various tasks that it hopes the Commission will perform and contributions that can be made using pillar one resources or policies. To be precise, a rational choice model would characterize joint actions as a two-step process of delegation: member states, each operating from a fixed view of their foreign policy interest, agree to delegate some task to the collectivity represented by the Council of Ministers; the Council of Ministers then chooses to parcel out various aspects of the task to a series of other actors, which may include the Commission, the Rotating Presidency, particular member states, special envoys and so on.

Member states will bargain with one another to lay down the instructions in the joint action. Rational theory would predict that they do so from fixed preferences. If there are any shifts in negotiating positions this will not be because any one government has convinced another to change its mind about its foreign policy interests. It will either reflect changed views of the means that are most likely to secure those interests, or forms of issue linkage in which governments are persuaded to lower or raise their price for agreeing to the joint action in exchange for concessions elsewhere. Given unanimous decision-rules, there should be no instance of a joint action that is is not pareto-improving: all joint actions should ultimately be explicable as part of a pattern of political behaviour that leaves all member states at least as well off as before. The analyst should, therefore, be able to identify clear evidence of the efficiency gain in any decision to pursue an action jointly through CFSP. Where those gains are unevenly distributed across members or outweighed by costs, the analyst should also be able to show that the joint action was accompanied by side-payments (compensations), or that those who lost out went along with the joint action because they would have been still worse off in terms of realizing their foreign policy preferences if a minority of member states had chosen to act on their own outside the CFSP framework.

So long as the pareto condition is satisfied in one of these ways, the rational approach would, however, predict that agreements on joint actions are likely to be closest to the ideal preferences of those member states with some combination of the following: a resource that is indispensable to the joint action; scope to achieve their own preferences by acting independently of the joint action; and a sufficiently intense preference for the joint action to dispense generous side-payments to achieve it. The first two conditions would tend to suggest that joint actions may tend to be closest to positions favoured by the larger member states.

A further implication of rational theory is that actors other than member states will only become influential in joint actions through 'agency loss' (Kiewiet and McCubbins, 1991). Each instance should be explicable as one in which the costs of enforcing obedience outweigh the costs of allowing the agent to exercise discretion. Both agents and principals can be expected to play this game to their advantage: the principals striving to attach a series of low-cost compliance mechanisms to those responsible for various tasks under joint actions, but otherwise accepting that some loss of control is the price that has to be paid for delegation; the agents understanding that they have some margin to pursue objectives of their own, but otherwise being careful to follow the terms of the mandate (Pollack, 1997). Amongst advantages to the member states is that they can at any stage amend or revoke the terms of policy delegation established under a joint action: as the Treaty puts it, the Council may review the 'principles and objectives' of the joint action if there is a 'change in circumstances'. As seen the Council also has scope to choose different patterns of policy delegation on a case-by-case basis. Requests to devise policy initiatives can, for example, be addressed to the Commission, Rotating Presidency or member states. Amongst advantages to agents, on the other hand, is that the Council consists of multiple principals.

Although rational theory would predict that actors only have 'calculative reasons' for keeping to their obligations under joint actions, or following the norms of CFSP more generally, it by no means follows that compliance is likely to be low, or that decisions to give agreements the formal status of a joint action under the Treaties has no effect on the probability of actors delivering on their promises. The very act of delegating a matter to CFSP under a joint action changes the pay-off matrix for each member state. Although withdrawal will be possible, it will, as was seen above, be free of cost.

Rational models have mixed implications for the coherence of the pillarization process. Actors who make good use of information should have little difficulty in co-ordinating their activities across the pillars in order to maximise pay-offs, especially when *ex hypothesi* joint actions are only likely to be agreed where they offer significant efficiency gains that are understood by all. A further point is that although pillarization departs significantly from practices of foreign policy-making through integrated command structures to be found in state bureaucracies, rational theory suggests that it remains hierarchical in one critical sense: for all the shifting loci of policy delegation, the member states – acting through the European and General Affairs Councils – are the principals and the rest agents in the process. On the down side, however, rational models might highlight a series of reasons why the pillarization structure might be expected to have a lower capacity to solve collective actions problems than more integrated Community structures: first, even where rational actors can identify all possible gains from co-ordinating policies across pillars, they may still be deterred by the transactions costs of arranging it; second, and most important, the absence of an enforcement mechanism in the intergovernmental pillars, will mean that many mutually profitable forms of co-operation may fail to develop because actors cannot remove uncertainty about the delivery of promises.

A policy network analysis of CFSP under pillarization

The starting point for this interpretation is that rationality is so costly to acquire that it only develops patchily amongst small groups of experts. Because informed policy-making often requires specialist knowledge, power slips away from top positions in political and administrative hierarchies to those who devote their professional lives to the study and management of specific policy areas. But because effective policy-making in pluralist societies also requires the co-operation of an increasingly wide array of different institutions and 'actor-types', the corrosion of vertical command structures within institutions is matched by a growing need for lateral links between them. This further reinforces the role of middle-level experts and policy-makers. Where co-ordination problems used to be solved by being 'passed up' the administrative hierarchy to some arbitrating body – often the core executive of a national government acting out the state's role as the final source of legitimate authority over all other relationships in society – they can now only be solved by those who are experts in particular fields making direct contact with one another across all kinds of institutional division: those between departments of the same government; those between different governments; those between supranational and intergovernmental bodies; those between governmental, non-governmental and quasi-governmental agencies; those between the private and public sectors.

In sum, therefore, the core of the claim that governance is being transformed into a web of policy networks is that because resources needed to achieve objectives are distributed between institutions, multiple layers of governance, and different kinds of actor, the real locus of decision-making can no longer be found in any one body (Peterson, 1995; Rhodes, 1996). Rather it lies in a series of networks set up to solve co-ordination problems between them. Individual network members rapidly acquire a measure of autonomy of their institution of origin; first, on account of their specialist knowledge; and, second, because only they can deliver the co-operation of the network in the institution's objectives.

Although the experts from all these bodies will only be able to solve their collective action problems by 'mixing their instruments' (Wessels, 1992 and 1997), the only basis on which they can do this is through mutual persuasion: no actor is in a position to compel compliance from another. Rather than negotiate agreements on a case-by-case basis they can, however, be expected to form themselves into policy networks or communities. These are likely to be minimum coalitions in the sense that they only include those with resources that are needed if other network members are to achieve their objectives. Their internal politics are likely to be characterized by a distinctive combination of consensus and competition (Héritier, 1997). The consensual aspect derives from the fact that members have a shared commitment to the same policy area, and are strategically interdependent if they are to achieve their individual goals. In some cases networks may even approximate to 'epistemic communities' where actors have shared standards of validity (what counts as good policy) and agreed views of the cause-effect relationships that link decision-making technologies in their area of special expertise to desired outcomes (Haas, 1992). Yet, absorption is never so complete that members cease to be motivated by a wish to promote the goals of their different institutions of origin, not least because of the power of the latter to reward or sanction their careers. Consensus about creating value thus coexists uneasily with potential for dispute about dividing value.

CFSP has several features that suggest specialist policy networks may have a significant role in shaping its outputs. The last chapter showed how even from the early stages of EPC, foreign policy co-operation drew actors together according to their expertise. Working parties and COREU linked desk officers with specialist understanding either of geographical regions in world politics or of technical issues such as disarmament. Collaboration between embassies in third countries or between delegations to other international organizations cemented contacts between those whose specialized concern was external representation or multilateral negotiation in specific contexts.

A further feature that fits the policy network model is that organizational boundaries become increasingly unclear with movement from the apex to the base of the CFSP pyramid. As seen, even the highest levels of decision-making are characterized by Commission involvement and a blurring of the formal institutional demarcation between the EC and EPC has been less than watertight. Second, working groups frequently seem to be obliged to treat their own work as only strand in a web that needs to be woven in with all kinds of other bodies stretching well beyond CFSP and even beyond the public–private divide. Third, the working groups not only have to draw in outside resources, there are also many instances in which they have had to subcontract governing functions to complex and variable actor configurations. Fourth, micro-CFSPs in third countries may involve collaboration on the ground that involves actors other than officials from member state embassies and from Commission delegations.

The absence of any pattern in these examples is also unsurprising from a policy network perspective, which implies that a different governance structure may well have to be assembled for the solution of each policy problem. Whatever the institutional formalities and their associated fictions as to how policy is made in some stable and repeatable fashion, the practice is that participation structures – and role allocations – have to be adjusted until they embrace a coalition of all those whose resources are needed for the delivery of goals in the specific policy area in question.

The policy community approach offers a distinctive interpretation of pillarization. The impact of formal institutional divisions either between the pillars or between the national and European levels will be softened by common membership of specialized policy communities that cross-cut them. Although joint actions are likely to be handled by a large number of bodies, the chances are that they will be managed by a small number of individuals, who are likely to be of comparable standing and experience, to be in constant communication across the administrative divide, and to operate from a shared knowledge base. They are also likely to see it as part of their professional commitment to network successfully, ensure policy delivery across agencies, and limit the need for decisions to be passed up the political ladder. If, it is true that the TEU mechanism for providing some central co-ordination of policy across the pillars – political directors from national foreign ministries prepare meetings of foreign policy Councils in full communication with the colleagues in COREPER responsible for pillar one Councils – has broken down (Ginsberg, 1997), the policy network approach suggests that a substitute source of co-ordination is possible, but at a level of middle-ranking officials with specific expertise, rather than administrative principals with frequent access to foreign ministers.

A 'garbage can' analysis of CFSP under pillarization

This model assumes that rationality is almost completely absent from organizational process with the result that outcomes develop through a mixture of chance conjuncture, inspired policy entrepreneurship and somewhat arbitrary devices for the making of decisions under conditions of extreme uncertainty. The starting point for the theory is that decision-making is characterized by uncertainties of preferences, technologies and of participants (Cohen et al., 1972; March and Olsen, 1984; Kingdon, 1984, 1995).

Actors are assumed to enter the policy process with only partially formed views of what they want. In so far as preferences are ever fully defined and stabilized, this is only as a consequence of debate, bargaining and feedback from policy experiments, not as as a prelude to these things. At Cohen et al. (1972) put it, preferences are formed through action and retrospective reflection on deeds and statements that are only imperfectly understood at the time of their making.

Nor do actors have a very good idea of the technologies by which their actions are translated into outcomes. The rules of the institutions in which they operate may be unclear. Cause–effect relationships that link actions to outcomes may shift constantly in a manner that is beyond their control or understanding. The result is that it is impossible for actors to come anywhere near the rational ideal of maximizing preferences subject to known constraints. To the contrary, cognitive studies into the political psychology of decision-making have highlighted the remarkable arbitrariness of methods used to guide public choice in frequently-found conditions of uncertainty. Simplifying doctrines, arguments from historical analogy, randomly selected experiences, and outright prejudice are everyday influences on policy (Kahnemann and Tversky, 1979; Nisbett and Ross, 1980). Some studies suggest that the conscious aspect of policy-making may almost disappear altogether, as actors adjust through a series of experiments and incremental changes that are only rationalized after the event (Simon, 1957; Steinbruner, 1974). Others point to systematic shortcomings in actor rationality or to persistent forms of bias in policy appraisal: a tendency for beliefs to persist even where the evidence that gave rise to them is disproved; a propensity only to notice that information which corresponds to pre-existing conceptual frameworks; exaggeration of the importance of agency over structure and context, including a tendency for actors to over-estimate their own importance either as originators or targets of policy.

Most curiously of all, actors may not even be sure of the identities of other participants in a decision-making process. Even in what is to outward appearance a well-defined institutional setting, attendance at particular meetings may be fluid, or interlocutors highly uneven in the attention that they give to one kind of decision rather than another. Overload, unclear role attributions, or confused division of labour are common causes of confusion as to who is doing what. This uncertainty will, moreover, compound the other two: if the preferences of others are part of the decision-making environment, it is necessary to know who other participants are before actors can maximize their own objectives; if preferences or understanding of problems and solutions are in part socially defined, the fluidity of interlocutors may mean that the policy process is only capable of punctured, disjointed equilibria.

The garbage can model predicts that agenda-setting and preference formation will be overlapping rather than sequential activities. Preferences are only transformed from vaguely desired states of the world to specifics as a result of active consideration of concrete options. In other words, the proposals come first and the preferences come later, with the implication that actor wants are heavily constructed within the policy process. This is in contrast to the rational view that actors only access institutions in order to ensure the delivery of largely predefined objectives. In circumstances in which preferences, technologies and participants are so uncertain it does not make sense for actors to invest much effort in making linkages between problems, solutions and opportunities, let alone to pursue the rational ideal of optimizing across the three streams. A tendency for problems, solutions and opportunities to develop independently will be reinforced by the political division of labour: elected politicians focus on the political opportunity structure, often without reading the fine print of technical solutions; and experts focus on working up solutions in their own specialist areas, without knowing exactly when they will be able to secure sufficient attention of politicians for the finance, legislation or other authorization of a technical initiative.

One consequence is that agenda-setting has an arbitrary quality. Many matters will fail to make it on to the agenda and the identity of those ideas that do receive active consideration will depend a great deal on the solutions that just happen to be around at the time that a problem arises. Such is the lead time in developing proposals that those actors who are able to respond to a pressing need with a ready-worked idea have a decisive advantage, even if the fit between problem and solution is less than ideal. Where there are windows of opportunity to launch new initiatives, agencies may likewise respond by simply dumping their pet projects into the policy process in the belief that the only sensible way of responding to fluid and unpredictable decision-making is to spawn as many initiatives as possible in the hope that some might get through. Yet, agenda-setting will not be governed by arbitrary linkages between problems and solutions alone. On the principle that in the land of the blind the one-eyed man is king, the failure of most actors to make plausible linkages between preferences and technologies may increase their dependency on policy entrepreneurship.

Of the models, the garbage can would probably have the most pessimistic implications for the prospects for coherence across the pillars. One obvious reason for this is that in spite of the sophisticated role attributions that are associated with the pillarization process, the latter falls a long way short of the arrangements that an integrated bureaucracy typically makes to overcome limitations on the rationality of individual actors (March and Simon, 1957): the emphasis is more on the exchange of information than on organising or testing it. In particular, there is no structured division of labour in analysis and assessment, or in the framing of problems and solutions. Rather there is open season on those tasks, which often seem to be conducted competitively with a view to capturing the CFSP process for national (or Commission) leadership, rather than with a view to accuracy. A second and related factors is that formal design of the pillarization structure may well be an invitation to policy overload. As seen, the TEU version of pillarization loads responsibility for the inter-pillar co-ordination on to the relationship between political directors – who do not even have permanent presence in the EU's political system – and COREPER. True, low- and middle-level policy networks may offer some compensation for shortcomings in co-ordination from the centre, but those networks are only likely to deliver inter-pillar coherence in the management of single foreign policy problems; they are less likely to deliver co-ordination across branches of foreign policy, or ensure that the sum total of CFSP activities blends into a consistent and effective attempt to achieve defined objectives. A third possibility is that pillarization approximates to the garbage model where it is associated with high uncertainty about patterns of participation in the policy process. Witness evidence suggests that there is some considerable unevenness in how far defined policy networks of those with all the necessary expertise to manage a problem stabilise around different functional or geographical arenas of foreign policy-making.

Using joint actions as case studies of pillarization

To recall from chapter 1 we offered two reasons why Joint Actions offer a particularly useful test of the TEU's pillarization structure. With this in mind, the remainder of this chapter provides a lead into the case studies.

An overview of joint actions taken since the TEU

Agreement of the circumstances in which joint actions would be used was not included in the TEU. It had to await a report to the Lisbon European Council of June 1992, which accepted that joint actions should be directed towards the settlement of international conflicts, the encouragement of stability and co-operation in other regions of the world, promotion of good government, support of democratic principles and institutions, assistance with international humanitarian efforts in emergencies, disarmament, regulation of the military technology transfers, and reinforcement of international restraints of nuclear proliferation, arms proliferation, terrorism and the narcotics

An Institutional Analysis of Pillarization   65

trade. The Treaty provision that joint actions should be developed where the members had 'interests in common' was made more specific by agreement that the latter would cover security threats to the Union, foreign policy problems in countries or regions contiguous to the Union, and other shared interests in the political or economic stability of a region (European Council, 1992).

At the time of writing, the TEU has been in force for some seven years. It is possible, therefore, to reach a preliminary overview of how joint actions have functioned. The following provided useful measures of their significance: the frequency with which they are agreed; the kind of foreign policy problem they are used to address; the areas of the world to which they are directed; the extent to which member states are prepared to commit resources to them; and the degree to which they engage with 'core' foreign policy issues. Needless to say, the last is the most difficult to assess, but, arguably, the most important of the list. Table 3.1 summarises data collected by the European Parliament on the frequency with which the various implements established by the TEU's chapter on CFSP have been used. Table 3.2 then categorises joint actions according to the areas of the world towards which they have been directed.

The following preliminary observations can be drawn from this data:

- Declaratory diplomacy remains the dominant mode of CFSP behaviour, dwarfing both common positions and joint actions
- Only modest resources have been allocated to joint actions, indicating that they are dominated by issues at the middling and lower levels of decision-making.
- Joint actions have been concentrated on particular regions. This could either suggest that the EU has a focused set of foreign policy interests, or that the legitimacy of its role is acknowledged more in respect of some theatres than others.
- There is, as yet, no indication of the frequency of joint actions growing with time, or that member states are prepared to move up the ladder from declarations to common positions and joint actions as they grow more familiar with the CFSP and confident in its operations.

To clarify the uses to which joint actions have been put and the problems they have encountered, it is useful to consider a few examples other than those which will be covered in our detailed case studies in chapters 4 to 6. In the joint action on humanitarian aid to

66 EU Foreign Policy beyond the Nation-State

Table 3.1 Frequency with which joint actions used in comparison with other instruments available to CFSP, 1994–97

	Joint Actions	Common Positions	Declarations
1994	14	8	110
1995	10	13	106
1996	21	10	116
1997	16	13	124

Source: European Parliament (1998).

Table 3.2 Areas of the world towards which joint actions directed, 1995–97

	1995	1996	1997
Africa	–	6	2
CIS	–	–	–
Middle East and Gulf	2	1	2
Central and Eastern Europe	5	6	4
Americas	–	–	–
Asia	–	–	–
Mediterranean	–	–	–
Others	3	8	8

Source: European Parliament (1998).

Bosnia-Herzegovina the Council decided in November 1993 to support the convoying of international aid, in particular through the identification, restoration and preservation of priority routes. In the joint action on the Palestinian Police Force, the EU committed itself to training police officers in the Gaza Strip and West Bank. A joint action decided in December 1993 aimed to support 'transition towards a democratic and multi-racial South Africa' by contributing a European Union Electoral Unit to election monitoring co-ordinated by the United Nations

A common feature of these three joint actions was ad hocery and confusion in financial arrangements. In the case of the joint action on humanitarian convoying in Bosnia-Herzegovina, ECU 32 million of the budget of ECU 48.3 m ended up being reallocated to financing the administration of Mostar. Conversely budgetary allocations originally intended for aid and development in West Bank were reassigned to the joint action on the Palestinian Police Force. In the case of election monitoring in South Africa an argument broke out between the British Government which argued that full costs for the joint action should come out of the Commission budget, and the Commission which successfully insisted on a 50:50 split between itself and the member states. It would, however, be a mistake to conclude that finance is the only resource available to joint actions. A 1996 joint action in support of Korean Peninsula Energy Development Co-operation illustrates the point. With a view to reducing risks to nuclear proliferation between the Koreas, the Council of Ministers decided not only to contribute to financing energy alternatives. It also agreed to make scientific expertise available.

A further example is the joint action on anti-personnel land mines agreed in May 1995. This promised the active co-operation of EU member states in the forthcoming conference to review the Convention on Prohibitions or Restrictions on the use of Conventional Weapons first signed in 1980. It also supported a moratorium on exports of anti-personnel mines. Two features of this joint action are worthy of note. First, it was one of the only occasions on which member states chose to make use of the Treaty provision allowing them to decide by consensus that they would apply majority voting to the subsequent development of a joint action. Second it illustrated a propensity to confuse joint actions and common positions: the Treaty envisages that common positions, and not joint actions, are the appropriate instrument for agreeing a CFSP ligne to be taken in other international organizations and conferences. A similar criticism might be associated with two further examples. A joint action was used to express support for the extension of the Non-Proliferation Treaty, and the main outcome of a joint action in December 1993 in support of a comprehensive Stability Pact in Europe turned out to be an international conference on consolidation of boundaries and rights of national minorities.

Other important examples are the joint actions adopted towards Rwanda and Burundi during 1994 and 1995. These were clear tests of the capacity of the Council to agree and develop joint actions under crisis conditions. In the Rwanda case, one member state, France, committed troops and much of the finance for the Joint Action. Yet the scale of the genocidal conflict on the ground was quite unequal to the willingness of member states to escalate their deployment of resources.

From the foregoing examples, it can be seen that joint actions have often been limited to uncontentious matters that are safely inside the value consensus of member states: humanitarian aid and election monitoring are obvious examples. Joint actions are also striking for the modesty of resources committed, and the difficulties of finding even limited sources of finance. With problems such as these in mind, Neil Winn (1997) has hypothesised that joint actions are only likely to emerge under the following restrictive conditions.

- The issue is relatively non-controversial and on a low level (European Parliament, 1997a, p. 7).
- The resources required are finite and time-limited (European Parliament, 1997b, p. 2).
- Coalitions can be mobilised between the member states (European Parliament, 1997c, p. 1).
- The 'receiving country' of the joint action is relatively content with EU intervention (European Commission, 1997).
- The EU institutions can agree on who pays and from what EU budget heading (Monar, 1997, pp. 57–8).
- Member states and EU institutions are able to agree on how the joint action should be implemented (European Parliament, 1997b, p. 5).
- Appropriate policy-networks can be set up ensure efficient policy-making and implementation (European Parliament, 1997a, pp. 6–7).

From the pool of joint actions undertaken between 1993 and 1999 we have selected three for in-depth case studies: the EU Administration of the town of Mostar (1994) in Bosnia; the EU's contribution to the implementation of the Dayton Accords (1995–98); and EU foreign and economic policy-making and implementation towards the Caucasus (1996–99). These cases were selected because they contain some interesting contrasts. On the whole, the joint actions involved different policy and organizational arenas, with the result that they were the responsibility of different personnel. In other words, the only common factor was the pillarization framework for the conduct of joint actions itself.

Case study methodology

Each of the three models has very different implications for more or less observable forms of policy behaviour: agenda-setting, patterns of actor participation, preference formation, political leadership, successful identification of means-ends relationships, implementation, the appraisal of feedback, and policy development and learning. This section, accordingly, develops a series of tests that will indicate which model bests fits particular case studies of joint actions. It then goes on to discuss our selection of case studies, our approach to difficult issues

An Institutional Analysis of Pillarization 69

of confirmation and falsification in case study research, and our use of interview material in gathering evidence.

Indicators suggestive of the the rational actor model:

(i) Agenda-setting is either explicitly led by the senior members of national governments (and the large ones at that), or, where other actors strive to put questions on the agenda, they do so within the known parameters of what is acceptable to the Council. Once again, Council preferences are both dominant and autonomous: they are not substantially influenced by other actors in the CFSP process. Moreover the preferences of individual members of the Council are bargained from relatively fixed preferences. They are not collegially formed through processes of mutual justification and shared learning.
(ii) The GAC can be said to dominate all other stages of the decision-making cycle through to implementation. A clear agency–principal relationship is discernible, with all other actors following the known preferences of the Council, if not its explicit instructions.
(iii) Joint actions are characterised by stable means–ends relationships: over the course of a joint action, objectives only change in response to developments that could not have been anticipated at earlier stages.
(iv) Joint actions are underpinned by efficient means–ends relationships. They make efficient use of the information available at any one time to identify those means most likely to provide optimal delivery of aims within prevailing constraints and resources;
(v) Preferences are exogenous to the process and well specified in advance. In other words actors do not form their objectives as a result of CFSP, the exposure it gives to the judgements of others, or to the 'psychic pay-offs' of consensus formation.

Indicators suggestive of the policy network model:

(i) At no stage of the policy cycle does any one actor-type dominate, political principals represented on the GAC or European Council included. This is because each actor-type needs resources that can only be delivered by others. Thus member states may need Commission co-operation where they wants to couple pillar 1 policies to the effective delivery of pillar two objectives.
(ii) Elements of shared analytical understanding develop between actors directly engaged in the delivery of the joint action regard-

less of the organization/administrative hierarchy to which they belong. There will, in other words, be shared causal assumptions of what policy instruments are likely to succeed or fail in the specialist context of the joint action, and why.

(iii) Although no one *actor-type* controls policy, there is a dominant *actor-level* in the formulation and execution of joint actions. Only middle-level policy-makers have the expert understanding and full-time focus to deliver policy objectives.

(iv) Those elements of epistemic community formed from within the network of middle-ranking specialists dominate the agenda-setting process. In other words, they frame the advice that is put before senior policy-makers. In place of supranational actors instructed by national actors, joint actions are critically shaped by the manner in which national decision-makers all receive strikingly similar advice from experts who constantly communicate with one another in stable policy networks.

(v) Preference formation is heavily endogenous. In contrast, to the garbage can model, however, preferences are well-specified and well-ranked, as a result of transnationally developed forms of expertise.

(vi) Communicative action dominates over strategic action. Actors are unable to shape joint actions by just bargaining national preferences. They are under continuous pressure to justify their preferences and proposals to one another as the best means of achieving widely agreed goals for the Union as a whole.

(vii) Coherence is achieved across complex actor configurations involved in the execution of the joint action, and that coherence is traceable to the networking activities of experts with shared professional commitments across formal institutional divisions.

(viii) There is an important element of path dependence both within the individual joint action and across joint actions. Joint actions are used as institutionalised contexts for shared learning about foreign policy problems. Policy networks of experts engaged in foreign policy-making have an interest in learning 'collectively' and not just 'individually'. This increases their future capacity for problem-solving and allows them to maintain control within their different governments/administrative hierarchies of origin. As there is, however, a cost of defecting from whatever are considered to be the shared lessons of the policy network, there is a classic pattern of path dependence: the costs of exiting from the policy rise with time, and actors may accept a substantial degree

An Institutional Analysis of Pillarization 71

of 'suboptimality', rather than damage their reputation as good partners, or sacrifice the steering/problem-solving capacities of a functioning and consensual network.

Indicators suggestive of the garbage can model:

(i) The preferences of key actors are not just heavily endogenous to the process, they are also problematic: that is, they change frequently and unpredictably throughout the course of a joint action; many actors do not have well-formed preferences in relation to important aspects of the joint action at all; there is little evidence that actors achieve a stable ranking between the preferences they use to justify a joint action, or that they anticipate ways in which preferences might have to be traded off against one another, unless and until choice is forced upon them;

(ii) Articulations of 'reasons' given for joint action grow are significantly vaguer in all foregoing senses before the decision moment than after it – that is, actors find out what they want through action, rather than act because they know what they want.

(iii) It is not even especially clear where joint actions come from: in other words, who thought of the idea first, when and why?

(iv) There is a good deal of confusion about both 'internal' and 'external' technologies. Confusion about 'internal' technologies means absence of clear and stable views about the procedures for joint actions themselves: confusion about who is to frame options and set the agenda; about the the appropriate scope of a joint action (that is, who is to be affected by the action); about levels at which decisions are to be made; and about rules that should govern decision-making including informal ones, such as when and where informal majority voting might be appropriate. There is even confusion about when decisions have been made and what they are.

(v) Confusion about external technologies means that attempts to specify means-ends relationships or resources are little more than guesses that bare little relation to subsequent evolution of the joint action.

(vi) There are fluid patterns of actor participation over the course of a joint action. Member states will vary in interest they give to a joint action. The locus of action will move between levels and agencies (Commission and Council, GAC and working parties of officials, even the EU itself and other International bodies) without such change being traceable to clear decisions on who should be authorised to act or take the initiative. As well as varying in their 'presence' across the course of a joint action, actors will vary in the intensity of their engagement, in the time, resources and interest that they give to it. This contrasts with the network assumption of continuously engaged experts.

(vii) In the absence of either well-specified interests (rational model), or shared understandings (network model), there is very little cross-pillar coherence in the formulation of joint actions

(viii) There is a disjointed pattern of path dependence within the joint action – that is, a pattern of 'punctured equilibrium'. *On the one hand*, radical uncertainty about preferences and the decision-making environment may lead to long periods of inertia in which joint actions remain much the same in their scope, means and resourcing, in spite of evident fluidity in what is expected of them, and unanticipated changes in circumstances. In contrast, to the network model there is little evidence of steady learning and adaptation within the joint action process. *On the other hand*, poor understanding of how issues are connected in the decision-making environment will often lead actors to destabilize or perturb the execution of the joint action without realizing what they have done until it is too late.

Approach to hypothesis testing

Karl Popper argued that a hypothesis could never be fully corroborated because of the impossibility of enumerating all instances of a phenomenon. Every swan that exists, has existed, or will ever exist must be found and examined in order to prove the hypothesis that all swans are white is true. In contrast, a single contrary instance is sufficient to falsify a hypothesis. The observation of one black swan is enough to falsify the claim that all swans are white (Popper, 1957). Many questions of social science are, however, as intractable to conclusive falsification, as they are to conclusive verification. This is, in part, the result of their probabilistic character; and, in part, because of their irreducible dependence on human judgement and observation, a point which is intriguingly acknowledged by Popper himself in a footnote to the *Logic of Scientific Discovery* (1957). With these problems in mind, we offer our own models and case studies as a kind of shared experiment with the reader. Although they are framed in positive language of verification and falsification, we acknowledge the dependence of our conclusions on judgements that we have made about goodness of fit. To attempt to do more than give full reasons for the judgements we have made, and invite the reader either to share or reject those appraisals, is in, our view, to pretend to a bogus science that is beyond the reach of case study research into policy-making processes that are non-reproducible.

4
The Mostar Joint Action, 1994: Agenda-Setting, Decision-Making and Implementation[1]

STAGE 1: CHRONOLOGY

Introduction

The Yugoslav conflict and its complexity challenged the international community to develop new strategies of conflict management and resolution, such as that evidenced by the unique European Union (EU) Administration in the central Bosnian municipality of Mostar. The Washington Peace Agreement of 18 March 1994, which forged a federation between the Bosnian Croats and Muslims, paved the way for the European Union's key new task. Following an invitation extended to the EU by the parties who signed the Washington Agreement, the Council formally decided on 16 May 1994 to carry out a major Common Foreign and Security Policy (CFSP) Joint action under the terms of Article J3 of the Treaty on European Union (TEU) to support the administration of the City of Mostar. On 23 July 1994 the European Union Administration of Mostar (EUAM) was established in the city, which had been heavily affected by the war. The EUAM's initial mandate was given for a maximum period of two years, with the aim of overcoming the city's ethnic division between Muslim Bosnians and Croats through a process of reconstruction and political and social reunification. This meant strengthening the implementation process of the newly created Muslim–Croat Federation. The City of Mostar, the former centre of a bloody ten-month 'war within a war' between the Bosnian Croats and Muslims, was to serve as a model of the obstacles which the Federation would have to overcome in order to ensure lasting peace in Bosnia and Herzegovina.

The following assessment explores the key question of the EUAM's capability to carry out its mandate of creating the conditions for democracy, economic reconstruction and human rights in Mostar. The objectives of the Joint action led to Council Decision 94/1790/CFSP of 12 December 1994 which advocated the creation of a single, self-sustaining and multi-ethnic administration of the City of Mostar under the supervision of the Council of Ministers of the European Union.

The chapter will also consider the extent to which the policy process in the case of the Mostar Joint action was characterized by varying degrees of rationality, bounded rationality, policy networks and/or garbage can agenda-setting, decision-making and policy implementation. The chapter also focuses on relationships between joint actions and related policies as an unusual policy-making method, actor behaviour, and policy outcomes.

Background

Before the war, Mostar was known for its ethnic diversity. With a population of 127 000, Muslims and Croats were nearly equal in population, and a sizeable Serbian minority comprised 19 per cent of the city's inhabitants. Mostar was representative of the multi-ethnic Yugoslavia Josef Tito strove for forty years to achieve (European Commission, 1997c). In May 1993, after the Croats and Bosnians jointly challenged the Serbian siege of Mostar, Croats turned against the Muslims and began a bloody ten-month conflagration. Both peoples defended Mostar as the place of their cultural heritage and used torture, forced expulsion, violation and murder to defend it. The Croats pursued the aim of controlling Mostar as the capital of their independent Republic of Herceg-Bosna. The result was the expulsion of 13 000 Muslims and the destruction of East Mostar (European Commission, 1997c).

When the EUAM began its work on 23 July 1994, Mostar, a city with a current population of about 60 000, was strictly divided up into the 70-per-cent-destroyed East, controlled by the Muslims, and the less damaged, Croat-controlled West. After three weeks of difficult negotiations with both military commanders of the town, demilitarization was carried out overnight under the auspices of Spanish United Nations Protection Force (UNPROFOR) troops, before the establishment of the EUAM. Since a Unified Police Force of Mostar was effectively not in existence and the mandate of UNPROFOR was too weak, the demilitarization of Mostar was already undermined by April 1995 (European Commission, 1997c). The EUAM team started working in difficult conditions, such as sporadic shelling of the city by Serbs from the mountains only 3 kilometres away from town, the decrepit state of most of East Mostar, the suffering of the population during and after the phases of open conflict, the breakdown of normal services and the collapse of the local economy. By June 1996, the leading British periodical the *Economist* referred to Mostar as being a 'Balkan Berlin' being divided by ethnic hatreds and by the presence of the Western powers along something like Berlin 'four-power' lines (*Economist*, 22 June 1996, p. 48).

Political assumptions

The *Invincible* peace talks

In September 1993, the Owen/Stoltenberg peace plan, which proposed a 'Union of the Republics of Bosnia and Herzegovina', consisting of three constituent entities, was negotiated on board the British warship HMS *Invincible* (European Commission, 1997c). For several months the three conflicting parties had not been able to reach an agreement on the questions regarding territorial boundaries, access to the Adriatic Sea, the Sava River, and the connecting passages between specified enclaves (Calic, 1995, p. 192). With the aim of finding an answer to these difficult questions, a document was drawn up proposing special administrative arrangements for the multi-ethnic, and, therefore, complicated Sarajevo district and the City of Mostar with the participation of the United Nations (UN) and the European Union. All three local parties in Bosnia and Herzegovina – the Bosnian Serbs, Bosnian Croats and Bosnian Muslims – accepted in principle that Mostar should be put under temporary EU Administration while a permanent solution to the problems of the city was being sought. The 'Agreement Relating to Bosnia and Herzegovina' stipulates that 'the period of European Community participation in the governance of the City of Mostar . . . is planned for two years' (United Nations, 1993).

In October 1993, while fierce fighting between Croats and Muslims was going on in Mostar, the Muslim Parliament rejected the Owen/Stoltenberg 'Confederation Plan'. They objected firstly to the percentage of territory allocated to them since it did not correspond to the Muslim percentage of the Bosnian population. Instead, it approved of the military situation on the ground.[2] Secondly, the Bosnian Serbs and Bosnian Croats were guaranteed the prospect of joining their mother countries later, while for the Bosniaks no similar opportunity existed (European Commission, 1997c).

The Bosnian-Muslim territories in the plural would have only a small chance of survival because its territory would be torn into several pieces linked by passages that were in dispute.[3] In addition to the rejection of the Owen/Stoltenberg peace plan, the 'Invincible Document', which established a European Administration in Mostar, also failed. The matter was left pending until the Federation of Bosnia and Herzegovina was founded a few months later. Following this failure of the 'Confederation Plan', EU Peace Mediator Dr David Owen, during a discussion with CFSP Commission of the European Parliament, expressed his disillusionment, saying that the scars from war atrocities might make separation along ethnic lines inevitable.[4]

The Washington agreement

Due to American peace efforts in February 1994, fighting ceased between the Bosnian Croats and Bosniaks. After a mortar shell struck the central market in Sarajevo, killing at least 68 civilians and injuring around 200 other persons, US President Bill Clinton launched a diplomatic initiative with the aim of preventing the spread of war in Europe. Also of special concern was the threatened 'strangulation of Sarajevo', by its Serbian besieger, and the interest in helping stem the destabilizing flow of refugees and displaced persons.[5] In addition, the credibility of NATO was in serious jeopardy (Rose, 1998). During the previous few months, the Bosnian Serbs had been outmanoeuvring the international force, without any determined reaction from NATO (Holbrooke, 1998).

After three weeks of intensive diplomatic efforts a skeleton agreement concerning the establishment of a Muslim–Croat Federation was mooted, and a later confederation with the Republic of Croatia was agreed. It was signed on 1 March 1994 by the Prime Minister of the Republic of Bosnia and Herzegovina, Haris Silajdzic, the Minister of Foreign Affairs of the Republic of Croatia, Mate Granic, and Kresirnir Zubak, the head of the Bosnian Croat delegation to the International Conference on the Former Yugoslavia (European Commission, 1997c). Under Title II, Part 8 of this agreement the idea of the *Invincible* peace talks, to put Mostar under EU Administration, was resumed (United Nations, 1994a).

Immediately a high-level Transitional Committee was established to work on: (i) the Constitution of the Federation; (ii) the Preliminary

Agreement of the Confederation between the Republic of Croatia and the proposed Federation; (iii) an agreement concerning military arrangements in the territory of the proposed Federation; and (iv) transitional measures to expedite the establishment of the Confederation and Federation. On 18 March 1994 the Constitution of the Muslim–Croat Federation, ensuring full national equality of the two constituent peoples, and the Preliminary Agreement concerning the later establishment of a confederation, were signed in Washington. President Clinton declared at the signing ceremony that these steps could help support the ideal of a multi-ethnic Bosnia and provide a basis for Muslims and Croats to live again in peace as neighbours and compatriots. Croats and Muslims who have fought with such intensity, President Clinton stated, 'must now apply that same intensity to restoring habits of tolerance and co-existence' (United Nations, 1994a).

In return for a Croat–Muslim Federation that would be tied economically, but not politically, to Croatia, the Bosnian Croats were required to rescind their declaration of the Republic of Herceg-Bosna, the independent Bosnian Croat state founded in autumn 1993. Supporting the idea of a Croat–Muslim Federation, Franjo Tudjman, the then President of Croatia, acknowledged the sovereignty and territorial integrity of the Republic of Bosnia and Herzegovina (United Nations, 1994b). In exchange for the waiver of a separate Croat Republic in Bosnia, the US pledged to help Croatia towards further integration into regional European economic and security systems and offered direct economic support as well. On 30 March 1994, the Parliament of Bosnia and Herzegovina unanimously approved the Constitution of the Federation, consisting of eight cantons, of which four were to be Muslim, two Croat and two mixed. Due to the lack of consensus concerning contested areas of formerly fierce fighting, it was concluded that the two peoples would have to share power in the disputed regions. One of those key contested regions was the Neretva Canton of which the City of Mostar was the capital (European Commission, 1997c).

Diplomats trying to bring an end to the conflict viewed the success of the Muslim–Croat Federation as *the* key to bringing a lasting peace throughout the region. There was the hope that the forging of the Federation would place pressure on the Bosnian Serbs, and would force them to accept a peace plan which would end the war (United Nations, 1994c). When the Bosnian Serbs refused on 3 August 1994, the division of Bosnia and Herzegovina into 51 per cent for the Muslim–Croat entity and 49 per cent for the Bosnian Serb entity, as proposed by the

International Contact Group[6] in July 1994, they definitively expressed their cancellation of membership of the Federation. Consequently, the 1500 Serb citizens of Mostar were excluded from the contract with the EU Administration (European Commission, 1997c).

The CFSP Joint Action in the Mostar case

Following the establishment of the Muslim–Croat Federation, the EU member states were of the opinion that their involvement in one of the cities most affected by the fighting between the Bosnian Croats and Bosnian Muslims, additionally the second largest city of the Federation, would help rebuild Croat–Bosnian co-operation and thereby strengthen the Federation (European Commission, 1997c). However, this would have to be achieved without exerting an overwhelming budgetary burden and workload on the small contingent of EU officials. Consequently, the Council of Ministers formally decided on 16 May 1994[7] to carry out a Common Foreign and Security Policy (CFSP) Joint action with the aim of supporting the administration of the City of Mostar.[8]

Within the Treaty of European Union (TEU) the Joint action was introduced as an instrument for pursuance and implementation of the aims within CFSP. Those aims include common values such as peace, the support of international security including the European Union and its member states, the promotion of international co-operation, the assistance of the principles of democracy and the rule of law, promotion of the principles of the market economy, and the safeguarding of human rights and fundamental freedoms.[9] With an agreed joint action, the member states bind themselves to active and unreserved loyalty and mutual solidarity.[10] A joint action is not only an attempt to agree upon the positions of the member states concerning specific issues. It is also an instrument to bundle all available means for its effective implementation together in order to guarantee a successful outcome, and therefore requires rigorous discipline among the member states (European Commission, 1992, 1997c).

The necessary preconditions for the realization of a joint action are an existing common interest (such as geographical vicinity of the concerned region or country), the existence of an important European issue that concerns the political or economical stability of a particular region or country, or the threat to EU member states' security. Since the Council has sole responsibility for declaring the general guidelines for EU action in international relations, adopting common positions and joint actions, and deciding on the financial means necessary for

80 *EU Foreign Policy beyond the Nation-State*

the implementation of the policies agreed,[11] it *theoretically* determines whether a matter should be the subject of a joint action, what the Union's general and specific objectives in carrying out such an action should be, and, if necessary, the means, duration, procedures and conditions for its implementation (European Commission, 1997c).

STAGE 2: MAPPING AGENDA-SETTING, DECISION-MAKING AND IMPLEMENTATION

Mapping the contributions of the different actors

The General Affairs Council (GAC) instructed the Commission to draw up a report on Mostar in August 1994 on the EU's Administration of Mostar. The report was presented to the GAC on 23 January 1995 and discusses the first six months of EU administration. The report noted that the town remained 'totally divided' between Bosnians in the East and Croatians in the West. The Croatians are blamed in the report for slowing down Muslim–Croatian joint police patrols. This prevented free movement between the two sides of the city. The report states that amongst measures taken since July 1994 have been the following: aid to 12 companies to the value of DM3 million; help to repair the telephone network; distribution of water and electricity supplies; re-opening of schools; and the distribution of meals. The GAC further discussed Mostar at the Rome meeting on 17–18 and 27 March 1996. It was decided to have an international donor conference for Mostar in particular and Bosnia in general. On 3 October 1996, a GAC meeting was held with Carl Bildt in attendance as High Representative and Sir Martin Garrod as EU Special Envoy in Mostar. A two-year strategy for implementing the peace was devised. ECU 231 million out of a possible ECU 306 million had been committed to Bosnia for 1996. On 26 October 1996, the GAC significantly laid down a 'regional approach' to cover Croatia, FRY, Bosnia, Albania and Macedonia. Mostar was to be a test case as an ethnically mixed city.

The European Union Commissioner for External Political Relations, Hans Van den Broek, was active in the following ways: The Commissioner met with the EU Representative in Mostar, Hans Koschnick, to review how ECU 150 million have been spent in Mostar on 19 January 1996. On 22 January 1996 the Commissioner placed conditions on FYROM to co-operate with the War Crimes Tribunal on Former Yugoslavia. This was also agreed with Hans Koschnick. On 26 January 1996 the Commissioner visited Croatia and had talks with President Tudjman on Mostar: he reported back to the EU foreign ministers. Then on 29 January 1996 Commissioner Van Den Broek issued a Joint Communiqué with the Bosnian Premier Izetbegovic. The EU committed ECU 63.5 million for new infrastructure projects. On 3 February 1996 the Commission committed ECU 600 000 for mine clearance in former Yugoslavia. In an important meeting on 23 February 1996 Van Den Broek and Koschnick met to discuss the free movement of persons in Mostar. Then on 26 February 1996 Bosnia-Herzegovina was included amongst PHARE recipient countries for the first time. This was happening against the backdrop of the 2nd International Donors Conference on Former Yugoslavia. Significantly on 12 June 1996 a Joint action was launched by the Commission and Council to support the electoral process in Bosnia-Herzegovina. On 14 June 1996 Hans Van Den Broek adopts a package of ECU 102 million for reconstruction in Bosnia. On 2 October 1996, the EU Commission invited refugees wishing refugees wishing to return to Mostar to register their interest with the High Representative's office.

On 24 January 1996 the EU High Representative in Bosnia, Carl Bildt, and the EU Representative to Mostar, Hans Koschnick, proposed 1996 splitting Mostar into sectors along the Berlin model developed by the four powers in the years following the Second World War. This was not well received by the Bosnian Muslims. On 27 January 1996 Carl Bildt made a preliminary report to the Council and Commission on the implementation of the Dayton Accords in Mostar. A policy of regional co-operation was to be prioritized on the ground. On 12 February 1996 Assistant Secretary of State Holbrooke criticized Carl Bildt over the deployment of a Croat police force in Mostar. Further, at the Rome Summit of EU Heads of Government held on 19 February 1996, a six-month extension to the EU Administration of Mostar was granted.

The EU Representative to Mostar, Hans Koschink, refused the division of Mostar into different ethnic zones on 8 January 1996. Carl Bildt instead announced a Joint Civilian Commission for Problems in Sarajevo as capital city. Nevertheless, by 24 January 1996 the EU Administrator in Mostar proposed splitting Mostar into occupation zones organized along ethnic lines. Then on 25 March 1996 Mr Perez Casado replaced Mr Koschnick as the EU Representative in Mostar. Throughout these developments, there was a continuity of policy generally, and a change of personnel did not lead to a change in EU policy on the ground.

On 12 February 1996, the Chair of the European Parliament Committee on Eastern and Central Europe, Doris Pack, demanded more efficient implementation of the civilian aspects of the Mostar accords on the ground. This could only be achieved with adequate security on the ground. In conjunction with the WEU, the EU contributed in 1996 to the training of a new police force for Mostar drawn from the different ethnic groups. A total of 380 officers were trained, with authority for the new force being formally handed over to the Republic of Bosnia on 15 October 1996. On 16 March 1996 the European Parliament approved ECU 95 million for extending the PHARE programme to Bosnia and Mostar in particular to back up political with economic reconstruction.

Mapping agenda-setting: the EUAM mandate in Mostar

Aims, objectives, and principles of the joint action

With reference to the invitation extended to the European Union by the parties who signed the Washington Agreement, the EU Administration drew its mandate from the Memorandum of Understanding (MoU). The MoU was signed on 5 July 1994, by the EU, the Western European Union (WEU) member states, and the various parties involved in the former conflict.[12] The MoU clearly sets out various aims and principles to be achieved by the EU binding the parties concerned. Article 2 of the MoU defines the objectives as follows:

- to give the parties time to find a lasting solution for the administration of the Mostar city municipality;
- to contribute to a climate leading to a single, self-sustaining and multi-ethnic administration of the city;
- to hold democratic elections before the end of EUAM;
- to assist in the return to normal life in the city;
- to restore public utilities;
- to ensure the protection of human rights;
- to enable the return of refugees and displaced persons;
- to assist in organizing and providing humanitarian aid;
- to prepare and implement programmes for economic reconstruction;
- to ensure the maintenance of public order;
- to re-establish all public functions;
- and to ensure the national, religious and cultural identity of all the people in the area under EU Administration in compliance with the Constitution of the Federation of Bosnia and Herzegovina. (WEU, 1997c)

Although the objectives in the MoU were not quantified, which makes the evaluation of progress difficult, they were wide-ranging and apparently ambitious vis-à-vis the situation of continuing conflict, ongoing mistrust and tension between the parties (European Commission, 1997c). Consequently, the aims and principles were further developed in a strategy document dated 13 May 1995 and prepared by the Administrator, the former Swedish Prime Minister Carl Bildt (European Commission, 1997c). Although the EUAM was not explicitly required to achieve a single administration for Mostar, the position of the member states leaves no doubt that a single administration remained its fundamental goal. The main criteria in the EUAM strategy document considered fundamental to the commonly accepted concept of a unified city included:

- a population willing to live under a common set of rules;
- a central municipal authority acceptable to the population;
- a common legal framework and guaranteed rights for all citizens independent of religion, language and culture;
- a common public service tax system;
- a common police force;
- and freedom of movement (European Commission, 1997c).

The principal assumptions against which the overall EUAM strategy document was prepared were that:

- the Federation between the Bosnians and the Bosnian-Herzegovinan Croats would remain intact and further developed;
- the United Nations Protection Force (UNPROFOR) would remain in the region with its existing strength unchanged;
- the shelling of Mostar by the Bosnian Serb Army (BSA) would not reach a level that rendered the task of the EU Administration impossible;
- and the EUAM would progressively build the confidence of the citizens of Mostar and not be obstructed in achieving its aims and objectives by any of the different parties (European Commission, 1997c).

The agenda of the proposed Joint Action, therefore, was subject to change between its initial conception, its development and final agreement. The action had to adapt to a number of exogenous and endogenous stimuli: member state bargains, specialist epistemic community influences, changes in personnel in key European and national bureaucracies, inputs from policy communities of experts, and daily changes on the ground in Mostar.

Agenda-setting: executive authority of the EUAM[13]

Article 4 of the MoU declares that the Mostar city municipality would be governed by the EUAM for a maximum of two years. The Administrator was to be the head of the Mostar city municipality (European Commission, 1997c). Former Swedish Prime Minister Carl Bildt was to have the powers necessary to fulfil the aims and principles of the EUAM while administering the Mostar city municipality appropriately, and efficiently, and in correspondence with the views and wishes of the local parties and population (Bildt, 2000, pp. 142–6).[14] In exchange, the receiving parties would assure their unrestricted commitment to support the EU Administrator in the exercise of his duties, as well as to work co-operatively towards the achievement of the aims and principles set out in Article 2 of the MoU.[15]

The Administrator received his instructions from the Council of Ministers[16] and operated in consultation and close collaboration with the local parties.[17] The Administrator was directly responsible for eight departments. Each EU official heading the eight departments[18] had 'two local Co-Heads, one Croat representative and one Muslim representative from the administrations in East and West Mostar, who were to be appointed by the Administrator'.[19] The Co-Heads did not have any operational responsibility within the EUAM itself. In addition, an Advisory Council, comprising five Muslims, five Croats and five representatives of other groups, out of which three were Serbs, advised the Administrator on all issues concerning the Mostar administration in weekly meetings. In terms of the daily workload the Administrator co-operated with the Principal Counsellors, the Mayors of East and West Mostar, and a Serbian representative.

After consulting with the Advisory Council and observing Part B, Chapter IX, Article 10 of the Federation's Constitution, the Administrator had the right to introduce regulations applicable in the area of the EU Administration if he deemed them necessary for the functioning of the EUAM (European Commission, 1997c).

A single police force, unified at all levels, was established under the authority of the Administrator. Following Article 13 of the MoU, the Unified Police Force of Mostar (UPFM) was entitled to organize, administer, direct, supervise and monitor some police functions, such as criminal investigations, public relations, handling of some sensitive inter-ethnic policing under supervision of the EUAM, routine patrols, traffic control, and the control of persons and goods. A Western European Union (WEU) police element provided the EU Administrator with information and offered advice on all aspects of public order (European Commission, 1997c).

Mapping decision-making

The role of the council presidency in decision-making: an agenda-setter in decision-making?

In accordance with the requirements of Article J5 of the TEU, and, as set out in the Council Decision of 16 May 1994, the Council Presidency decided upon the practical orientations of the operation, assisted by an Advisory Working Party of Member State Permanent Representatives and in association with the European Commission. In actuality, the Advisory Working Party acted as the de facto management body responsible for preparing the work of the Council and for carrying out the tasks assigned to it by the Council, as referred to Article J11 Part 1 of Title V of the TEU (European Commission, 1997c).

The Presidency also determined the precise actions required to meet the needs identified by the Administrator and decided upon the release of funds to the account of the Administrator. The Administrator was required to report regularly to the Council Presidency on his requirements, and in turn the Presidency kept the Working Party informed. Despite the fact that operational funding was provided from the EU General Budget, the EUAM was not specifically required to report on its progress to the European Commission (European Commission, 1997c).

Decision-making: pillarization and resources

The main decision-making stage revolved around relations between the EU institutions, individual European- and national-level middle-range civil servants, and an ad hoc group set up by the Council. The GAC provided a degree of leadership from above. Nevertheless, the Advisory Working Party acted as an interlocutor between the various institutions and EUAM personnel in Mostar.[20] Economic and political questions were dealt with, as Michael Smith has written elsewhere in more general policy terms, in a coherent manner across the pillars (M. Smith, 1996, pp. 247–62). Pillarization – the problem of different decision-making rules, contexts and related policy domains – was not a particular problem in this case.

On 15 April 1994, before the formal Council Decision on the Joint Action was taken, a three-person Advance Party – sent out by the Ad-Hoc Council Group – arrived in Mostar to prepare for the arrival of the administration. There was no formal Council Decision mechanism in place at the time to ensure that adequate funding was provided for the advance operation (European Commission, 1997c). To fund the Advance Party actions, during June and July 1994, loans totalling ECU 32 600 from the European Community Monitoring Mission (ECM) were arranged. Further cash amounts totalling ECU 53 000 were financed from the German federal budget. The Council then made a payment of ECU 100 000 from its administrative budget, which enabled the Advance Party to repay the EC's earlier loans. The Council classified the expenses of the Advance Party as administrative expenses under the terms of Article J11 of the TEU.[21] This decision made out of general principle was endorsed by the Council on 11 July 1994 (European Commission, 1997c).

The European Parliament has since pointed to the need for care in defining administrative and operational expenditure with respect to CFSP Joint actions, and in deciding from what part of the European Union budget such expenditure should be financed (European Parliament, 1997a). Since the work of the Advance Party formed part of the establishment of the action, the nature of the expenditure incurred can be regarded as operational. Such expenditure by the European Commission in other areas of the budget is normally financed from operational appropriations of the EU budget (European Commission, 1997c).

Until the Advance Party had succeeded in its mission, it remained unclear which department or individual within the Council or the Presidency was responsible for overall co-ordination (Court of Auditors, 1995, 1996). The Advance Party submitted separate reports to the Council Presidency. Nevertheless, many questions raised by the Advance Party at the time, when the Ad-Hoc Council Group negotiated the assigned mandate went unanswered (European Commission, 1997c).

While the Advance Party was laying the foundation for the EU's Administration of Mostar, the member states nominated expatriate staff on the basis of proposals for the organization of the EUAM made by the German delegation, including a suggested allocation of posts (European Commission, 1997c). The senior management team designed to implement the programme was established by allocating the posts between the then 12 member states, as well as Switzerland,

Sweden and Austria. There was no assessment of alternative candidates at the Council level, nor was the Administrator of the organization able to influence the composition of the team. The EUAM, including the ombudsman's office, was to be staffed by 39 expatriate civil staff, 6 additional staff, and a WEU police element eventually numbering 182 officers (European Commission, 1997c). The arrival of the staff in Mostar was not adequately co-ordinated with the Advance Party and this resulted in logistical problems. For example, without reporting to the Administrator, two humanitarian advisers were sent to Mostar, one from the European Community Humanitarian Office (ECHO) and another from Denmark. The two worked in parallel for three months until the Administrator obtained the approval of the Council Presidency for the appointment of a single humanitarian co-ordinator from Denmark (European Commission, 1997c).

A problem area in pillarization policy-making terms is related to the issue of finance. As Jorg Monar has written elsewhere, the problem of coherence and different decision-making rule systems in the first and second pillars exacerbates already difficult discussions on finance (Monar, 1996, 1997). In effect, decision-making takes place within the context of bureaucratic and rule-based dysfunctionalities that can encourage lack of coherence in decision-making, garbage-can-like decision-making, and bureaucratic problems of democratic control of decision-making. Nevertheless, as is stated above, in this case there existed a good deal of cross-pillar coherence in the decision-making stage of the Joint Action. The European Parliament attempted in the early- to mid-1990s to influence CFSP budgetary politics, but has failed to do so in the longer run. The CFSP budget is now under the 1997 CFSP Inter-Institutional Agreement, which gives the EP powers of consultation and information only. Nevertheless, in this particular case, a good degree of coherence did exist between second-pillar policy objectives and how they were implemented by first competencies.

The Council Decision of 16 May 1994 indicates the provisions for the EUAM budget as follows: the Administrator shall 'assess the requirements' and the 'means necessary' for the support actions of financing and shall communicate those particulars to the Council Presidency (European Commission, 1997c). On the basis of those particulars the Presidency, assisted by an Advisory Working Party,[22] issued guidelines, determined what measures were needed to meet those requirements, and decided to release the amounts necessary to finance them one *tranche* at a time.[23] The Council Decision also provided for an initial set-up budget of up to ECU 2 million to be used to finance the initial establishment and the subsequent joint actions relating to the new European Union Administration of the City of Mostar. Out of the ECU 32 million, ECU 15 million was initially made up from the Community budget.[24] The remaining ECU 17 million was provided by direct contribution from the member states, assessed according to the GNP24 key. On 31 December 1994, 4.9 million out of ECU 17 million owed by the member states (representing 15.2 per cent of EUAM's 1994 budget) was still unpaid (European Commission, 1997c).[25]

The 1995 budget for the EUAM was set at ECU 80 million and was entirely financed from the EU General Budget (European Commission, 1997c).[26] During 1995 the EUAM made revisions to its original budget in response to changes in the overall political situation. The most significant change was a reduction of the health and social services budget by ECU 12 million, which mostly represented funds no longer required for the completion and equipment of the Bijeli Brijeg central hospital, because of the absence of satisfactory guarantees regarding free access to it for all Mostar citizens (European Commission, 1997c). Budget provisions for transport and infrastructure projects were reduced as plans for two new bridges were postponed from 1995 until 1996. In contrast, public utilities and housing repair programmes, which had made more rapid progress than had been expected, had their budgets increased. In the wake of those budget revisions the procedure (based on Commission procedures normally applied to individual projects) was adopted by the Council, to transfer funds in three stages (European Commission, 1997c). However, the implementation of the new procedure led to cash-flow problems. One consequence was that the EUAM requested the advance of the second and third *tranches* of the 1995 budget before justifying the use of the advance of the first *tranche*, so that it could commit new projects and obtain funds (European Commission, 1997c). Finally, following a request from EUAM supported by the EU Court of Auditors, it was decided to simplify procedures by regarding all three budget years (1994, 1995, 1996) as one continuous project (Court of Auditors, 1995, 1996).

The 1996 EUAM budget (which covered a seven-month period up to the planned final end of EUAM operations) amounted to ECU 32 million and was again entirely financed from the EU General Budget. However, subsequent decisions increased the total available budget to ECU 144 million, amounting to ECU 2400 per person in Mostar – based on an estimation of 60 000 citizens (European Commission, 1997c). At an additional estimated indirect cost of nearly ECU 35 million, ECU 585 per person could be added to that sum. This represents an unusually high concentration of assistance compared to other assistance programmes in the world. International staff were supplied by member states, with staff monthly salaries and living costs paid directly by their countries of origin (European Commission, 1997c). The cost of these expatriate staff and police officials is estimated at approximately ECU 16.8 million per annum, excluding from the budget of the EUAM.

Mapping implementation: bottom-up and top-down perspectives

In considering policy implementation the analysis will focus on the means used to achieve implementation, on the issue of resources, and on shifts in objectives of the major actors involved in implementation. The analysis will then go onto consider some cases of implementation in the context of the Mostar Joint action.

Policy implementation in the Mostar case tended to be from the bottom up. Implementation structures emerged for a number of reasons. First, via resources exchange. In this case resources were made available by the member states and the Commission to achieve effective policy implementation by DG1A of the Commission on the ground in Mostar. Second, via power dependency. In this case the national governments were dependent on the Commission and vice versa for implementation. Additionally, official national and supranational institutions/actors were in turn dependent on their specialist advisers to make sense of policy. Third, through policy feedback and policy learning. Policy-makers adjusted policy at the core and the margins in order to implement something akin to a coherent policy – often depending on policy networks of experts to do so. Fourth, ad hoc implementation structures occasionally occur in that individuals are instrumental. They can often serve as the glue holding together a diverse network of actor interests.

However, so-called 'implementation gaps' emerged periodically. This is the gap between intention and reality in terms of what goes into the public domain in public policy terms. Such gaps can occur by accident, by intent or can emerge when an impasse occurs between policy actors. As Jeremy Richardson (1996, pp. 280–5) points out, a number of criteria need to be achieved in order to achieve perfect implementation (which rarely or never happens): external constraints need to be manageable; time and resources need to be adequate; the type of resources need to be appropriate for the task; there should be a valid theory of cause and effect in implementation; dependency relationships need to be minimal; objectives need to be clear and transparent; tasks need to be sequenced; communication is good; and those in authority can theoretically attain compliance by using authority and power. The following cases of policy implementation are liberally drawn from Sarah Reichel's recent excellent study on the European Administration of Mostar (European Commission, 1997c).

Implementing the Mostar Police Force and the question of public security: a key joint action implementation aim[27]

According to Articles 12 and 13 of the MoU, a Unified Police Force of Mostar (UPFM) was to be established with the support of 182 Western European Union (WEU) police officers to ensure public safety and freedom of movement in a unified city (European Commission, 1997c). Co-ordination of the UPFM was the first task the EU had delegated to the WEU since the ratification of the Maastricht Treaty (TEU), which called on the WEU to 'elaborate and, implement decisions and actions of the Union which have defence implications' (WEU, 1995). The WEU sought to restore and maintain peace, confidence, and individual civil rights within the overall mandate of the EUAM (WEU, 1995). Furthermore, the WEU was to build a framework which would ensure a smooth transition of the UPFM to local control when the WEU and the EU mandate expired. Further details were to be set out in a separate document as detailed in the MoU.[28] Due to resistance from the Croat side this important document of September 1994 was never signed.[29]

The WEU has been involved in Mostar since May 1994 when it sent a small police force to assess the possibilities of a larger operation (European Commission, 1997c). In June and July 1994, following reports from the advance force, the WEU began planning its operations. The result was a three-phase plan leading progressively to a unified autonomous police force. The following section heavily relies on Sarah Reichel's excellent recent study of the implementation aspects of the EUAM (European Commission, 1997c).

Phase I, the implementation stage, began in May 1994 when the WEU initiated its advance work. This phase had been scheduled to last five months, during which the WEU would define its responsibilities, begin recruitment, select and train the local police officers and implement the prearranged operational structure. Furthermore, it planned to establish combined patrolling, and a Joint Operations Centre. Due to Croat security reservations only very slow progress was made toward the establishment of the Joint Operations Centre. After fruitful talks between the Administrator and high-ranking diplomats of the Republic of Croatia and the Muslim–Croat Federation (concurrent with the first anniversary of the Washington Agreement in March 1995) most of the objectives of the first phase had been achieved by November 1995, though not the recruitment of local police officers (European Commission, 1997c).

Phase II, the operational stage, was due to begin in December 1994 and run for 15 months until March 1996. The objectives during this phase were to put police stations into operational use, develop links between the UPFM and legal bodies, and to extend integration from the command level to the operational level (European Commission, 1997c). On 18 September 1995 an agreement on the implementation of Phase II was reached and signed by the mayors and police officers of Mostar East and West, but due to Croat objections no progress was achieved.[30] When in the midst of the Dayton peace talks in November 1995, Franjo Tudjman, the President of Croatia, and the Bosnian President, Ali lzetbegovic, reached an agreement to strengthen the core of the Federation (NATO, 1995), Mostar was seen as the weak link (European Commission, 1997c).

There the agreement included a plan to accelerate the political integration of the city. The goals of ensuring freedom of movement, holding free elections in the city and the establishment of joint police patrols, at the heart of the operational stage, were set forth. This was one year later than the schedule proposed in the WEU document (European Commission, 1997c). Some violent incidents in early January 1996, following the deaths of Croat and Muslim police officers, underlined the problems the WEU had with the implementation of the joint patrols, which were to begin in January together with the establishment of complete freedom of movement (European Commission, 1997c). The violence, however, set back this schedule. At a February 1996 summit in Rome, the parties agreed to begin deployment of the joint patrols on 20 February 1996. To aid the WEU with unification of the police force, Croatian President Tudjman offered 100 police officers, and to balance those forces the Bosnian government also agreed to send 100 officers (European Commission, 1997c).

From then on, the typical Joint Patrol was composed of two officers from the WEU, one Croat, one Bosnian Muslim, one Mostar Croat, one Mostar Bosniak, and one interpreter. The Croat and Bosnian police, together with the WEU officers, helped to heal the tension among the Mostar police force, so that after their 20 February 1996 implementation, the joint forces functioned relatively smoothly (European

Commission, 1997c). In late April 1996, in accordance with the Dayton Agreement, the WEU opened the Joint Police Headquarters. Although the final phase concerning the transition and withdrawal was due to begin in March 1996, and end when the EUAM's mandate expired on 22 July 1996, Phase II was still running well into 1996 (European Commission, 1997c).

In Phase III, following an intensive training programme for the local police officers, the WEU was to be withdrawn and control of the police force gradually handed over to the local officials (European Commission, 1997c). Furthermore, the WEU police chief would be replaced by an elected police chief.[31] The UPFM would then theoretically be able to continue the same independent and self-sufficient role following the withdrawal of the EU Administration and the WEU Police (European Commission, 1997c).

Implementing freedom of movement in Mostar: a key issue of security

Due to Croat resistance, freedom of movement was from the beginning a stumbling point, beyond which no meaningful progress was made for one-and-a-half years (European Commission, 1997c). As a result, until 1 December 1995, the City of Mostar was almost totally divided. Because freedom of movement is essential for fulfilling the mandate laid down to bring life back to normal in Mostar, and to unify the city, its absence represented a serious obstacle to many of the objectives of the EUAM (United Nations, 1994c).

With the exception of military-age men (those between 16 and 60 years of age), only 250 persons in the entire history of the EUAM had received permission to cross the former front line on a daily basis (European Commission, 1997c). In addition, a small number of people had been able to obtain identification cards enabling them to cross to the other side for professional reasons. The EUAM tried hard to achieve more progress in the area of freedom of movement, but the Croats constantly objected for security reasons. West Mostar police had even obstructed access for East Mostar citizens to the EUAM Headquarters (in the Hotel Ero), situated in West Mostar (European Commission, 1997c). However, the Croats had no incentive to make any concessions of their own, since they occupied the destroyed *and* the less-damaged part of Mostar. The Bosnian Croats also had free access to both Bosnia and Herzegovina and to Croatia proper.

After 1996 there were three police agencies in the city, East and West Mostar Police and the UPFM, which was passed over to the responsibility of the Cantonal Ministry of Interior on 15 October 1996 (European Commission, 1997c). Although UPFM officers have authority across the whole city, local commanders only allow them to operate within the central zone.[32] Since the Neretva Canton has neither a constitution nor an administrative structure, this additionally hampers the growth and development of an UPFM (European Commission, 1997c). This has made implementation of the Joint Action almost impossible in certain parts of Mostar: hence the Joint Action had to adapt to strange circumstances, as did the objectives of the main Western actors. This changed the nature of the implementation stage of the policy process.

One recent study has realistically concluded the following with regard to free movement of persons in Mostar: 'Few heterogeneous towns remain, such as Mostar and Tuzla, and even in these, the ethnic groups have been separated, as in Mostar where the Croats and Muslims now live on different sides of the Neretva river. A formal split seems likely' (von Hippel, 2000, p. 157; Deprez, 2000).

STAGE 3: EVALUATION

General conclusion

Thinking empirically

According to Sarah Reichel the EUAM has been a trial case for the EU's Common Foreign and Security Policy in at least three different respects (European Commission, 1997c). First, as a long-term engagement it has been a test of the coherence and homogeneity of the political will among the member states. Secondly, the number and the nature of tasks entrusted to the Administration has brought European foreign policy for the first time into the field of post-conflict peace-building, testing the consistency of a strategy to deal with such tasks (Jorgensen, 1997; Lucarelli, 1997). Finally, the management of the Joint Action has revealed the capacity of the procedures and mechanisms set forth in Article J3 of the Treaty on European Union to guarantee an effective and efficient handling of broad and long-term policy action (European Commission, 1997c).

The Council rushed into the Mostar Administration without any preliminary doctrine or systematic plan on how to deal with post-war reconstruction or peace-building activities. The six-month rotation of the Council Presidency, however, has shown evidence of being ill-adapted to the need for continuity in management of a joint action such as Mostar (European Commission, 1997c). The personnel responsible for the ultimate decisions and their execution change every six months, and, as is the norm with the functioning of the Presidency of the Council, not only does the apparatus shift from one member state capital to another as the Presidency rotates, but each Presidency sets different priorities. This leads to a lack of coherence in dealing with particular issues. In addition, the assisting Working Party did not provide a suitable permanent structure for the overall supervision of the Joint Action (European Commission, 1997c). The officials that made up the Working Party had numerous other responsibilities and frequently decisions were carried over from one meeting to the next, reflecting the need to refer back to member state capitals. This slows up decision-making, especially concerning the release of funds to the EUAM. An effective permanent structure and operational procedures capable of assuring continuity in the management of future CFSP Joint actions are needed (European Commission, 1997c).

This first major CFSP Joint action was undertaken under the extremely difficult circumstances of ongoing conflict in Bosnia and Herzegovina. The objectives that were set for the EUAM were extremely ambitious, and the EUAM did not itself control the key elements that influenced whether or not the objectives (such as for example the repatriation of refugees) could be achieved (Court of Auditors, 1995, 1996). Considerable progress was, however, achieved in the areas of rehabilitation, reconstruction and redevelopment. Seeing Mostar as a test case for how well economic support leads to political unification, the EUAM set about prioritising its objectives towards rebuilding Mostar's infrastructure and assisting in the return to normal life (European Commission, 1997c). The majority of projects proceeded smoothly, but a number were delayed for various political and technical reasons, leading to a time lapse between project initiation and execution. Notwithstanding these problems, the reconstruction of the city was ultimately a relative success in terms of the objectives set for the EUAM (European Commission, 1997c). The far more difficult objective was to unite the city economically, politically and socially in order to prepare its residents for self-administration. The Croats constantly rejected any progress towards political reunification of the city, even though they had committed themselves long-term with Article 3 of the MoU to support the EU Administration. The existing gap between the living conditions in East and West Mostar resulted from the Croats not being provided with a material incentive to reunite the two halves of the city. It is uncertain, however, that a material incentive could ever serve as leverage, for compliance (European Commission, 1997c).

One of the principal assumptions of the overall EUAM strategy document of May 1995, was that the EUAM would progressively gain the confidence of the citizens of Mostar. In practice, the Croats' reluctance to co-operate constantly hampered the EUAM's work during the whole two years of its mandate (European Commission, 1997c). The fundamental concern of the Croats of Mostar was that the EU Administration would institutionalize a Muslim majority in the city, leading to what they refer to as a 'silent occupation' of Mostar by the Muslims (European Commission, 1997c). This fear lies at the heart of Croat intransigence and obduracy toward anything the EUAM initiated to bring the parties into closer collaboration, from the unified police force, to freedom of movement and joint use of public facilities such as hospitals and schools.[33] Knowing that the EUAM was accepted by most Bosnian Croat leaders, but only under the pressure of the international community, together with the political support of Croatian President Tudjman, the local Croats' behaviour was not surprising (European Commission, 1997c). The Council of Ministers realized in May 1995 that a maximum amount of political pressure is often necessary in order to force compliance (European Commission, 1997c).

Consequently, diplomatic steps in Brussels, Washington, London, Paris, Bonn, Sarajevo and especially Zagreb were constantly needed to kick-start the political dialogue concerning the future status of Mostar.

Thinking about preference formation

The EUAM was not designed as a protectorate. Since the Administration was not provided with real executive powers, it was completely dependent on the receiving parties political willingness to co-operate. As this chapter has demonstrated above, the idea for the Joint Action came from the Council working with the Commission, the GAC Advisory Working Party, and NGOs in a network-like fashion. The agenda changed from its initial conception of adapting to events on the ground and to the policy predispositions of all the participating actors in the policy process. The Joint Action was closely specified at the agenda-setting stage: its main aims and objectives, resource allocations, and delegation of duties/responsibilities were specified at this stage of the policy process. The first major change in preference structures occurred on 13 May 1995: the former Swedish Premier Carl Bildt prepared a Strategy Document that scaled-down the ambitions of the original 16 May 1994 Joint Action. Indeed, key clauses in the original Joint Action on human rights, public order, the free movement of persons, and criminal justice were thought to be too ambitious. The former Swedish Premier had the luxury of being able to gauge the situation on the ground in order to tailor solutions to problems.

The agenda for the Joint Action came from the Commission External Political Relations Directorate and the GAC Advisory Working Party in early November 1993 in conjunction with middle-range policy specialists and the Permanent Representatives Advisory Working Group. The Joint Action was initially proposed by Desk Officer Balkan area specialists working on the Bosnia desk of DG1A. The Mostar Joint Action was then set at the level of desk officers in DG1A of the Commission, and key participants in the policy process included the Commission, Council, its Advisory Working Party, successive EU Presidencies, the Permanent Representatives Advisory Working Group, NGOs, international lawyers and technical specialists. Policy was the product of interactions between small groups of mid-level national civil servants, EU officials and policy specialists producing specialist reports on the main Joint Action issues: humanitarian relief, economic aid, human rights, infrastructure project management and so forth. These issues are covered in sections 1 and 2 above, and in a series of reports by the interested international organisations and their key institutions (European Parliament reports and resolutions, 1997a–d; European Commission, 1996a–g; European Commission, 1997a–c; European Council, 1994; Court of Auditors, 1995, 1996). Suffice to say, the key omission of war criminals from Carl Bildt's 13 May 1995 Strategy Document showed the degree to which the policy preferences of the main actors had to change to meet the realities of the situation on the ground in Mostar. The aims and objectives of the original 1994 Joint Action – related to basic democracy, human rights and market capitalism – had to be scaled down to a more *practical* agenda.

The main style of discourse was ad hoc in small groups led by policy specialists from the national Presidency civil service, Eurocrats and private sector advisers. Temporary policy communities focusing on specialist matters were set up at various stages in the course of the policy-making process. The dominant form of decision-making was non-hierarchical and multi-level oriented. In order to consider agenda-setting it is necessary to consider sub-variables: the levels of decision-making (low, medium and high); and types of decision-makers (national civil servants, Eurocrats in the Commission and European Parliament; and nationalities of decision-makers).

In this particular case agenda items were typically placed on the agenda in a semi-structured fashion according to the degree of importance attached to each item by Commission desk officers advising higher-level national civil servants, Eurocrats and politicians. Political decisions were taken by politicians within the context of information and advice provided by European-level desk officers in the various external relations directorate generals of the Commission. The agenda-setting style, therefore, was driven from the middle ranges of power upwards, being reified at higher levels. This may be termed 'filtering up' of policy preferences in order to achieve a certain outcome. Again, however, means and ends had to change in order to meet the realities of the situation on the ground: for example, increases in the 1995 and 1996 EU/CFSP budget allocations for Mostar generated new priorities in themselves and decidedly changed previous preference structures.

In the decision-making stage, the preferences expressed by the key actors (Council, Commission, Parliament, GAC Advisory Working Party, CFSP Working Groups) were similar from the outset and emphasized human rights, free movement of persons, the rule of law, and ethnic reintegration when possible. The preferences of all the major actors were not fully complete at the outset of the Joint Action decision-making stage, but matured into completeness as the action progressed via mutual adjustment and participation in networks. This policy learning approach to decision-making influenced the stances taken by the major actors. The Council, for instance, acted more like an umpire from below than a dictator from above. The Commission and Parliament likewise co-operated with the Council to aid the passage of the Joint Action with as few problems as possible. Nevertheless, preference structures were flexible to cope with problems as they arose. For example, in 1995, without reporting to the Administrator, as is highlighted above, two specialist humanitarian advisers were sent to Mostar: one from ECHO and one from Denmark. They worked in parallel duplicating each other's work for three months. In the end the Council nominated the Danish national to carry on with his job.

The Council Presidency was key to setting the agenda of Joint action via the Advisory Working Party. In this case the decision-making style was typically one of policy learning and communicative action. Shared norms and values permeated all levels of decision – existing hierarchies were challenged by expert networks informing and in some cases structuring policy. The Presidency was keen to share information in order to achieve the overall goal of freedom of movement and convoying humanitarian aid to Mostar. Due to Croat resistance, freedom of movement was from the beginning a stumbling point, beyond which no meaningful progress had been made in over two years. Then EUAM tried hard to fulfil the original Joint Action aim of free movement of persons to no avail. Preferences were contorted and various interested Western actors bent over backwards to ensure this important aim could be met. In the end, they failed due to the differences between the ethnic groups. The quality of the decision-making itself on the Western side had actually been efficient, being in line with the preferences stated in the original Joint Action and the modifications suggested by Carl Bildt on 13 May 1995. Mutual justification and an adjustment of preferences was constantly occurring during the policy-making process. The Presidency made use of policy experts to guide its agenda-setting and decision-making during the evolution of the Joint Action. Nevertheless, the decision-making phase was characterized by networks of interested actors all working together to achieve common goals. The Council acted as the 'giver' of authority to initiatives which came from the bottom up rather than the 'controller' of the decision-making phase from the top down. The result was a highly non-hierarchical decision-making stage. Indeed, the structure of preferences were multi-level and operating across levels at the same time.

The EUAM experienced major difficulties in achieving progress towards the UPFM. In responding to this lack of progress, the EU had to change its implementation objectives in conjunction with the actors involved. Despite this having been earlier identified as one of the most important tasks agreed in the MoU, notwithstanding the fact that the force was designed without any real executive powers, local forces in West Mostar steadfastly opposed the speedy development of such a body. What limited progress there was required international pressure on local Croats from the highest political level in Zagreb. The output criteria defined in the IWU document of September 1995 as handing over a reliable, well-trained, well-equipped and well-led UPFM able to provide a full range of police services and to maintain law and order, took some considerable time to achieve (European Commission, 1997c).

Thinking theoretically: a case of expert policy networks

The Mostar case is a classic example of the policy network model in action. At no stage of the policy cycle did any one actor dominate the policy process, the General Affairs Council or a sub-set of member states included. The General Affairs Council set the parameters of the Joint Action. In the agenda-setting stage this gave the Council a great deal of structuring power in determining what was to be discussed. Nevertheless, the Council was dependent at all times on the Commission, European Parliament, the EU member states, the OSCE, and NATO for the delivery of resources needed to meet the objectives of the Joint Action. The agenda-setting phase, therefore, was influenced by a range of actors at various stages of its genesis. The Council and the member states relied heavily on specialist advice from elsewhere during the agenda-setting phase. Priorities moved up and down the wish lists and changed to accommodate new information supplied by specialists. Additionally, specialists influenced the Council and member states to remove items from the agenda that were thought to be either obsolete or beside the point. As is stated above, the GAC had input into the Joint Action via the Advisory Working Party. In effect, this Working Party helped to set the parameters for the Joint Action policy process. However, it found that is could not work alone entirely. The other key actor – or, more accurately in this context, figure – Carl Bildt, the EUAM Administrator. His Strategy Document of 13 May 1995 had the effect of scaling down expectations in the preference structures of the key Western actors. Less emphasis, for example, could be given to war criminals when the main priority had to be economic and political reconstruction. This was a cultural change of some significance vis-à-vis the stated objectives of the Joint Action.

Additionally, the member states constantly needed Commission co-operation when required in order to couple pillar one policies to the effective delivery of pillar two objectives. The resources required to deliver pillar two objectives could only be mobilised either: (i) from the member states; (ii) from pillar one, or (iii) by a combination of the two. Hence no one institution or decision-making system could dominate the agenda-setting phase of the policy process. This is best illustrated with reference to budget allocations from the CFSP general budget for Mostar. It was clear by May 1995 – one year into the Joint Action – that extra resources would need to be allocated to Mostar as the situation on the ground was getting worse not better. 'Minimalist' member states did not wish to commit more resources to the action, and therefore, gave permission for the Commission to appropriate funds from other headings of the EU budget to achieve the objectives of the Joint Action. This was illegal and was commented upon in a Court of Auditors judgement on the funding side of the EUAM in 1996.

Furthermore, high-level decision-makers of all kinds (in the Council, Commission and the member states) were highly dependent on the expert understandings of middle-ranking public and private sector specialists. The EU institutions made extensive use in this case of NGOs, think tanks, academics, journalists, and those with local knowledge of Mostar. This helped to shape the policy agenda in a decisive fashion at critical junctures of the agenda-setting cycle. To deliver objectives set in the Council the core institutions displayed ingenuity and called in policy experts, advisers and regional specialists. For example, in drafting his Strategy Document of 13 May 1995, Carl Bildt was advised by an expert on water supplies, an architect, a police force commander, academic experts on the ethnic communities an accountant and an economist.[34]

Elements of epistemic community – meaning shared understandings of policy – formed early in the agenda-setting and decision-making phases of the policy process between actors directly engaged in the delivery of the Mostar Joint Action. This became particularly apparent in the evolution of policy towards free movement of persons, policy on refugees and displaced persons, and policy towards the creation of the Mostar police force. In other words, there were agreed shared causal assumptions of what policy instruments were likely to succeed or fail in the specialist context of the Joint Action. In this case, the specialists advised the EU to use a mixture of carrot diplomacy (aid and trade agreements) with a heavy Western military presence to enforce law and order (necessary stick diplomacy). For example, in the case of the setting up of the proposed Mostar Police Force the EUAM took advice from New Scotland Yard and the New York Police Department on approaches to multi-ethnic civilian policing.[35]

In a cognitive sense, the middle-range policy specialists broadly shared normative views of what counted in any particular situation as being desirable/undesirable, good/bad policy, appropriate/inappropriate agenda-setting, and so on. For example, in the Mostar case it was decided that the protection of human and minority rights was to be treated as a major policy objective. Other identified priorities included the creation of a multinational police force in Mostar, the protection of refugees and displaced persons, the return of refugees and displaced persons to their original abode, and the general re-education of Mostar's citizens to accept a multi-ethnic city. On the latter point, expert advice was taken from local chieftains/leaders who were sympathetic to the EUAM's principles. Local teachers were also approached by Carl Bildt's office to explore the possibilities of reaching young people's attitudes via the classroom.

As the Mostar case highlights, although no one *actor-type* controlled policy, there was a dominant *actor-level* in the formulation and execution of the Joint action. In the Mostar case, the combined effect of (i) no one actor-type dominating agenda-setting nor decision-making; and (ii) shared understandings of policy in an epistemic community, handed control of agenda-setting and decision-making to networks of middle-level policy-makers, united by their expert understanding and full-time specialism in the issue in question. Interestingly, this was case even though the specialist middle-range actors came from a wide range of different administrative hierarchies: national/supranational, public/private, official/unofficial and so forth. Indeed, as has been stated above, Carl Bildt talked to a whole range of policy specialists to improve the EUAM policy process where possible.

As was pointed out at the outset of this analysis, the main EU institutions and the member states called for the Mostar Joint Action. Those elements of epistemic community formed from within the network of middle-ranking specialists tended to dominate across the whole policy cycle: they framed the advice that was put before senior policy-makers; they structured the agenda of choice available to policy-makers. Indeed, the policy-makers were often cognitively predisposed to take on board agendas and broader policy advice from the likes of specialist advisers, NGOs in Mostar, technical specialists, and international lawyers. A further illustration of such 'open' policy-making concerns the key EUAM policy aim of free movement of persons. In September 1994, the office of Carl Bildt, which was ceded considerable powers in this area from the GAC, began speaking to local warlords about opening up Mostar for reconstruction. He was advised by specialists in urban geography, architects, town planners and so forth.

As in the rational model, as was indicated in the opening theoretical chapter, but unlike in the garbage can model, preferences were well-specified and accurately ranked. This was the effect of the domination of policy-making by experts with full-time concentration on the specialist issue areas in the Mostar case: refugees, economic reconstruction, aid and trade regimes, police force training and so forth. Indeed, as the chapter has illustrated above, each sector of the EUAM policy process was given expert inputs into the policy process in order to ensure that decisions were made with as much technical information as possible. This was a guiding preference contained in the original 14 May 1994 Joint Action and in the modifications of the action carried out by Carl Bildt in his 13 May 1995 Strategy Document.

Unlike in the rational model, preferences are formed endogenously. Will formation in the Mostar case was almost entirely traceable to transnational expert networks associated with CFSP. In place of supranational actors instructed by national actors, the Mostar Joint Action was critically shaped by the manner in which national decision-makers' received strikingly similar advice from experts who constantly communicated with each other in stable policy networks. For instance, on the issue of the MoU signed on 5 July 1994, each of the parties stated that they were to be explicitly advised by policy experts in order to help to fulfil the objectives of the MoU.[36] This is a key defining document on the EUAM.

Unlike in the rational model, communicative action dominated over strategic action. In the Mostar Joint Action, interested actors were unable to shape the agenda by just bargaining 'egotistical' preferences. All actors were under continuous pressure to justify all proposals as an appropriate means of achieving collective benefits for all: security, peace and economic reconstruction. In this case, the need to demonstrate 'appropriate means' required continuous appeal to the goals and norms of CFSP, the original Joint Action of 14 May 1994, the MoU document of 5 July 1994, and the Carl Bildt Strategy Document of 13 May 1995. Each of the above documents are important in the sense that they either explicitly adopt language stated in the TEU, or, as implicitly developed through policy precedents, and/or contemporaneous perceptions of the EU's international role. 'Collective benefit' in the Mostar case required the interested actors to demonstrate that 'payoffs' will not just accrue to particular member states but to the overwhelming majority of the Union.

Like in the rational model, as is stated above, the Mostar Joint Action was characterized by a high degree of cross-pillar coherence. Pillar one competencies were efficiently used to implement pillar two objectives relatively smoothly in most instances. Means–ends relationships were efficiently organized across the pillars. Policy goals were well integrated across a complex range of actor configurations that were involved in the execution of the Joint Action. For instance, on the issue of finance the EU Mostar Administrator, Carl Bildt, had to take into account the needs of economic reconstruction as his first priority, and then all other policy sectors as second-order priorities. His recommendations – heavily influenced by experts – then had to be 'translated' into the political system of the EU in an efficient manner. The political system of the EU then had to efficiently manage cross-pillar competencies, different decision-making rules in pillars one and two, the member states' requirements, and resource requirements *in association with* the expert and non-expert advice. Furthermore, communication in general was efficient. Surprisingly few policy problems arose due to the relatively efficient co-ordination of policy. A high level of cross-pillar coherence characterized the decision-making stage: means–ends relationships were efficiently organized across the pillars. Communication was efficient as was policy co-ordination between the different actors. Indeed, the EU acted as an efficient international actor achieving a good degree of coherence in policy-making terms.

Unlike in the rational model this coherence is, however, traceable in this particular case to the domination of policy by networks of experts that cross-cut the plurality of agencies involved in the Joint Action, and to the shared assumptions they bring to policy-making. Additionally, normative assumptions held on the part of all actors lead to the expectation that major policy decisions will involve policy experts. As we have demonstrated, this was the case: (i) in the formation of the Mostar Police Force. Expert advice was sought from New Scotland Yard and the New York Police Department; (ii) in general economic reconstruction projects advice was sought by Carl Bildt from agronomists, economists, accountants, and NGOs with experience of post-war reconstruction; (iii) in terms of physically rebuilding the city of Mostar advice was taken from town planners and architects; (iv) in relation to the resourcing the Joint Action advice was taken from DG1A, ECHO, specialized NGOs and the EUAM Administrator's office.

Unlike in the rational model, there was an important element of path dependence both within the individual Joint Action and between all the Mostar Joint Actions. Policy networks of experts engaged in foreign policy-making have an interest in learning 'collectively' and not just 'individually'. In the Mostar case, individual experts – engaged in civilian police work, economic reconstruction, rebuilding the infrastructure of the city, and so forth – worked together in a stable fashion. This increased their capacity for collective problem-solving and allowed the various experts to maintain control, and enrich their experience, within their different governance/administrative hierarchies of origin. As there is, however, a cost of defecting from the shared lessons of the policy network (for example, in the areas of co-operation on refugee resettlement, economic aid and political reconstruction), there is a classic pattern of path dependence. The costs of exiting from the policy rise with time. In the Mostar case, actors tended to accept as a matter of course, a substantial degree of 'sub-optimality', rather than damage their reputation as good partners, or sacrifice the steering/problem-solving capacities of a functioning and consensual network.

Notes

1 The following chapter heavily relies on Sarah Reichel's excellent study of the European Union Administration of Mostar (EUAM) prepared for the Directorate General for External Political Relations of the European Commission. *Factual* information relating to the EUAM is liberally drawn from Sarah Reichel's descriptive-factual piece on the EU Administration of

104 *EU Foreign Policy beyond the Nation-State*

    Mostar: Sarah Reichel, 'The European Union Administration of Mostar', Report Prepared for DG1A, External Political Relations, Commission of the European Union, 1997c.
2 In 1992, 43.7 per cent of the population in Bosnia and Herzegovina were Muslim.
3 The Bosniak Republic would have consisted of some territory in central Bosnia. The West-Bosnian region around Bihac and some 'islands' around Gorazde, Zepa and Srebrenica.
4 Lord Owen's discussion with the CFSP Commission of the European Parliament on 7 October 1993.
5 Speech given by US National Security Adviser Anthony Lake at the Johns Hopkins University in Baltimore, MD. 7 October 1993.
6 Due to a Russian initiative, a International Contact Group on Bosnia-Herzegovina was established consisting of the US, the UK, France, Germany and Russia. Its aim was to prevent military escalation with diplomacy acceptable for all sides.
7 Council Decision (94/308/CFSP) of 16 May 1994.
8 This decision followed an earlier Joint action to support the convoying of humanitarian aid to Bosnia and Herzegovina. However, the Joint action was never realised due to continuous Bosnian Serb harassment of the convoys.
9 TEU. Article J.1.4.
10 TEU. Article J.1.2.
11 TEU. Article J.1.4.
12 The Memorandum of Agreement (MoU) was a product of the continuing tensions between the different parties until a substantial cease-fire was reached in October 1995 at Dayton, Ohio. The representatives of the former conflicting parties included the President of the Republic of Bosnia and Herzegovina, Alija Izabegovic. At the national level Harris Silajdzic represented the Muslims and Jadranko Prlic represented the Bosnian Croats. At the local level the mayors of East and West Mostar respectively, Safat Oruccvic and Mijo Brajkovic, represented local interests. See European Commission, 1997c.
13 The following section heavily relies on: European Commission, 1997c.
14 MoU, Article 7. Part 1 and Article 3.
15 MoU, Article 2.
16 MoU, Article 7. Part 1.
17 Structure as described above.
18 MoU, Article 9. Part 3.
19 MoU, Article 9.
20 Interview, Desk Officer, DG1A, Brussels, November 1997.
21 The Council considered that in certain circumstances *administrative* expenditure *could* include such expenditure in crisis situations. Additionally the rules provides that where the Council decides unanimously that operational expenditure of a joint action is charged to the EU budget. The budgetary procedure laid down in the treaty establishing the European Community shall be applicable. Without consulting the Parliament the Council Presidency modified this budget procedure to its sole responsibility, in accordance with Article 3 of Council Decision (95/123/CFSP) of 6 February 1995. This had been fiercely contested by the Parliament securing

its budgetary rights. The 1997 Inter-Institutional Agreement on Financing CFSP removed the Parliament's powers in the area of finance in foreign policy. Since 1997 the Parliament has had powers of information and consultation only.
22 In association with DG1A of the Commission. Interview, Desk Officer, DG1A, Brussels, January 2000.
23 Budget Line B7-010.
24 More often than not the Community budget provides its share of funds on time. The member states provide funds according to GDP, but often fail to deliver their shares on time, thereby disrupting the implementation of the Joint action. Some 'minimalist' member states perceive that Joint actions are the first practical achievement of CFSP and do not want them to succeed and provide possible spillover effects for future EU foreign policy plans.
25 The last of the member states' contributions were paid in February and April of 1995 respectively.
26 This was made up of (i) ECU 20 million provided in the second supplementary budget of 1994 by the Parliament for the Mostar hospital (ii) ECU 60 million from the 1995 budget comprising ECU 10 million on the operational budget line (B8-100) and, (iii) ECU 50 million in the reserve budget. On 18 July 1995 this ECU 50 million reserve was transferred to the budget line Bg-100.
27 The following section heavily relies on: European Commission, 1997c.
28 MoU, Article 12.
29 Interview, Desk Officer DG1A, Brussels, December 1997.
30 Interview, Desk Officer DG1A, Brussels, December 1997.
31 MoU, Article 15.1.
32 Following an official suggestion by the SDA (Bosnian Serbs) on 10 July 1996.
33 Interview, Desk Officer, ECHO, January 2000.
34 Interview, Desk Officer, DG1A, Brussels, December 1997.
35 Interview, Desk Officer, ECHO, Brussels, January 2000.
36 Interview, Desk Officer, ECHO, Brussels, January 2000.

5
Implementing the Dayton Agreements, 1995–98: Agenda-Setting, Decision-Making and Implementation[1]

STAGE 1: CHRONOLOGY

Introduction

This chapter provides an assessment of the situation in Bosnia and Herzegovina with reference to the implementation of the Dayton Agreements between 1995 and 1998. The chapter aims to test the various theories of agenda-setting, decision-making, and implementation from a pillarization perspective that were set out in the introductory chapter. The chapter also specifically focuses on process, relationships between joint actions as an unusual policy-making method, actor behaviour, and policy outcomes. It will do this by considering key European Union Joint actions vis-à-vis the implementation of the Dayton Agreements of October and November 1995, which were formally signed in Paris on 14 December 1995.

On 5 February 1994, a Bosnian Serb mortar attack on the central market in the Bosnian capital of Sarajevo killed 69 civilians and wounded 200. The European Union (EU) and United States (US) were galvanized into action after three years of general war in Bosnia-Herzegovina. This led the Western powers to instruct the North Atlantic Treaty Organisation (NATO) to bomb Bosnian Serb positions in the hills surrounding Sarajevo. On 8 May 1995, another Bosnian Serb attack on the central market in Sarajevo led the Atlantic Alliance to launch further air attacks against Bosnian Serb positions. In July 1995, thousands of Muslim men were hunted down and murdered by Bosnian Serb forces under General Ratko Mladic at Srebrenica in the single worst atrocity of the Bosnian war. Srebrenica is infamous for also being the site of the single worst war crime on European soil since the Second World War. At the time of writing, the Red Cross is still seeking information on the whereabouts of 7380 men (Both and Honig, 1997; United Nations, 1999). The Atlantic Alliance continued to bomb Bosnian Serb positions in Bosnia-Herzegovina into submission. As a result of renewed Western military and diplomatic pressure the leader of all Serbs, President Slobodan Milosevic, signed the Dayton Agreements on 14 December 1995 in Paris with his Croatian and Muslim counterparts to formally end the war in Bosnia-Herzegovina (NATO, 1995).

The Dayton Agreements: objectives and contents

The Dayton Agreements were designed to provide the basis for a unified, reconstructed, democratic and capitalist Bosnia-Herzegovina. The Western powers set the following general priorities for the postwar reconstruction of Bosnia-Herzegovina: arms control; law and order; human rights; democratization; elections; freedom of movement; repatriation of refugees and displaced persons; arrest of war criminals; postwar economic and political reconstruction; a market economy; reconciliation; education; and mine removal.

The Dayton Agreement contained 10 articles, 11 annexes, and 102 maps. It maintained a 51:49 per cent territorial division between the Croat-Bosniac Federation and the Republika Srpska within a unified state, with Sarajevo being the unified capital of the state. Dayton allowed special access for Bosnian Serbs and Bosnian Croats to Serbia and Croatia respectively. It confirmed the right of refugees to return to their original place of residence. Dayton also banned those accused of war crimes from holding office. Article I guaranteed freedom of movement throughout Bosnia-Herzegovina. Article II promised to protect individual and group human rights. Article III of Annex 4 set out responsibilities of the government. Article IV outlined a 15-person upper-house legislative chamber, and a 42-person lower house. Article VI set out a Constitutional Court. Annex 4 specified a three-person executive presidency, with representation from each ethnic group. Article VII of Annex 4 set up a Commission for Displaced Persons and Refugees. United Nations (UN) forces were replaced by a 53 000-strong NATO Implementation Force (IFOR), which was in turn replaced by a NATO Stabilization Force (SFOR) on 20 December 1996 (von Hippel, 2000, pp. 152–4).

Key European Union 'Joint Actions' and Dayton

In the context of implementing Dayton the EU launched a number of key Joint actions which were coterminous with the Dayton Agreements contents. Key Joint actions were launched in the following areas that were identified at Dayton as being important for the purpose of democratizing and rebuilding a multi-ethnic Bosnia-Herzegovina, and are listed below with some background context: persons responsible for committing violent acts; war criminals; local elections and democracy; economic reconstruction and development; and, free movement of persons.

The European Union launched a Joint action on 10 February 1997 against persons who have perpetuated violent acts against the principles of the Dayton Agreements in Joint action 97/153/CFSP.[2] Indeed, many suspected and indicted war criminals hamper the implementation of the Dayton Agreement while denying large parts of the population any role in economic and political developments which are essential for the reconstruction of the country. This has been recognized as a key policy aim of the European Union in Joint action 97/224/CFSP.[3]

This is prescient in the case of suspected war criminals who are also national political and/or military leaders. In 1998, the General Affairs Council passed a Declaration condemning the infiltration of suspected or actual war criminals into positions of power in Bosnia-Herzegovina, thereby preventing key clauses of the Dayton Agreements from being implemented. This was especially applied to Slobodan Milosevic, Radovan Karadzic and Ratko Mladic.[4] This was put forward in Council Decision 98/196/CFSP. In 1998, the EU passed Joint action 98/117/CFSP, undertaking to implement the war crimes sections of the Dayton Agreements.[5]

In terms of local elections in Bosnia, the European Union has opted for a democracy and transparency agenda in line with Dayton. The European Union's policy has been to support local democracy where it is feasible in conjunction with the Organization for Security and Cooperation in Europe (OSCE).[6] In the West's view, democratic elections can never lead to the unbridled exercise of power by the winner. Real democracy means being elected to exercise power while allowing others to hold that power in check. This was recognized in Joint action 98/302/CFSP. Furthermore, Joint action 97/625/CFSP was passed against persons who had undermined the peace process and elections.[7]

In terms of economic reconstruction and development, the EU's view is that bilateral relations, the granting of commercial preference and exchanges, economic co-operation and financial aid would only be possible with the parties to the Dayton Agreement respecting democratic principles and the rule of law, human rights and the rights of minorities, the principles of a market economy and regional co-operation.[8] This was recognized in the General Affairs Council Decision 98/737/CFSP.

With reference to the free movement of persons – a key policy objective of the Dayton Agreements – the Council adopted Common Position 97/193/CFSP to guarantee freedom of movement in Bosnia-Herzegovina in order to be in line with the free movement sections of the Dayton Agreements.[9]

Towards an assessment of Dayton

A series of ministerial meetings of the North Atlantic Council and the Peace Implementation Council Steering Board in Sintra, Portugal, at the end of May 1997, provided an appropriate opportunity for a serious assessment of the situation in Bosnia and Herzegovina (WEU, 1998b). These meetings appear to have been a general turning point since none of the authorities involved saw any good reason to conceal the truth any longer (WEU, 1998c). In their final communiqué of 29 May 1997, Ministers of the North Atlantic Council first made mention of some progress in the implementation of the Dayton Agreement, stating:

> We recognise that important and demonstrable progress has been made in the overall effort to implement the Peace Agreement since we last met. Municipal elections are scheduled, the sensitive Brcko decision is being implemented, and there have been positive developments in the initiation of joint institutions, the return of refugees and displaced persons and in economic reconstruction. We are greatly encouraged by the effective cooperation between SFOR [the NATO-led Stabilisation Force] and the High Representative and the international organisations and agencies. (WEU, 1998c)

In the following paragraph, however, the ministers made it crystal clear that in fact there was little reason to be satisfied, and mentioned a whole list of items in respect of which the parties had failed to meet their obligations, expressing their opinion as follows:

> Nevertheless, significant challenges remain and the failure of all the parties to the Peace Agreement to comply fully with their commit-

ments cannot be tolerated. Reaffirming our commitment to the full implementation of the Peace Agreement, we express our serious concern at the lack of determination by the authorities in Bosnia and Herzegovina to honour their obligations and strongly urge them:
- to establish functioning central institutions;
- to ensure freedom of movement, freedom of communication and freedom of the press;
- to respect human rights, the rule of law and the right of all refugees and displaced persons to return freely;
- to cooperate fully with the international community in preparing, conducting and implementing the municipal elections;
- to cooperate with the International Criminal Tribunal for the former Yugoslavia in The Hague in the apprehension and bringing to justice of war criminals;
- to implement fully the provisions of the arms control agreement;
- to adopt and implement the economic measures needed for the functioning of Bosnia and Herzegovina as a single state; and,
- to develop democratic, restructured police forces. (WEU, 1998c)

The final communiqué of the ministerial meeting of the Steering Board of the Peace Implementation Council (PIC) was even more outspoken in expressing discontent with the situation. The Steering Board 'unanimously agreed that all the authorities of Bosnia and Herzegovina are failing to live up fully to their obligations under the [Dayton] Peace Agreement, and that this is unacceptable' (WEU, 1998c).

As a result of the PIC meeting in Sintra, Bosnia and Herzegovina's political leaders were given a checklist of laws to be passed, with deadlines set and the threat of penalties for any failures. The first deadline, 1 August 1997, caused a showdown between the parties (WEU, 1998c). The central government had been told to agree on the appointment of joint ambassadors, common citizenship and passports, and the reopening of airports by that date. When the deadline was not met, a number of countries suspended relations with the embassies of Bosnia and Herzegovina. In 1997, an agreement was reached on the appointment of ambassadors and broader diplomatic relations, but a whole range of other problems have not to date been satisfactorily resolved (Radha, 1997, pp. 22–34).

After the negative assessment of the implementation process, with the September 1996 municipal elections in sight, and a difficult decision to be taken on what to do after the end of the SFOR mandate, the United

States realized that it was vital to step up pressure on the three parties (Holbrooke, 1998). Since then, progress has been made but at a relatively slow pace. In June and July 1997, the US Secretary of State and the British Foreign Secretary each visited Bosnia and Herzegovina and instructed the various political leaders in very straightforward and undiplomatic language to comply with the Dayton Agreements (WEU, 1998c).

At the beginning of August 1997, it was the turn of Richard Holbrooke, the US envoy to former Yugoslavia, to visit the signatories of the Dayton Agreement to try to accelerate the process and keep it moving forward (O'Hanlan, 1998, pp. 41–4). At the request of the US, the Presidents of Croatia and Bosnia and Herzegovina met in Split on 6 August 1997. They promised to co-operate in order to promote peace, establish a cooperation council, create border controls according to international standards at their common border and facilitate the return of refugees (Holbrooke, 1998).

The Dayton Agreement was never intended to be perfect. All the parties involved in its genesis were aware of this, as well as of the fact that many of its signatories had blood on their hands (being, in some cases, indicted war criminals). Under the given circumstances, however, with each party pursuing different objectives, it was probably the best available solution (WEU, 1998c). But it should be remembered that the Agreement is an intricate jigsaw puzzle in which all the pieces are interdependent. If the civilian parts are not fully implemented, there is little doubt that the fragile peace will collapse as soon as the foreign military peace implementation forces have left (Chandler, 1999). The importance of implementing the civilian provisions of Dayton is clear, among other things by promises of badly-needed economic aid if the various parties on the ground comply (WEU, 1998c).

Since the Dayton Accords were signed in 1995 the main obstacles to their implementation remain obstructive leaders in Republika Srpska (some of whom are indicted war criminals), in particular Radovan Karadzic (WEU, 1998c). Inter-ethnic relations remain on a knife-edge and impede progress. In fact, none of the joint institutions as stipulated in the Dayton Agreement is working effectively, and many of the suggested supporting institutions are not even being established (Bass, 1998, pp. 95–107). One author has realistically referred to the Dayton Accords as confirming the existence of a 'Balkan chill' in terms of inter-ethnic relations in Bosnia-Herzegovina and, inter alia, in terms of relations between the Western powers and the various ethnic factions in former Yugoslavia (Crawford, 1998–99, pp. 84–5). Other respected authors have gone much further and written that Dayton 'entrenches the ethnic divisions that gave rise to the conflict in the first place' (Borden and Kaplan, 1997, p. 231). Indeed, 'Bosnia's post-Dayton reality is a complex one . . . Nationalist politics and ethnic differences continue to dominate every aspect of daily life' (Daadler and Froman, 1999, p. 106).

STAGE 2: MAPPING AGENDA-SETTING, DECISION-MAKING AND IMPLEMENTATION

Mapping the contributions of the different actors

On 15 January 1996, the UN intervened with troops in Eastern Slavonia to enforce the human rights aspects of the Dayton Accords and to seek out possible war criminals. The effects of this action were dashed on 1 February 1996, when, 300 mass graves were reported in former Yugoslavia, from an examination of American spy satellite information. Previously, on 20 January 1996, Javier Solana, the NATO Secretary-General' praised NATO troops in former Yugoslavia for keeping law and order in the context of the Dayton Agreements.

On 22 January 1996, Hans Van Den Broek – the Commissioner for External Political Relations – placed political conditions on FYROM to co-operate with the War Crimes Tribunal on former Yugoslavia. A series of events persuaded the Commission of the need to adopt a framework approach to implementing the Dayton Accords. However, by 23 January 1996, a tuberculosis crisis in Serbia triggered Commission aid of ECU 300 000. On 26 January 1996, Van Den Broek visited the President of Croat Franjo Tudjman in Zagreb and reported directly to the foreign ministers of the European Union member states via shuttle diplomacy. On 27 January 1996, the EU High Representative in Bosnia, Carl Bildt, was requested by the Commission to make a preliminary report on the implementation of the Dayton Accords on the ground in actual practice. Based upon this report – highlighting the degree of non-cooperation on all sides – the Commission decided to adopt a 'framework' approach to implementing the Accords. This approach emphasised a regional approach towards problems on the ground as they emerge – adopting *geographical* and *thematic* approaches to problem-solving. By the end of January 1996, Commissioner Van Den Broek had offered ECU 63.5 million for infrastructure projects in Bosnia, dependent on each party implementing the Dayton Accords.

Significantly, on 2 February 1996, at a meeting of the International Contact Group on Former Yugoslavia, it was reported that 150 000 Bosnian, Croat and Serb soldiers still had to be mobilized to fulfill the conditions of the Dayton Accords. Following up, on 7 February 1996, the European Parliament Committee on Eastern and Central Europe demanded much higher standards in the implementation of the civilian aspects of the Dayton Accords. To provide a much-needed 'carrot' for reconstruction in Bosnia the Parliament approved an extension of PHARE monies for the fiscal year 1996–97 to ECU 95 million. At the same time the Parliament called for a Joint action on land mines.

Then, on 27 March 1996, the General Affairs Council of the EU approved an international donor conference for Bosnia. The EU stated that it would commit resources in proportion to its member states' contributions and other non-EU states. Finally, on 26 April 1996, Bosnia-Herzegovina was included as a PHARE recipient as a result of pressure from the European Parliament.

By the end of May 1996, the Muslims had decided to boycott regional elections in Bosnia in direct contravention of the Dayton Accords. A major objective of the Dayton Accords is/was to introduce properly validated elections to Bosnia. This was followed up on 12 June 1996, with a Joint action in support of the electoral process in Bosnia (Agence Europe, 12 June 1996, p. 2). By 20 May 1996, the European Union was openly calling for the Bosnian-Serb leader Radovan Karadzic to surrender himself to the International War Crimes Tribunal in The Hague. By the end of June 1996, the European Parliament highlighted the need for humanitarian aid to Bosnia-Herzegovina.

From the beginning of 1997 onwards, the EU's strategy revolved around three objectives: war criminals, democratization, and respect for human rights. On 1 January 1997, the EU endorsed a report by Felipe Gonzales on the local elections in Serbia, which were held on 17 November 1996. The EU and OSCE called on the Serbian authorities to implement reforms suggested in the Dayton Accords on free elections, press freedoms and civil liberties. Within the same context, on 10 January 1997, the Deputy Director General of DG1A Francois Lamoureux, commented on the need for Republika Srpska to respect human rights and democracy within the context of the Dayton Agreements. On 5 February 1997, the Serbian President Slobodan Milosevic accepted the findings of the Gonzales report in principle, but not in practice.

On 20 February 1997, the EU dispatched a fact-finding mission to Belgrade to oversee implementation of the Gonzales report. This was to prove – typically – difficult and problematic. Additionally, the EU pressed forward with its 'regional approach' to implementing the Dayton Accords. PHARE monies were to be linked to progress in human rights and democracy. To give extra weight to the EU mission, the Danish Foreign Minister Niels Helvig Peterson and Mr Van der Stoel – Chair of the OSCE group on minorities – presented the Western powers' case to the Serb leadership. Both men then reported directly to the EU Council of Ministers.

On 14 April 1997, the European Parliament adopted a resolution condemning a tax of DM70 for those wishing to leave Republika Srpska. This was a direct contravention of the free movement clause of the Dayton Agreements. The situation was so serious that the European Parliament asked Carl Bildt to remain as the EU High Representative in Bosnia until further notice. The EU had a basic choice when dealing with the Bosnian Serbs at this time: First, the 'stick' approach of sanctions, bombings and so forth. Second, a 'carrot' approach emphasizing rewards for good behaviour. The General Affairs Council of the EU chose to concentrate on the 'carrot' approach for the time being. By the end of April, preferential trade measures were announced for Serbia with conditions attached: local democracy, freedom of movement, and human rights to be actively promoted and respected by the Bosnian Serbs.

Nevertheless, by 9 May 1997, the Bosnian Serbs were refusing to meet with Klaus Kinkel, the German Foreign Minister, and with Hans Van Den Broek, the European Commissioner for External Political Relations. The 'carrot' approach was beginning to fail. This was depressingly confirmed when the 3rd International Donor Conference on the Former Yugoslavia, due to be held on 21 June 1997, was postponed due to a lack of progress in implementing the Dayton Accords. By 30 July 1997, the Secretary-General of NATO, Javier Solana, called on the leadership of Republika Srpska to make a commitment to halting acts of violence against Croats and Muslims. Indeed, the Bosnian Serb leadership was actively propagating acts of violence at this time. Interestingly, by 8 August 1997, Germany cut diplomatic ties with the Bosnian Ambassador to Bonn for similar violations of human rights and democracy. However, by 11 August, the Luxembourg Presidency of the Council of Ministers recommended reinstatement of diplomatic contacts to create a new political dialogue between all the parties in Bosnia and the EU.

By the end of August 1997, violent Serb-inspired riots against IFOR in Brcko and Bijeljina were condemned by the EU, NATO and OSCE.

SFOR had to use massive force to quell the riots. On 2 September 1997, President Milosevic condemned SFOR actions in Republika Srpska, and also reiterated his support for Radovan Karadzic over Mrs Plavsic. This was a sign that the Serb leadership in Belgrade was unwilling actively to co-operate in the implementation of the Dayton Accords on the ground. On 13 September 1997, Mrs Doris Pack led a delegation of the European Parliament to monitor the Bosnian local elections.

By 20 September 1997, the full European Parliament demanded a monitoring of the settling in of new mayors in Bosnia and Herzegovina as a result of the local elections of the previous week. The local mayors were likely to be highly influential figures in the implementation of the Dayton Accords. On 3 October 1997, an EU Joint Declaration stressed the responsibility of President Milosevic as the main influence on events in ex-Yugoslavia. This is significant because the EU had chosen to single out Milosevic and Serbia as main perpetrators of the war. Somewhat more embarrassing for the EU, however, was the finding of the European Parliament Committee on Budgets which pointed out failings in the operational relationship between the European Commission and the Office of the EU High Representative for Bosnia. Indeed, communication was often so awful that multiple 'EU policies' were emerging from both Brussels and Bosnia with equal occurrence. This made policy coordination almost impossible.[10]

By 22 January 1998, the EU had decided to follow up on the 'carrot' approach towards Republika Srpska. A *tranche* of ECU 15 million was made available to FYROM from the Commission. This was followed up on 24 January by a Troika mission led by British Foreign Secretary Robin Cook to assess the implementation of the Dayton Accords on the ground. The EU High Representative to Bosnia, Carlos Westendorp, called for the return of Bosnian refugees to Bosnian-Serb-held territory. On 29 January 1998, Hans Van Den Broek, the EU Commissioner for External Political Relations, called on the Bosnian Serb leadership to respect the human rights aspects of the Dayton Accords.

On 6 June 1998, the European Parliament Committee on Budgets voted ECU 90 million for reconstruction work in former Yugoslavia to ensure the implementation of the Dayton Accords. By the end of July 1998, the EU Troika travelled to Belgrade to meet with President Milosevic in Belgrade and to press home the need for implementation of the Dayton Accords. The situation was complicated by the parallel happenings in Kosovo at the time. The European Parliament decided to withdraw ECU 200 million from the Phare programme due to corruption on the ground and bad investment risks.

By the end of 1998, the Implementation Council of the Dayton Agreements demanded higher standards from all sides in implementing the Dayton Agreements. In testimony to the European Parliament on 3 December 1998, Carlos Westendorp highlighted the situation in Bosnia and Herzegovina: First, there was a need for refugees and displaced persons to have the right to return to their former homes in accordance with Dayton. Second, there was a need for more cross-border patrols by SFOR troops to ensure adherence to the human rights clauses of the Dayton Agreements. Third, there was a need to cut out corruption and prevent fraud of EU funds on the ground. As a key 1996 Court of Auditors Report on Mostar had indicated EU controls on the ground were no match for local warlords who appropriated funds almost at will (Court of Auditors, 1996).

Mapping agenda-setting

This section of the chapter focuses on the origins and development of key areas of agenda formation in the context of key joint actions and related policies towards the Dayton Agreements: refugees, displaced persons, war criminals, local elections, resourcing of policies, and coherence in the EU's pillar structure. The analysis draws heavily on a key WEU report 'European Security in Stages: Implementing the Dayton Agreements' for *factual* aspects of the agenda-setting stage of the Dayton policy process (WEU, 1998c).

Refugees and displaced persons: mid-range priorities and agendas

Of all the annexes to the Dayton Agreement, Annex 7, the Agreement on Refugees and Displaced Persons, has proven to be the most difficult to implement (WEU, 1998c). It should be noted that refugees are persons who went to another country after leaving their home or having been expelled from their home. Displaced persons are those who left or were expelled from their homes but stayed within the borders of Bosnia and Herzegovina. This has been recognized by the European Union as a key policy aim vis-à-vis Dayton.[11] The basic principles of this agreement are formulated in Article I of this Agreement which stipulates: 'All refugees and displaced persons have the right freely to return to their homes of origin.' (WEU, 1998c).

The Agreement further contains many guarantees for a return home for refugees and displaced persons in safety and without any risks. SFOR (UN Bosnian Stabilization Force) figures dating from August 1997 (quoted in WEU, 1998c) make it clear how little progress had been made in this field during the first two years after Dayton. (This pattern has been replicated since 1997–98, although encouraging local election results in Bosnia and Herzegovina in the autumn of 2000, concluded with non-ethnic-based political parties in the majority for the first time since 1995.) Agenda-setting at the national and European levels in the West had been consistently undermined by the intransigence of local Muslim, Croat and Serb warlords protecting localised and parochial interests (WEU, 1998c). An 'implementation gap' was emerging between Western rhetoric and reality. Progress in this particular area was – and is – extremely slow. According to recent SFOR figures, there were 800 000 refugees and 800 000 displaced persons in 1998. Around 400 000 refugees were in Western Europe, with the vast majority in western Germany (WEU, 1998c). An estimated 70 per cent or (1.12 million of the total 1.6 million) should – according to the Agreement – return to areas where their ethnic group is in a minority. For most of these persons, there is little or no chance of returning to their original homes. Many of those returning are being 'relocated' (WEU, 1998c).

In 1996 and from January to July 1997, for example, a total number of 53 039 refugees returned to Bosnia and Herzegovina (cited in WEU, 1998c). Of these, only an estimated 27 000 returned to a minority area, with 78 per cent going to the Bosnian-controlled part of the Federation, 18 per cent to the Croat-controlled part of the Federation and 4 per cent to Republika Srpska. According to figures from the Office of the Special Envoy of the United Nations High Commissioner for Refugees, only 1 per cent returned to minority areas in Republika Srpska in the period 1 January to 31 July 1997 (cited in WEU, 1998c).

In its Declaration of 30 May 1997, the PIC rightly stated that unless and until a process is set in train to facilitate the return of refugees and displaced persons to their pre-war homes in a peaceful, orderly and phased manner, there will be continued instability in Bosnia. EU and UN progress in this area has been hampered by Bosnian Serb intransigence to a great degree to fall in line with the Western agenda of resettlement of refugees and displaced persons (WEU, 1998c). The Declaration further mentioned that steps had to be taken to permit various ethnic groups to return to Drvar, Sarajevo, Brcko, Banja Luka and numerous other cities. It insisted that current property laws place insurmountable legal barriers in the path of anyone returning to his/her home, and called for the Federation and Republika Srpska to amend their property laws (WEU, 1998c).

On 2 and 3 August 1997, for example, a number of violent incidents in and around the town of Jajce again demonstrated that the return of refugees to their own homes is one of the most thorny issues (WEU, 1998c). The series of incidents started when a threatening crowd of Croats besieged the headquarters of the UNIPTF of the region. Following this event, a total number of around 1000 Muslim refugees were expelled from their homes to which they had returned one week before in accordance with the Dayton Agreement (WEU, 1998c). The UN, SFOR and the EU stated that they had information suggesting that the local Croat police force had played a role in these events. After these incidents, the Croat and Muslim authorities, under strong international pressure, signed an agreement to set up a joint police force in the area from 30 August 1997 (WEU, 1998c).

Missing persons in a humanitarian perspective: a key item on the joint action agenda

In Bosnia and Herzegovina 20 000 individuals are still missing (cited in WEU, 1998c). After the conclusion of the Dayton Agreement, it was realized that the issue of missing persons is one of the stumbling blocks hindering reconciliation. The issue was placed on to the top of the agenda in late 1995 and has remained there ever since. Policy has tended to be controlled by high-level diplomats and Eurocrats with expertise in this specialist field. Implementation has been left to the Commission and particularly to the specialist European Community Humanitarian Office (ECHO).[12]

In the summer of 1996, as a result of joint EU and US pressure, an International Commission on Missing Persons (ICMP) in former Yugoslavia was established under the chairmanship of the former US Secretary of State, Cyrus Vance (Holbrooke, 1998). The objective of this Commission is to assist the families of persons listed as missing as a result of the conflict in former Yugoslavia and to persuade the governments concerned to intensify their efforts to solve cases of missing persons. The Commission is financed by donations. An ICMP office under the direction of a permanently based Chief-of-Staff was opened in Sarajevo in autumn 1996 and the governments of the region have designated officials as their representatives to the ICMP (WEU, 1998c).

The programme of the International Committee of the Red Cross was suspended in 1996 and efforts to restart it have not made much progress (WEU, 1998c). A programme of the office of the High Representative has been blocked since April 1997 and an agreement on continuation is still a long way off (WEU, 1998c). The International

Criminal Tribunal for Yugoslavia (ICTY) has performed in excess of one thousand exhumations to support evidence of war crimes, but financial problems hamper further progress.

Political power struggles between the entities of Bosnia-Herzegovina, and a general lack of co-operation on the part of the political authorities of Republika Srpska in particular, are the most obvious stumbling blocks in the efforts to make real progress on the issue of missing persons (Holbrooke, 1998). The ICMP has noted that international organizations should press local politicians to stop obstructing the identification process and convince local authorities to support the professionals committed to carrying out this work (WEU, 1998c). The European Union launched a joint action on 10 February 1997 against persons who have perpetuated violent acts.[13]

War criminals: the political and administrative agenda

When SFOR took over from IFOR, its mandate did not include setting up search parties to go after indicted war criminals. According to Article IX.9 of Annex 1-A to the Dayton Agreement, the responsibility for arresting indicted war criminals lies with the signatory parties to that Agreement (WEU, 1998c). SFOR's task was to apprehend indicted war criminals when it came across them in the course of carrying out its duties. This reluctance on the part of the foreign forces, whose main task is to ensure a secure environment for the further implementation of the Dayton Agreement, has understandably met with increasing criticism. Many of the indicted war criminals openly continue to wield political and economic influence with impunity (*Economist*, 29 June 1996, p. 47). In addition to offences committed during the conflict itself, many indicted war criminals are suspected of continuing extortion and blackmail. They also represent an ongoing threat to inter-ethnic reconciliation, economic development and to the Dayton process itself (WEU, 1998a). Indeed, many suspected and indicted war criminals hamper the implementation of the Dayton Agreements while denying large parts of the population any role in economic and political developments, which is essential for the reconstruction of the country (WEU, 1998c). This has been recognized as a key policy aim of the European Union.[14]

After many hesitations and objections, even the members of the Peace Implementation Council became convinced that a more active policy had to be adopted. In its political declaration of 30 May 1997 at Sintra, it confirmed that co-operation of all the signatories of the Dayton Agreement with the ICTY remained a key part of the peace implementation process (WEU, 1998c). It expressed particular concern over the situation in Republika Srpska, 'where Mr Radovan Karadzic continues to influence the political decision-making of the Entity in violation of both the letter and the spirit of previous undertakings'. (The European Union's policies were in line with this sentiment.)[15] The declaration noted that persons co-operating with, or condoning the role of, indicted persons should be denied visas to travel abroad. It supported the High Representative's recommendation to deny further economic assistance to those municipalities which continued to tolerate indicted persons working in a public capacity and said it would follow this up (WEU, 1998c).

Finally, it reminded the Federal Republic of Yugoslavia and the Republic of Croatia to honour their obligations as regards war criminals (Holbrooke, 1998). They were also reminded of their obligation to use their close ties and economic support to help obtain the surrender of indictees, especially in Republika Srpska and the predominantly Croat areas of the Federation. By the end of June 1997, for example, only 8 out of 75 publicly indicted war criminals had surrendered or been arrested (WEU, 1998c). Only one guilty verdict had been given, while two more trials had then just started. Soon after the more energetic approach agreed at Sintra was made known on 29 June 1997, the indicted war criminal, Slavko Dokmanovic, was arrested in Eastern Slavonia. Mr Dokmanovic was mayor of the Croatian town of Vukovar in November 1991, when the Yugoslav army troops and Serbian paramilitaries allegedly abducted and killed 260 personnel and patients from the local hospital (WEU, 1998c).

A few days later, on 10 July 1997, SFOR Special Forces mounted an operation against other indicted war criminals in Prijedor, in which Milan 'Mico' Kovacevic was arrested and transferred to The Hague and Simo Drljaca was killed when he opened fire on SFOR soldiers (WEU, 1998c). Mr Drljaca was forced to step down as Prijedor's police chief in 1996, but he continued to wield political influence. He took part in the black market which enables Radovan Karadzic to finance his unofficial authority and was in charge of cloaking other indicted war criminals by providing them with false documents and safe houses (WEU, 1998c). Mr Kovacevic was the political chief of Prijedor during the war and at the time of his arrest was a hospital director. Both men were the subject of sealed indictments issued by the War Crimes Tribunal and were accused of participating in genocide (*International Herald Tribune*, 12–13 July 1997). The Tribunal's Chief Prosecutor, Louise Arbour, announced in early 1998 that she planned to keep indictments secret in the future to avoid tipping off suspects about possible arrests (WEU, 1998c).

Political leaders in Republika Srpska and the Federal Republic of Yugoslavia immediately protested fiercely over the operation in Prijedor, which was followed by bomb and grenade attacks against Western targets in Bosnia and harassment of SFOR troops. The then Russian Foreign Minister, Yevgeni Primakov, criticized the firmer attitude SFOR was taking towards Bosnian Serbs. He called it 'counterproductive' and said he would prefer not to see similar operations in the future (WEU, 1998c). When visiting Sarajevo on 30 July 1997, SACEUR Wesley Clark declared that reprisals by Bosnian Serbs following the more active operations would not deter SFOR from continuing its new policy.

Notwithstanding these operations, SFOR and NATO officials insisted that the SFOR mandate had remained unchanged. It was at this point in July 1998 that the EU passed its key joint action undertaking to implement the war crimes sections of the Dayton Agreements.[16] Apparently, however, the interpretation of the mandate has been widened and there is more willingness to exercise it fully (WEU, 1998c). It has been made clear, however, that in weighing future similar operations, several important factors will be considered, such as the probability of success in capturing suspects with minimal civilian casualties, the possibilities of deterring Bosnian Serb retaliation and the value of any operation in destroying the power base of the hardline leadership in Pale (WEU, 1998c).

On 15 July 1997, the ICTY sentenced the Bosnian Serb war criminal Dusan Tadic to 20 years' imprisonment (*International Herald Tribune*, 20 July 1997). He was the second person to be sentenced for war crimes and crimes against humanity. Bosnian Serb authorities criticized the verdict as unjust and said it proved an anti-Serb bias on the part of the court. After heavy pressure had been exerted by the United States, ten indicted Bosnian Croat war criminals – including Dario Kordic, one of the most wanted suspects – were turned over to the ICTY in The Hague on 6 October 1997 (WEU, 1998c). They had surrendered in exchange for assurances that they would not have to wait for more than five months before going on trial. This leaves only one known indicted Croat war criminal, Ivica Rajic, at large.

The few spectacular arrest operations which have now taken place since June 1997 will have to be followed by others. By 1998, for instance, the Bosnian Government had handed over all the publicly indicted Muslims. Croatia more or less acted in the same way. The

Serbs consider that the ICTY in The Hague is part of a greater international conspiracy against them. The Dayton peace process, which aims at a unified Bosnian state, has stalled mainly because of the continuous sabotage and opposition of the Bosnian Serbs, in particular Mr Karadzic and his supporters (WEU, 1998c). It has been pointed out repeatedly by Western authorities that arresting Mr Karadzic is an option, but not necessarily the only one. There is also a possibility that he will be marginalised by new political developments. In particular, until her arrest in 2001, Mrs Plavsic's emergence as an alternative was seen by some as a more attractive way of removing Mr Karadzic from power (Daadler and Froman, 1999). Interestingly, in conclusion, on a visit to Sarajevo on 30 July 1997, the then NATO Secretary-General, Javier Solana, declared that all indicted war criminals will be brought to trial in The Hague before the international community leaves Bosnia-Herzegovina (WEU, 1998c).

Local elections: a democracy and transparency agenda

The establishment of democracy involves a long learning process. In the Balkans, elections have long been considered as a means to legitimize the power of the rulers (Malcolm, 1994). The main parties in power at present have a nationalist and ethnic stance and are in control of the media, employment, housing and the economy. The European Union's policy has been to support local democracy where it is feasible in conjunction with the OSCE.[17] Policy has been largely determined within small groupings at the highest levels of political organization. Implementation of policy has been carried out by the humanitarian and external relations DGs of the Commission in consultation with the OSCE.[18] Nevertheless, unexpected external policy developments have meant that EU actors' policy preferences have had to change – sometimes violently – to meet new circumstances. The fluidity of the situation prevented planning for implementing policy beyond a rudimentary level.

In the West's view, democratic elections can never lead to the unbridled exercise of power by the winner. Real democracy means being elected to exercise power while allowing others to hold that power in check (WEU, 1998c).

The local elections which should have taken place on 14 September 1996 were postponed several times for a number of reasons (*Economist*, 3 August 1996, p. 44). In November 1996, the political leaders of the Muslim–Croat Federation asked the OSCE to supervise the local elections in 1997, which at the time were still being rejected by the political leaders of Republika Srpska. However, on 1 December 1997, the OSCE announced that the President of Republika Srpska, Biljana

Plavsic, had formally agreed to local elections, requesting the OSCE to prolong its mission in order to supervise them (WEU, 1998c).

After many complaints, calls to boycott the elections, requests to postpone them and other attempts to undermine the process, municipal elections finally took place on 13 and 14 September 1997 in the whole of Bosnia and Herzegovina. President Slobodan Milosevic had convinced the SDS (Serb) leaders of Republika Srpska not to boycott the elections, stating that 'nobody may meddle with the legitimate right of the citizens to vote for their representatives' (WEU, 1998c). The OSCE sent 2450 observers. In order to be able to ensure maximum security, SFOR increased its strength from 30 000 to 36 000 troops, while the US sent six F-16 aircraft to the Italian air base at Aviano for reinforced surveillance of Bosnian territory during the elections. On the eve of the elections, NATO's Secretary-General, Javier Solana, made it clear that SFOR would 'not tolerate any violence or threat of violence' and he warned the media 'whose output is in persistent and blatant contradiction of either the spirit or the letter of the Dayton Peace Agreement' (WEU, 1998c).

The OSCE proclaimed the elections a success and a major milestone in the peace process (von Hippel, 2000, pp. 154–67). It recognized that there had been minor irregularities but these had not had a significant influence on the overall process. More than 70 per cent of the 2.5 million registered voters went to the polls. Results highlighted that the three nationalist parties – SDA (Muslim), SDS (Serb) and HDZ (Croat) – secured the largest number of votes, but both in the Federation and in Republika Srpska their popularity is waning and there is a shift in favour of a heterogeneous opposition (WEU, 1998c).

In Banja Luka, the SDS won only 7 of 70 seats, while a number of parties which had pledged their support for Mrs Plavsic won 45 seats. In Brcko, the Serbs held the majority in the municipal council but in Srebrenica, Muslims won 25 seats against 20 for the two main ultra-nationalist Serb parties. The current mayor of Srebrenica has rejected the results. The main problem will now be to implement the results of the elections, in particular in those municipalities where the majority is a result of the votes of refugees who cast their votes elsewhere (WEU, 1998c). The OSCE has announced that independently of the results of the vote in each community, a multi-ethnic administration will be established in order to control the tension that still exists. There will, however, be little chance for Muslims to return to such towns as Srebrenica or for Serbs to return to Drvar as long as these remain 'occupied' by Serb and Croat extremist nationalists respectively (WEU, 1998c).

Theoretically, much depends on the political will of the foreign countries committed to the peace process and to the election results to implement the results and use the means at their disposal (WEU, 1998c). It is not quite clear what this would mean in practice. The OSCE can of course try, with the assistance of SFOR and the EU, to enforce the election results in those municipalities where the elected municipal council does not have the same ethnic composition as the current inhabitants, but that would lead to a splendidly artificial situation. It will certainly not lead to the establishment of democracy, which was one of the key objectives of the Dayton Agreement (Woodward, 1997). Since 2000, however, local politics has been organized less along ethnic than party political lines.

Pillarization: financial and economic aid for reconstruction

Economic and financial aid and trade between the EU and Bosnia-Herzegovina is within the domain of pillar one. However, increasingly, political decisions taken in pillar two have had economic spill-over effects for pillar one. Decisions, as is mentioned below, have tended to be advocated from the 'top down' by national politicians and implemented by ECHO and the external relations DGs of the Commission. As is stated above, arguments surface from time to time concerning whether the member states or the Commission ought to pay for Joint actions. Since the Inter-Institutional Agreement of 1997 operational expenditure has been charged to the Community budget as non-compulsory expenditure unless the Council decides otherwise.[19] The member states have continuously failed to pay their share of Joint action monies on time. The foreign donor countries and also the Croats, Muslims and Serbs agree that economic integration and a strengthened relationship with the international business community is the only possibility for lasting peace and development in Bosnia and Herzegovina. The key actor in this respect is the EU (Woodward, 1997). Undoubtedly, the country needs foreign aid for reconstruction, but this aid can only be effective if there is an administration with enough know-how and a satisfactory framework of legislation to guarantee the smooth running of the state and its economics. As long as these are lacking because of the reluctance of the different entities to inject energy into the establishment of government machinery which they were forced to accept under the Dayton Agreement, foreign aid can only be moderately effective. The fragile political situation deterring foreign private investors for whom the alternatives in neighbouring countries in Central Europe are less complicated and more attractive.

Implementing the Dayton Agreements 125

In April 1997, the Council of the European Union declared that its commercial relations with Albania, Bosnia and Herzegovina, Croatia, the Federal Republic of Yugoslavia, and FYROM were subject to certain *conditions* (WEU, 1998c). Policy debates at the EU level have been driven by questions of political conditionality by national politicians, civil servants and European civil servants. The EU's view is that bilateral relations, the granting of commercial preference and exchanges, economic co-operation and financial aid would only be possible with countries respecting democratic principles and the rule of law, human rights and the rights of minorities, the principles of a market economy and regional co-operation.[20]

The lack of internal agreement in Bosnia and Herzegovina caused the repeated postponement of an international donor conference. The United States insisted on postponement until the Serbs agreed on legislation which would facilitate investments in the country (this is also linked to human rights records). This legislation was to comprise laws on the payment of foreign debt, the creation of a central bank, a common currency, customs arrangements and a privatization programme. Europeans wanted this conference to take place on the condition that aid to Republika Srpska would be blocked until they agreed to the new legislation (WEU, 1998c).

The central Bosnian Government announced on 15 April 1997 that it had agreed to establish a central bank and a common currency. No sooner was this agreement concluded than the Bosnian Serbs withdrew their approval, bringing everything back to square one. In June 1997, the Parliament passed laws to create a central bank and a common currency but their implementation appears to be causing problems (WEU, 1998c).

Finally, an international donor conference on Bosnia took place on 23–24 July 1997, under the auspices of the European Union and the World Bank, with 30 organizations participating. The participants pledged a total of $1.22 billion in aid to support industry, repair the infrastructure and get the local economy moving (*International Herald Tribune*, 28 July 1997). The conference chairman, Hans van den Broek, the EU Commissioner for External Political Relations, said that aid could not be justified to parties who 'oppose and frustrate' the goal of post-war reconstruction in Bosnia and Herzegovina (WEU, 1998c). He added that humanitarian assistance to Republika Srpska would be continued, but that the overall political and economic influence of indicted war criminals in the republic 'is such that it would be irresponsible to continue spending public funds for reconstruction purposes' (WEU, 1998c).

The conference issued a declaration in which it denounced the critical situation in Republika Srpska, noting the anti-democratic climate, terrorist actions and violations of the authority of the police (WEU, 1998c). The granting of non-humanitarian aid was not excluded, but as long as the Republic did not meet its obligations under the Dayton Agreement, it would only concern aid which would promote its integration into Bosnia and Herzegovina without ending up in the pockets of indicted war criminals (WEU, 1998c).

In 1997, the United States blocked two World Bank and International Monetary Fund loans to Croatia and threatened it with diplomatic isolation if it did not comply with the obligations of the Dayton Agreement (European Commission, 1997b).

Mapping the decision-making stage[21]

International stabilization force (SFOR)

The growing consensus over the need for a successor force to IFOR was consistently voiced in the chancelleries of Western European states in the course of 1996. The European Union launched a series of joint actions in 1997 and 1998 vis-à-vis the Bosnian situation, each of which was dependent on a successful international presence in the region to prevent war breaking out.[22] The EU suggested that a semi-permanent military force should be operational in Bosnia-Herzegovina.

The EU's main input into the SFOR policy-making process is via the Consultative Task Force on Bosnia which comprises the main Western military powers, the UN, NATO, WEU and EU (European Commission, 1997b). This consensus became even stronger when the head of the OSCE electoral mission, Robert Frowick, announced on 22 October 1996 that the municipal elections in Bosnia and Herzegovina, scheduled for November after having been postponed several times, were to be postponed until spring 1997 (WEU, 1998c). Among the reasons for this fresh delay were the irregularities noted during enrollment on electoral lists, and the lack of freedom of movement which was closely connected with the activities of nationalist leaders to promote separation.

On 7 November 1996, General William Crouch, head of the Allied Land Forces Central Europe (AFCENT), took over the command of IFOR. Elements from headquarters AFCENT were deployed to form the nucleus of a new headquarters for the command and control of IFOR (WEU, 1998c). Although the main mission of the new headquarters was to assume responsibility for organizing the IFOR withdrawal, it was no secret that it might also become the headquarters of the IFOR successor force (WEU, 1998c).

Later, on 27 November 1996, the NATO Permanent Council agreed on most of the political directives for the military authorities to plan for an IFOR successor force, named SFOR (WEU, 1998c). After having replaced IFOR on 20 December 1996, SFOR was, in principle, to stay for a period of 18 months until 20 June 1998 (under pressure from the US Congress). It was also agreed, in principle, that the initial contingent of 31 000 troops would be reduced as soon as possible, depending on the circumstances, and that the definitive duration of its mandate would depend upon reviews of the situation after six and twelve months of its mission (WEU, 1998c).

SFOR was to provide assistance in the municipal elections planned for the summer of 1997 and the possibility of sending more troops during the election period was kept open. Like IFOR, SFOR was not to perform any police tasks and, as a consequence, it was not to pursue war criminals indicted by the International Criminal Tribunal for Former Yugoslavia (ICTY). This was a task taken on more forcefully by the EU in conjunction with the ICTY.[23] SACEUR Wesley Clark emphasized that SFOR would concentrate on the main military tasks and provide a safe, secure environment and that it would have the same rules of engagement (von Hippel, 2000, pp. 154–67). After the adoption of UN Security Council Resolution 1088, which gave NATO a mandate to carry out operation Joint Guard on the basis of Chapter VII of the UN Charter, NATO's defence ministers approved the operational plans for SFOR on 17 December 1996. SFOR became operational on 20 December 1996, having taken over from IFOR (WEU, 1998c).

Mapping the implementation stage[24]

Implementation structures: SFOR, NATO, the EU, democracy and legitimacy?

Theoretically, implementation of the combined joint task forces (CJTF) concept would provide Europeans with the possibility of deploying an SFOR successor force under the responsibility of WEU and under a European command. Most NATO, EU and WEU officials have rejected this option as being beyond WEU's capabilities. In principle, WEU is capable of mounting a military operation of the 'Petersberg type', involving no more than 10 000 troops (Jorgensen, 1997). Policy developments in 1997 and 1998, which resulted in the decision to maintain

SFOR at its reinforced level until an unspecified date, clearly indicated that the situation in Bosnia and Herzegovina required the presence of a substantial force for a long period of time (WEU, 1998c, Part 2). In terms of implementing Dayton, the 'EU' Europeans will not deploy a successor force to SFOR on their own (WEU, 1998c), despite the announcement in November 2000 of a European Rapid Reaction Corps designed exactly for this kind of eventuality. The EU and its member states still rely on an American presence in Europe to maintain crisis management and Petersberg capabilities on the continent of Europe (The Independent, 30 November 2000). The purpose of a foreign military presence in Bosnia and Herzegovina is to ensure the secure environment which is needed for the full implementation of the Dayton Agreement. This complicated Agreement, even if its theoretical framework is based on earlier European peace initiatives, was drafted by the Americans, who have also made great efforts to convince the warring parties that they had no choice other than to sign (Chandler, 1999). The US will therefore at least have to assume its full co-responsibility to ensure there is a secure environment for implementation of the Agreement (Glitman, 1997–98, pp. 5–18). Indeed, as is stated above, the Europeans lack the necessary credibility to implement to the Agreements without US backing (Holbrooke, 1998).

Implementing Operation Joint Guard: The Four Phases (Cited in WEU, 1998c).

I: transition: a period from 20 December 1996 to 3 February 1997, to fully deploy SFOR with 32 participating countries;

II: stabilization: from February to June 1997, the aim being to prevent further hostilities until after the municipal elections planned for June 1997 – this was SFOR's main task;

III: deterrence: from June 1997 to spring 1998, during which time SFOR, with a reduced strength would still have to dissuade parties from starting a fresh conflict;

IV: end of mission, with the complete withdrawal of forces at the end of June 1998 (troops are still in Bosnia to prevent a return to inter-ethnic conflict (Chandler, 1999)).

In spring 1997, soon after the full deployment of SFOR, it became increasingly clear that the implementation process of the Dayton Agreement had come to an almost complete standstill in many respects. Both the NATO Council and the Steering Board of the Peace Implementation Council, meeting in May 1997, decided to stabilize the situation on the ground by greater NATO presence (WEU, 1998c).

Inevitably, this approach would only be effective if accompanied by a more assertive stance on the part of SFOR which was reinforced for this purpose.

In preparation for the municipal elections in Bosnia and Herzegovina, SACEUR Wesley Clark called for a temporary reinforcement of SFOR with six battalions from 20 August to 20 October 1997 in order to guarantee an environment of security and provide logistics and communications support which was accordingly authorized (Holbrooke, 1998). The NATO Council discussed the first six months' review of the SFOR mission on 27 June 1997 in consultation with the 20 non-NATO countries contributing to SFOR (which included several EU member states). A statement on the six-month review noted in particular the following: 'While the Parties remain in general compliant with the military provisions of the Peace Agreement, there are still serious concerns about the deficiencies remaining in the overall [civilian] implementation of the Peace Agreement' (WEU, 1998c).

At its meeting at the end of July 1997, the Permanent NATO Council called on its military authorities to study several options for transition from Phase II (stabilization) to Phase III (deterrence), which in the original plan entailed a considerable reduction in troop numbers – from 30 000 to less than 20 000 (WEU, 1998c). At the same time, the Secretary-General of NATO, the SFOR Commander and a number of Western governments issued firm warnings to political leaders in Republika Srpska that more terrorist attacks against SFOR and other international personnel in the Republic could lead to punitive action (WEU, 1998c). This forceful sentiment was backed by the EU's High Representative in Bosnia and Herzegovina, Carlos Westendorp.[25]

At an informal meeting of NATO's defence ministers in Maastricht on 1 and 2 October 1997, no formal decisions were taken on SFOR, but consensus was reached in favour of an ongoing SFOR presence in Bosnia and Herzegovina (WEU, 1998c). At the same time, ministers thought that as SFOR was at its maximum strength, and that the situation must be used to support the pro-Dayton forces and make maximum progress in stabilizing Bosnia and Herzegovina (WEU, 1998c).

STAGE 3: EVALUATION

Conclusion

Thinking empirically[26]

In spring 1997, the Clinton Administration, acknowledging that the Dayton peace process was in danger, started to advocate and take more active steps to make parties meet their obligations. The President had previously pledged that United States ground forces would leave Bosnia and Herzegovina at the end of the SFOR mandate in June 1998 (Agence Europe, 14 January 1997). President Clinton and his closest foreign policy advisers recognized full well that without the presence of foreign military forces (especially American forces), progress in the implementation of the Dayton Agreement would be almost non-existent (WEU, 1998c). Both the Secretary of State, Madeleine Albright, and the craftsman of the Dayton Agreement, Richard Holbrooke, were sent to the region in order to give fresh impetus to the peace process (Holbrooke, 1998). Widespread consultation with the Western European NATO allies was carried out at the bilateral level and in the EU context. A similar exercise was carried out in 1996, when remarks attributed to Richard Holbrooke caused a stir in transatlantic relations and hampered consultation. Holbrooke publicly stated – it turns out incorrectly – that Western European officials were preparing for the partition of Bosnia and Herzegovina (Agence Europe, 17 June 1996, p. 24).

SFOR was instructed to become more actively engaged while, at the same time, it was reinforced with extra troops. It very soon became clear, however, that even this more active foreign involvement in getting the Dayton Agreement implemented would never result in a situation which would allow foreign troops to leave Bosnia and Herzegovina by June 1998 without any risk of a resumption of hostilities between the parties (Chandler, 1999).

In a series of meetings with NATO in Brussels during late 1997 and early 1998, both the EU High Representative, Carlos Westendorp, and the Head of the OSCE Mission, Robert Frowick, stressed the need for a long-term international commitment while pointing out that substantial progress had already been made in implementing the Dayton Agreement (WEU, 1998c). Advisers close to Mr Frowick made it clear that it was absolutely essential for the international community to remain in Bosnia for an unspecified length of time, including a 'significant and credible commitment, especially by the United States'.[27]

Although for some time, the United States Government tried to maintain the impression that it was determined to withdraw its ground troops from Bosnia and Herzegovina in June 1998, this was never a policy option in the light of developments in that country, in Kosovo and in NATO (R. Cohen, 1998, pp. 106–11). Nevertheless, a shift in opinion is clearly apparent in the attitude of the US Congress. In June 1997, for example, the House of Representatives adopted an amendment to cut off funds for US peacekeeping troops in Bosnia after June 1998. Members of the House said that this deadline provision should serve notice on European allies to be prepared to take on greater responsibility in Bosnia by that time (WEU, 1998c; von Hippel, 2000).

In September 1997, several US authorities started to prepare the public for a continuation of close US involvement in Bosnia. Sandy Berger, President Clinton's National Security Adviser, criticized those politicians and analysts who had argued in favour of giving up the peace process under the Dayton Agreement. Admitting that progress in the Dayton peace process was painfully slow, he said there was nevertheless positive change and that the conditions were being created for a lasting peace. He added that a failed Dayton would almost certainly result in a new conflict which could extend into south-eastern Europe. This would undermine NATO's credibility at a critical moment. The United States, he concluded, had an important interest in the establishment of a lasting peace in Bosnia (WEU, 1998c).

In preparation for the meeting of NATO defence ministers in Maastricht on 1 and 2 October 1997, the then NATO Secretary-General, Javier Solana, declared that the priority for SFOR was not to concentrate on full implementation of the Dayton Agreement (WEU, 1998c). As regards to the possible end of the SFOR mission in June 1998, Mr Solana affirmed that the international community would not abandon Bosnia but said it was too early to discuss a follow-up to SFOR in concrete terms (WEU, 1998c). He did not believe that any country, including the US, would leave Bosnia-Herzegovina completely.

The Western European NATO allies all expressed the opinion that in any post-SFOR configuration, US ground troops would have to participate on the territory of Bosnia and Herzegovina. The EU and the US had decided in 1997 to share the economic and political responsibilities for managing the situation in Bosnia through SFOR (WEU, 1998c). Nevertheless, the EU's economic contribution (not including Western European contributions to SFOR) since 1996 has amounted to ECU 2 billion (von Hippel, 2000).[28] The majority of Western European states have also declared that their troops would leave the country if the US forces were to do so. Further fissures were revealed in EU policy towards Bosnia in 1997 when the British Defence Secretary George Robertson stated that if a new follow-on force in Bosnia was agreed 'it will have to be NATO-led, with NATO-led credibility, and with all the major players sharing the risks on the ground' (WEU, 1998c).

Thinking about preference formation

In terms of preference formation the agenda-setting stage of the Dayton Accords phase was set by low- to middle-level desk officers and low- to middle-level politicians on the ground in Bosnia-Herzegovina.

Policy preferences typically formed around significant policy areas in an almost unplanned and haphazard 'garbage can' manner in some cases. Several examples of this form of agenda-setting style can be gleaned from the key Dayton-related case studies empirically set out above, and summarized in conceptual terms below, in the following key Joint action areas: refugees, displaced persons, war criminals, and local elections.

Agenda-setting was typically a product of the need to solve problems that required solutions rather than finding problems to apply ready-made solutions to them. Hence decision-making consistency was reactive as opposed to proactive in the majority of cases. Policy initiatives tended to be grounded in practicalities. The main idea for the majority of the Joint Actions under scrutiny came from the member states through the General Affairs Council. However, means–ends relationships were not properly specified and uncertainties in technologies meant that agenda-setting was endogenous to the policy process. The agenda of the Joint Action changed from its initial conception to the final product of the agenda stage. This was mainly due to actor preferences changing erratically during the formation of the agenda phase. This contributed to producing a 'garbage can' policy process.

For example, with reference to the free movement of persons – a key policy objective of the Dayton Agreements – policy has tended to be controlled by high-level diplomats and Eurocrats with expertise in this particular area. As is stated above, implementation has been left to the Commission and particularly to ECHO.[29] Nevertheless, the implementation did not always run smoothly. Means–ends relationships were not always adequately specified; the fluidity of the agenda meant that preferences of the major actors had to change to suit circumstances; the aims and objectives of the Joint action were often confused leading to confusion in implementation.

Preference formation in terms of decision-making in this case was *theoretically speaking* based on strategic action from the level of leaders downwards maximizing policy preferences, but the practice was very different. A good deal of muddled debate had produced a semi-structured policy-making environment with some partisan mutual adjustment of policy preferences at the margins of policy. However, the main decision-making stage was dominated by uncertain means–ends relationships, uncertainties of technologies, and indecisiveness on the part of the major Western actors in Bosnia. For example, as we have stated above, with reference to refugees and displaced persons, Annex 7 of the Dayton Agreement was never implemented. Policy changed to meet the realities of the ethnic divide in Bosnia-Herzegovina as was the case in the specific instance of the Mostar Joint action (as discussed in chapter 4). This induced a muddling of preferences in Western policy not knowing how to react to the situation. Decisions were made as they went along.

Further examples of such muddled Western preference structures exist. The Western – especially EU – response towards war criminals was one of indecisiveness: indeed, the Council and Commission initially failed to combine with the member states to produce a solid decision-making basis for implementing a joint action on war criminals. The EU also failed to make explicit policy linkages with NATO and the OSCE. Preferences were often incomplete and not well worked out, leading to confusion and strained relations with the US. Additionally, some actors held on to redundant preferences when it would have been more rational to ditch them.

For example, the European Parliament was keen to have direct inputs into the local election process in Bosnia and Herzegovina (European Parliament, 1997a). Democratic accountability and elections in Bosnia – linked to the Parliament's parallel conception of its *own* role in the EU – has been relatively high on the agenda for EU policy-makers in former Yugoslavia. Indeed, restoring democracy to the Balkans is a key objective of the Dayton Accords. Nevertheless, the EP's inputs into this process after 1997 have been restricted. The European Parliament, in democratic accountability terms, following the Inter-Institutional Agreement of July 1997, has powers of information and consultation in CFSP only (this not being conducive to proper democratic audit or accountability).[30] Without direct inputs from the EP into CFSP – the EP is an institution that understands how to build democracy incrementally from a low starting point – the Western policy towards elections in Bosnia has not been as vigorous or rational as it could have been. The result has been mixed policy preferences and indecision on the part of Western decision-makers. Policy has tended to be made up as the process has gone along.

Thinking theoretically: a case of garbage cans

In the course of the agenda-setting, decision-making and implementation phases of the policy cycle, the Dayton Accords were influenced to varying degrees by rational choice, policy network and garbage-can-like policy-making. The dominant form of policy intercourse, however, tended to be influenced by key factors which were endogenous to the policy process. The preferences of key actors were heavily endogenous to the process.

This is common to the policy network and garbage can models. However, the complicated situation presented by the Dayton Agreements was far more complex than this and resembled a garbage can.

Unlike in the policy network approach, actor preferences were extremely problematic in a garbage can-like manner. Actor preferences changed frequently and unpredictably through the course of the Joint action to keep up with the often bewildering behaviour of the various indigenous ethno-political groupings. It is clear that in order to be flexible many Western (that is, Western European and American) actors did not have well-formed preferences in relation to important aspects of the Joint action at all. Indeed, there is little evidence here that the main actors achieved a stable ranking between the preferences they used to justify a particular joint action, or that they anticipated ways in which preferences might have to be traded against one another, unless and until choice was forced upon them. The articulations of 'reasons' given for the various Joint actions' growth over time were significantly vaguer before the decision moment than after it. Actors found out what they wanted through action, rather than acting according to a ranked list of what they preferred.

For example, with reference to the return of displaced persons and refugees to their homes, which is also a key objective of Dayton, the EU has been slow to put forward a clear strategy. Due to divisions between the EU member states, policy preferences have been fluid and not very stable over time. Additionally, the member states have tended to leave this area of policy to NATO and the UN.[31]

It is not even especially clear in this case where the various joint actions came from in the first place. The Council *did* take a lead in initiating the various joint actions. It is also clear that the Commission played a leading role in the agenda-setting and implementation phases of the policy process. However, it is much less clear who thought of the idea first, when and why. During the agenda-setting phase, the idea for the various joint actions above came from the Council. Nevertheless, at key phases of the agenda-setting process the Council failed to give leadership in response to the fluidity of the situation on the ground in Bosnia. The muddled, imprecise and stilted policy preferences of the key EU actors failed to change in order to meet the new realities of the changing situation in Bosnia. Smoking guns (that is, external shocks) emerged to force preference changes. It was at this stage that the lack of preference ranking of actors came into evidence.

In another example, with regard to EU policy on missing persons – a key policy objective of the Dayton Agreements – the EU's policy process was characterized by uncertainty and indecision in the Union's institutions, and in the member states. Whilst supporting the objectives of the ICMP, which was set up in the summer of 1996, the Union lacked a coherent view of its own collective policy in this area. This can also be tied in with the indecisive EU inputs into the work of the allied ICTY. A lack of proper priorities, corresponding decisive policy-making and implementation in the EU has produced something akin to garbage can policies.

In terms of the agenda-setting and decision-making stages of the policy process, the Commission and Council held similar preferences towards the case (those of facilitating free movement of persons; facilitating human rights; bringing to book indicted war criminals; reconstructing Bosnia and Herzegovina after the war; and conducting local elections in order to legitimize the political system). However, preferences were not at all well worked out. A series of unforeseen external shocks meant that the incomplete preferences of the main actors were unable to deal with the fluid situation on the ground. The preferences of the main actors became more complex as the Joint Action progressed, but the gap between the normative values implied by these complex preferences, and their actual utility was cruelly exposed by the fluidity of the situation. This also implies that the preferences were ill-informed and had not been well worked out. Additionally, means–ends relationships were badly operationalised, and uncertainties as to technologies made it difficult to plan for making and implementing policy.

For example, with reference to the Union's policy towards indicted and suspected war criminals, the EU has aligned its policies in line with those pursued by SFOR, NATO and ICTY. Nevertheless, the Union has lacked a corresponding normative vision of its place in this process (Delcourt and Remacle, 1997, pp. 74–87). Brussels has allowed other international institutions and actors to drive this important process and has lacked correspondingly well worked out preferences in order to place a coherent 'EU view' on the bargaining table (Laignel-Lavastine, 1998, p. 47).

In the period of the Joint Action, there was a good deal of confusion about both 'internal' and 'external' technologies. Confusion about 'internal' technologies means the absence of clear and stable views about the procedures for the Joint Actions themselves. Confusion and disagreement reigned as to: (i) who was to frame and set the agenda; (ii) where the appropriate domain of the Joint Action ought to be (in other words, on whose behalf it is conducted); (iii) the appropriate scope of the Joint Action (that is, who is to be affected by the action);

(iv) rules that should govern decision-making including informal rules; (v) when decisions have been made and what they are. Additionally, confusion about 'external' technologies did not help. Attempts to specify means–ends relationships or resources in advance amounted to little more than guesses that bore little relation to the subsequent evolution of the Joint Action.

For example, with reference to local elections the EU's policy was underdeveloped. As stated above, the EU institutions constantly vied for policy hegemony. The EP – the natural institution to have input into any democratic experiment in Bosnia – was sidelined in the EU's policy process. Indeed, inter-institutional disagreements between the Council, Commission, Parliament, and with member states, produced a messy policy process devoid of structure and coherence. Indeed, policies were based more on crude guesses than on well-researched preferences. The end result was confused and confusing to the parties in Bosnia, NATO and the US. In the latter instance, Washington took EU indecision to reflect a malaise in policy-making in Brussels, thereby straining transatlantic relations.[32]

There were also fluid patterns of actor participation over the course of the Joint Action. Some member states were far more interested in the Joint Action than others, sometimes to the point at which a joint action emerged as the 'pet project' of particular member states, while being virtually ignored by others. The locus of action shifted between levels and agencies (Commission, Council, GAC and working parties of officials, even the EU itself and other international bodies) without such change being traceable to clear decisions on who should be authorized to act or take the initiative. Actors of all kinds drifted in and out of the Joint Action, or showed marked variation in the time, attention and resources they expended. All of this contrasts with the policy network assumption that policy is dominated by continuously engaged experts.

For example, with regard to its relations with SFOR the EU did not have a clear policy. The EU's main input into SFOR was via the Consultative Task Force mentioned above. Nevertheless, some states were much keener than others to contribute to collective European diplomacy via CFSP joint actions. The British and French were keen in this regard, whereas Belgium and Germany were not at all keen. It was not clear, therefore, whether Britain and France could or should speak for the EU in the Consultative Task Force. This produced indecision in EU policy, fluid participation and a lack of rank-ordered European-level preferences. In the end, Britain and France decided to adopt national

Implementing the Dayton Agreements 137

foreign policies towards the Consultative Task Force at least in part due to the lack of a coherent alternative in the EU.

In the absence of either well-specified interests (as in the rational model), or shared understandings (as in the policy network model), in this particular case there was very little effective cross-pillar coherence in the formulation of joint actions. Each pillar acted according to its own organizational, procedural and legal rules in relatively splendid isolation from the other pillars.

For example, as stated above, in terms of having inputs into Operation Joint Guard in 1996 and 1997 the EU failed to present a coherent cross-pillar consensus in policy. The Council did not take the lead in suggesting EU inputs of resources into the policy process. Indeed, neither did the Commission, but the Parliament did. Due to a standstill in developments on the ground in Bosnia, the EU and its member states did not change their preferences in a fluid dynamic manner. The end result was a failure to comprehend the wider dynamics of Operation Joint Guard, which relied on the EU for its success to some degree. The main EU policy failure was not to adequately provide resources for Operation Joint Guard that were distinct from national member state resources. This was reflected in poor cross pillar co-ordination.

The whole series of Dayton-related joint actions highlighted a disjointed pattern of path dependence – a pattern of 'punctured equilibrium'. On the one hand, radical uncertainty about preferences and the decision-making environment led to long periods of inflexibility in which the joint actions remained much the same in scope, means and resourcing, in spite of evident fluidity in what was expected of the various actors, and despite large changes in circumstances. This was what happened, for example, in the case of Operation joint Guard. On the other hand, poor understanding of how issues were connected in the decision-making environment often led to the unintentional destabilization of particular joint actions. This was the developing situation, for example, in the case of the local election Joint action where the various EU institutions competed for policy hegemony, thereby failing to grasp important inter-institutional policy linkages, whilst unintentionally destabilizing the decision-making environment of the Joint action.

Critical decisions were often made at the highest levels of national governments and implemented through WEU, NATO and EU structures. First-pillar structures in the EU were utilized – somewhat ineffectively – for resourcing purposes to give concrete meaning to decisions

138 EU Foreign Policy beyond the Nation-State

made at the national and European levels in a 'high politics' context (that is, in a second-pillar context). Nevertheless, during the implementation stage cross-pillar coherence was ineffective and inefficient, due to fluid patterns of EU actor participation. Additionally, communication between the pillars was not generally efficient and effective due to the lack of properly formed sets of aims/objectives and means/ends. By this late stage of the policy process, EU policy was being driven from the ground in Bosnia reacting to events, but the corresponding necessary changes to ensure efficient preference structures in EU policy-making were not made.

The result of all this is that the various joint actions under scrutiny tended to be made up by the actors as they went along: analysis shows that it is very difficult to trace eventual outcomes back to initial intentions, via stable and agreed procedures for framing joint actions, and means–ends relationships that were anticipated in advance.

Notes

1 The following chapter heavily relies on Western European Union, 'European Security in Stages: Report on the Former Yugoslavia and the Implementation of the Dayton Agreements', Brussels, WEU, 1998c, for *factual* interpretations of the Dayton Agreements' implementation. *Factual* information relating to the implementation of the Dayton Agreements – and their historical and political context – is liberally drawn from the report.
2 Joint action 97/153/CFSP.
3 Joint action 97/224/CFSP.
4 Council Decision 98/196/CFSP.
5 Joint action 98/117/CFSP.
6 Joint action 98/302/CFSP.
7 Joint action 98/625/CFSP.
8 Council Decision 98/737/CFSP.
9 Common Position 97/193/CFSP.
10 Interview, Desk Officer, DG1A, January 2000.
11 Bulletin, EU 6–1998, Common Foreign and Security Policy, 11/31.
12 Common Position 97/193/CFSP.
13 Joint action 97/153/CFSP.
14 Joint action CFSP 97/224/CFSP.
15 Council Decision 98/196/CFSP.
16 Joint action 98/117/CFSP.
17 Joint action 98/302/CFSP.
18 Interview, ECHO Desk Officer, Brussels, December 1997.
19 Bulletin 7/8–1997, points 1.4.1. and 2.3.1.

Implementing the Dayton Agreements 139

20 Council Decision 98/737/CFSP.
21 This section of the analysis heavily relies on WEU (1998c, Part 2).
22 Successive reports have been produced by the European Parliament's Committee on Foreign Affairs on CFSP Joint actions since November 1993. See the bibliography for further precise details.
23 Joint action 97/193/CFSP was aimed at persons having perpetrated violent acts in Bosnia and Herzegovina. Joint action 97/625/CFSP was against persons who had undermined the peace process and elections.
24 This section of the analysis heavily relies on WEU (1998c, Part 2).
25 OJ L 259, 22.9.97.
26 This subsection of the conclusion heavily relies on WEU (1998c, Part 2).
27 Interviews, Desk Officer, DG1A, Brussels, November 1997.
28 In May 1998 the Fourth Bosnia and Herzegovina Donor Conference was held in Brussels. It is made up of the main SFOR participating states, the EU and UN. Bulletin EU. 5–1998. Point 1.3.76.
29 Common Position 97/193/CFSP.
30 Bulletin 7/8–1997, points 1.4.1. and 2.3.1.
31 Interview, Desk Officer, ECHO, Brussels, January 2000.
32 Interview, Desk Officer, DG1A, Brussels, January 2000.

6
The European Union's Policy towards the Caucasus, 1996–99[1]

STAGE 1: CHRONOLOGY

Introduction

The following chapter seeks to analyse the European Union's (EU) main political and economic policies towards the Caucasus. In particular, the chapter will focus on key joint actions and related political and economic policies. The specific focus of the chapter, however, is on EU policy towards emerging markets in oil and gas production in the Caucasus. The Union's policy vis-à-vis the Caucasus is primarily driven, as the evidence below highlights, by economic and technical considerations. This will form the major area of inquiry of the present analysis. The chapter will also consider EU policy-making towards the Caucasus with special reference to agenda-setting, decision-making and the implementation of key joint actions and related policies. Specifically, the chapter focuses on process, relationships between joint actions and related policies as an unusual policy-making method, actor behaviour, and policy outcomes. Finally, the chapter will test the extent to which the policy process was characterized by degrees of rationality, bounded rationality, policy networks and/or garbage can agenda-setting, decision-making, and policy implementation.

Western Europe's interest in the developments in the Caucasus is of recent date, having emerged since the birth of newly independent states situated between the Black Sea and the Chinese border (WEU, 1998b). All of the Caucasus states used to be part of the former Soviet Union and are now members of the Commonwealth of Independent States (CIS). Until the break-up of the Soviet Union most of them had never genuinely known independence (Herzig, 1999).

Because of its geostrategic position, vast natural resources, ethnic diversity and variety of cultural and religious traditions, the entire Caucasus and Central Asian region is of considerable interest to the neighbouring major powers and especially to Russia, to which most of the newly independent countries belonged before the 1917 revolution (WEU, 1998b). Many regional conflicts have broken out in these areas and equitable solutions to some of them have not yet been found. The nineteenth-century power struggles between Russia and Great Britain are now consigned to history (WEU, 1998b). The number of other powers taking an interest in this part of the world has considerably increased since the dissolution of the Soviet Union. Without listing them comprehensively, mention might be made of the United States, Turkey, Iran, China, Pakistan and several European Union member countries, including France, Germany and the United Kingdom, while international organizations such as the Organization for Security and Cooperation in Europe (OSCE), the North Atlantic Treaty Organization (NATO), the United Nations (UN), the Council of Europe and the EU have begun to devote part of their political activity to the countries of central Asia and the Caucasus (European Report, 1999).[2] The Western European Union (WEU), which has responsibility for security and defence matters, has so far merely kept a watchful if increasingly interested eye on the situation, without taking any practical action (WEU, 1998b).

The WEU Council has thus made several statements on the ongoing disputes in Nagorno–Karabakh and Chechnya in support of the attempts made by the OSCE and the EU to arrive at a peaceful settlement of the conflicts (WEU, 1998b). In its document *European Security: a Joint Contribution*, adopted by the 27 WEU countries in November 1995, the WEU Council devoted a special chapter to Europe's world economic interests, which noted, inter alia, that:

> Most European countries are largely dependent for their supplies of energy and raw materials on countries whose political and economic stability over the medium term cannot be taken for granted. Gas and oil are conveyed, at least in part, through pipelines crossing countries of uncertain stability. In the event of a major crisis, the disruption of those supplies is a distinct probability and maritime transport routes could be vulnerable. The flow of gas and oil to European markets through reliable pipeline and maritime routes hold great political and strategic significance! (WEU, 1995)

As far as the Caucasus and the countries of Central Asia are concerned, the WEU Council stressed that it was in Europe's interest to encourage fruitful co-operation with the countries of the region and to ensure that any conflicts that divided it were settled by peaceful means, according to the principles defined by the United Nations Charter and by the OSCE. The Council furthermore confirmed its support for sovereignty and independence for all CIS member states (WEU, 1998b).

The Western European countries involved in the region generally share similar political objectives to the United States and have consequently drawn up political, commercial and aid programmes similar to the American programmes for the region. The main Western European and American policies towards the Caucasus revolve around economics (European Commission, 1996a). Strong competition to obtain shares in the consortium exploiting energy resources in Azerbaijan, for example, accentuates the different positions adopted by Western states (Herzig, 1999). There are major differences between the United States and European Union countries when it comes to the question of what attitude should be taken vis-à-vis Iran (WEU, 1998b). Some international organizations, such as the World Bank and the European Bank for Reconstruction and Development (EBRD), could play a bigger role in the future of the region. The World Bank has set up projects designed to help some of the countries around the Caspian Sea develop their energy infrastructure and legal systems (WEU, 1998b). The European Union provides the Caucasus and Central Asia with quite considerable humanitarian and technical aid and has further plans for assistance in the gas and oil sectors (European Commission, 1996a).[3] While the EU is, however, currently studying the construction projects for the Burgas–Alexandroupolis (Russia–Greece–Bulgaria) oil pipeline, it will have to weigh the advantages and disadvantages of all the solutions and not support just one project (European Commission, 1996a).

The countries of the Caucasus (Armenia, Azerbaijan, Georgia) are locked in by three regional powers – Iran, Russia and Turkey – and by two seas – the Black Sea and the Caspian Sea. Because of its strategic location, the region has, throughout history, been a battlefield for the empires of the region – Achaemenid, Greek, Roman, Parthian, Byzantine, Arab, Mongol, Ottoman, Persian, Russian (WEU, 1998b).

With the coming of *glasnost* and *perestroika* in 1986, the countries of the region saw their opportunity to exact further autonomy (Herzig, 1999). Georgia quickly laid claim to sovereign status and Armenia to the Nagorno-Karabakh region. These demands brought an explosion of violence in their wake (WEU, 1998b). The Armenian campaign in Nagorno-Karabakh to unite the enclave with Armenia led to confrontation in 1988, followed by anti-Armenian demonstrations in Azerbaijan. In April 1989, in Tbilisi, Georgian nationalists responded to Abkhazi agitators demanding greater autonomy by staging their own demonstration. This initially anti-Abkhazi demonstration soon took on the flavour of an independence rally and was quashed by the Soviet army. The Soviets were also responsible for the violent break-up of a demonstration in Baku in January 1990. These incidents strengthened Azerbaijan's determination to speed up the independence process. The hand of Moscow was automatically assumed to be at work in any separatist movement in those countries (WEU, 1998b). In each of them nationalist forces assumed power after the failed Moscow coup in 1991. The existing power structures established by the Russians collapsed, leading to instability and internal power struggles (WEU, 1998b, Part 1).

In 1996, the European Commission put forward a Joint action Plan for Russia and the Caucasus region (European Commission, 1996a). The Joint action Plan has guided general EU and member states' policies towards the region. The Joint action Plan had four main priorities which have been consistent with Union Joint actions towards the region: First, the modernization of nuclear facilities. Second, the fight against organized crime in the former Soviet Union (soft security issues under pillar three headings). Third, for the EU to put in place policies to prevent – and realistically stem – the flow of refugees from the CIS into Western Europe. Fourth, the integration of Russia and the Caucasus into the EU's research and development programmes. A related policy priority was for the EU to have preferential market access for developing Caucasus energy production in oil and gas. This latter economic policy priority has been *the* major driving force behind General Affairs Council and Commission policies towards the Caucasus since 1996.[4] The present analysis will therefore particularly focus on the area of emerging energy markets in the Caucasus, and the EU's policies towards those markets.

STAGE 2: MAPPING AGENDA-SETTING, DECISION-MAKING AND IMPLEMENTATION

Mapping the contributions of the different actors

In the course of 1998, the EU adopted two further Joint actions which were relevant to its overall regional approach to the CIS and the

144   *EU Foreign Policy beyond the Nation-State*

Caucasus: First, a Joint action on election monitoring for the Caucasus region to encourage greater democracy (Agence Europe, 28 September 1998, p. 4). Second, the EU adopted a Joint action on small arms to prevent the accumulation of dangerous handguns and semi-automatic rifles in the Balkans, CIS and elsewhere (Agence Europe, 30 December 1998, p. 4).

The major questions, however, remained economic and were contained in framework meetings and documents of the EU. On 18 September 1998, an EU Ministerial Troika met with Boris Yeltsin in Moscow to discuss the economic crisis in Russia and the Caucasus. In the previous months the stock market had lost 25 per cent of its value, inflation was on the rise, the rouble was in a tail spin on international money markets, and Russia was again posturing towards Chechnya. This was problematic for Western strategy and specifically for EU strategy as outlined above. The Troika made clear to Yeltsin that Russia would have to continue with its dual strategy of market reforms and democratic governance. This was despite massive discontentment in Russia with the general thrust of the Yeltsin reforms.

On 30 September 1998, a Joint EU–Russian twice-yearly summit was announced. This was designed to complement existing structured and unstructured Political Dialogues between the Commission and the CIS. The emphasis – as in NATO's Partnership for Peace – was on consultation without the West committing resources. Nevertheless, Russia was seen to be given a place at the top table of international summitry.

By mid-November 1998, the Commission proposed to the Council that the Caucasus region be provided with aid totalling ECU 60 million for infrastructure projects. This was to be topped up with Tacis aid where applicable. On 12 December 1998, an agreement on 32 cooperation projects between the EU and the CIS was signed in Brussels totalling ECU 122.2 million. This money was to be spent on energy projects – that would hopefully lead to a pipeline supplying cheap oil and gas to Western Europe.[5] The United States was livid that the EU had attempted to fill a policy vacuum in the Caucasus region without prior consultation. There were those in the Washington policy community who – as with the Siberian pipeline incident in 1981 – wanted to blacklist Western European companies from US markets for going ahead with a project that they perceived was possibly destabilizing for transatlantic relations.[6] To top things off, Azerbaijan was voted ECU 10.85 million under Tacis for technical economic assistance.

By early 1999, the EU was welcoming Turkmenistan's moratorium on executions for capital crimes as a sign that its reforms were taking hold in difficult circumstances. As a carrot for further 'good behaviour' the Commission released ECU 800 000 to cover basic health care in Kyrgyzstan in January 1999.

By January 1999, the EU had launched the Royaumont Process for Stability in South Eastern Europe and the CIS. The aim was to bring together the main military powers from the East together in order to discuss their differences. The Royaumont process was also one of inculcating the values of democracy, capitalism and human rights to the participants. In that sense, it is a significant part of the EU's 'regional' approach towards economic development and conflict resolution in Eastern Europe and the former Soviet Union.[7] Significantly, on 29 April 1999, a Stability Pact for Eastern Europe and the former Soviet Union was discussed at an EU Council Experts Conference in Petersberg, Germany. This was significant, as Moscow was about to launch renewed attacks on Chechnya – thereby jeopardizing EU investments in the Causasus and Central Asia.

Mapping agenda-setting

The European Union's main involvement in the Caucasus is in the economic-technical field. The European Union's main involvement is in the Traceca project, whose purpose is to establish rail and sea links between the Georgian Black Sea coastline and central Asia (European Commission, 1996a). Many EU member countries are involves in economic consortia in the region. But what is missing in Europe is a coherent political view of affairs. The agenda in Brussels has been dominated by technical and humanitarian concerns. This has somewhat gone against the EU's aim to influence and exploit the opportunities presented by energy politics in the regions concerned. Agenda-setting in policy has been mainly been the preserve of the Commission and its Directorates General (DG). Turf battles between the European Community Humanitarian Office (ECHO) vision of humanitarian policy and DG1A's more aggressive commercial take on policy have often resulted in a rational, if sometimes muddled, outcome for the overall agenda. Increasingly, however, the Joint Action agenda, in particular, has been dominated by energy politics and what benefits that might bring to European countries.[8] Policy preferences have been confused and have resulted in a mixed and uneven policy agenda which is characterized by bounded rationality.

Indeed, partially due to a mixed and incoherent policy agenda in Brussels, to date the European Union countries have had only a relatively small role in the strategic decisions concerning energy matters. Nevertheless, the EU has developed a coherent policy that emphasizes a strong correlation between means and ends, coherence between and within technologies, and effective cross-pillar communication. As one insider specialist stated:

> In 1990, at the earliest possible opportunity, the European Union drew up the basis for a treaty text in the form of the European Energy Charter (which was signed in December 1991) covering the whole of Europe, the former Soviet Union and all other Western industrialised countries. Its purpose was to establish a common code of conduct for the exploitation of energy resources and their transport, thus providing a legal guarantee for investors in particular, but also to set environmental standards.[9]

By 1994 an Energy Charter Treaty had been negotiated whose provisions make this code of conduct binding on the signatories under international law. Although the United States and Canada have not signed this Treaty, all the European countries and Soviet Union successor states have done so. However, the ratification process is still under way and the Treaty is not yet in force. There is everything to suggest that the European Union and its member states, which have no political counter-interests in the region, will push for the process to be completed and enhance its political value. After all, it does nothing less than replace an era of order by diktat with an era in which the same rules apply to everyone, thereby imparting valuable lessons in the rule of law and democracy in the Caucasus (WEU, 1998b).

By 1999, the General Affairs Council of the EU set down its broad strategic objectives for EU policy towards the Caucasus region. The Commission operationalized these priorities via a series of Partnership and Cooperation Agreements between the Community and the Caucasus states dated 1 July 1999. On 21 June 1999, the General Affairs Council stated the following: 'The EU should promote sustainable economic development, bilateral and regional cooperation. The [existing] Political Dialogue . . . should be used to reinforce this process, and, the Council makes clear, a greater degree of *conditionality* should influence EU assistance' (European Report, 1999, p. 1).

As is stated above, Brussels lacks a coherent political view for the region as a whole. Tacis projects such as Traceca, and more general rehabilitation projects, help to underpin the region via confidence-building measures. The key areas, however, are trade and investment.

There's the rub – the Commission DGs covering external economic relations and external political relations compete for policy space in setting the EU's policy agenda. Reforms on the ground in the Caucasus have been retarded due to an uncertain policy agenda in Brussels that is confused between organizational interests, functional requirements, levels of responsibility *within* and *between* DGs, clashes of personality between external relations/trade Commissioners, and between the EU and its member governments. Nevertheless, preferences have been generally rational to varying degrees as a result of planning, good means-ends relations, and a sound understanding of technologies by the actors in the agenda-setting stage of the policy process.

Mapping decision-making

European Union policy towards Central Asia and the Caucasus is driven by the economic and political pillars of the Union (European Commission, 1996a). EU policy has been largely subject to the pillar structure of the Union: pillar one has provided the policy reality for decisions taken in pillar two. To some degree, however, pillar one priorities, preferences of the differing actors, and institutions have not always been coterminous with pillar two priorities and institutions.[10] There have been problems of internal and external co-ordination between the External Political Relations and External Economic Relations DGs of the Commission. Nevertheless, there existed a good deal of cross-pillar coherence between means and ends, preference wish lists, due to the main actors effectively working as 'agents' of the GAC. This was also underpinned by a high degree of member state input into to actions/policies from an early stage in the decision-making process. Variations in preference formation were tempered by the overarching presence of the GAC in decision-making.

The EU and its member states are keen to democratize and economically restructure the former Soviet Union in order to create conditions of stability in that region: they also generally agree on the means and ends of how to set about achieving this lofty objective (European Commission, 1996a). Structural weaknesses in the economies of the region have been endemically serious for most of the twentieth century, and especially pressing since 1992. These structural difficulties include weak legal and regulatory frameworks, poor industrial restructuring and privatization, vulnerable currencies and poor revenue tax collection. Since 1992 the European Commission has provided technical and economic support to the former Soviet Union via the Tacis programme. EU policy towards Central Asia and the Caucasus is subdivided into a key number of sub-policies: macro-financial assistance; exceptional financial assistance; food security assistance; rehabilitation assistance; humanitarian aid; and special programmes (European Commission, 1996a).

Typically, policy has been the product of high-level transactions between Eurocrats and national civil servants. Policy ideas have been generated by desk-officer-level European and national civil servants that fit within the parameters of decisions made by politicians in the GAC. DG1A of the Commission has had particular input into the EU's policy process via TACIS, TRACEA and other such technical assistance programmes. Policy has mainly been decided upon at the national or bilateral diplomatic level and then implemented at the European level by EU structures derived from pillar one of the Treaties. Nevertheless, policy has also been influenced decisions taken in the second- pillar institutions associated with the common foreign and security policy. This makes the present case a particularly interesting snap shot of pillarization in the EU.

Specialists estimate that Central Asia and the Caucasus contain the world's third largest oil and natural gas reserves after the Gulf region and Siberia. Oil resources are estimated at 200 billion barrels (WEU, 1998b). The European Union has been extremely keen to exploit the commercial possibilities in the regions under scrutiny, aiming to provide inexpensive gas and oil to Western European consumers. This it has done via a number of collective and individual co-operation agreements with the states of Central Asia and the Caucasus. The most extensive fields have been located in Kazakhstan (European Commission, 1996b), and Azerbaijan (European Commission, 1996c). Other lesser reserves and oil exploitation sites are to be found in Georgia (European Commission, 1996d), Uzbekistan (European Commission, 1996e), Turkmenistan (European Commisssion, 1996f) and Armenia (European Commission, 1996g). It has been possible in the post-Soviet era for Western companies to establish themselves in the area, bringing new technologies with them. Geological surveys using sophisticated equipment have shown that reserves are probably much larger than earlier surveys carried out under the Soviet regime (now some 40 years out of date) had suggested. The strategic importance of the region is increasing as more oil is discovered (WEU, 1998b).

According to industrial analysts, Kazakhstan, with over 60 billion barrels, has the largest oil and gas deposits of all the countries of the former Soviet Union (European Commission, 1996b). Azerbaijan has a much greater potential for production than Soviet geologists had predicted (European Commission, 1996c). Turkmenistan, whose main resource is natural gas, ranks third among the oil-rich nations of the regions, with estimated reserves of 46 billion barrels (European Commission, 1996f). Uzbekistan has 230 oil and natural gas fields (European Commission, 1996e). Georgia also has energy resources, although not on the same scale as its neighbours (European Commission, 1996d). The reserves to be found in Armenia, Kirghizstan and Tajikistan are smaller. Despite their enormous oil potential, the countries of the Caucasus and Central Asia, suffer from inadequate infrastructure development which restricts economic growth and leaves them vulnerable internationally.

Macro-financial assistance can offer flexible and swift responses to external economic shocks to the Central Asian and Caucasus economies. However, it has important constraints. First, pillar one financial assistance, involving direct balance of payments or budgetary support, is *conditional* upon satisfactory implementation of International Monetary Fund (IMF)-supported programmes (European Commission, 1996a). Second, eligibility for macro-financial assistance is subject to strict geographical criteria and several states (Kazakhstan, Kyrgyzstan, Uzbekistan and Turkmenistan) are unlikely to benefit from such support.

In the cases of Armenia and Georgia, at the time of writing a framework Council decision for exceptional financial support of ECU 255 million has already been adopted (European Commission, 1996a; WEU, 1998b). This has been achieved via a combination of grants and loans to be disbursed over a six-year period. However, full use of this assistance would normally be made possible only if the Budgetary Authority confirms the amount to the Council. All financial decisions are scrutinized by the Court of Auditors. It was decided in 1998 to include Tajikistan on a preliminary basis in the 1988–89 Agreement with an assistance package of ECU 100 million through grants and loans.

The Commission has been implementing a major assistance programme for food security aiming to respond to insecurity caused by serious food shortages in the region. Food aid programmes do not, in principle, fall within the Tacis programme, except during a serious crisis. Assistance is subject to prior agreement between the government of the individual country, the IMF and the EU Commission. The programme provided for direct budgetary support for agricultural sector reform in Central Asia and the Caucasus. ECU 142 million, for example, have been set aside for this particular food assistance programme for 1999 and 2000. Implementation of EU monies has often been delayed as individual countries have often failed to meet strict conditional IMF targets for reform. This is a classic case of political conditionality of one international institution conveniently tying the hands of another international institution: an implementation gap then emerges.

The EU has also been implementing a programme that focuses on the rehabilitation of damaged infrastructure. Since 1997, as a complement to the Tacis programme the Council decided that the rehabilitation programme should cover the Caucasus countries and Central Asia. In 1997–98, for example, an amount of ECU 20.5 million was allocated for Azerbaijan, Georgia and Tajikistan. This was decided upon at the highest levels of national governments and in the humanitarian DGs of the Commission. Implementation has been the responsibility jointly of the European Community Humanitarian Office and DG1A of the Commission.[11]

In terms of humanitarian assistance, the most important operation in 1998–99, for example, was in Tajikistan. ECHO funded substantial food and medical projects worth ECU 16 million. This money was used to help civilian victims of the civil war in that country. Another ECU 11 million was allocated in the continuation of ongoing operations in the three countries of the southern Caucasus (mainly focusing on refugees). For security reasons, operations in the northern Caucasus (in Chechnya and Dagastan) had to be suspended in early 1998. This decision was taken by the external relations and humanitarian DGs of the Commission and the Council collectively.

ECHO carries out its operations through humanitarian agencies (non-governmental organizations, UN agencies and the Red Cross). The number of humanitarian agencies differs from country to country. ECHO is reassessing its strategy in line with the need for: (i) greater accountability of funds spent in the carrying out of joint actions and humanitarian projects. The Court of Auditors has pointed out that ECHO's appalling auditing system militates against resources reaching their intended targets; (ii) changes in personnel at all levels in 1999 coinciding with the departure of ECHO Commissioner Emma Bonino from her job.

The current TACIS programme provides technical assistance aimed at bringing about the transition to a market economy and reinforcing democracy. For example, in 1997–98, the TACIS programme allocated ECU 257 million to the former Soviet Union. Where possible, ongoing Tacis programmes have been adapted to finance urgent joint actions.

This involves a great deal of co-ordination – between the responsible DGs of the Commission, between the Commission and the Council, and between the Parliament and the Commission. Decisions in the financial field are increasingly predicated against rules published by the Court of Auditors on the spending and appropriate use of funds. This ensures some degree of decision-making scrutiny, but after the fact.

The pipeline battle: a question of decision-making styles[12]

In the period 1996–97 the EU developed various co-operation agreements with Central Asia and Caucasus states (European Commission, 1996a–g; European Commission 1997a). The main tenor of the agreements was one of supporting the independence, sovereignty and territorial integrity of the newly independent states to create conditions conducive to democracy, human rights and the market economy (European Commission, 1996a). The key provisions of the agreements, however, concerned provisions on trade in goods and services, and, especially related to reciprocity in most favoured nation (MFN) status (European Commission, 1997a). From a Western European viewpoint, the agreements were initiated to develop various forms of economic activity that might benefit the European Union in the long term. As one Commission desk officer states:

> The agreements meant that tenders were flying about all over the place for Western [public and private] companies to exploit available new markets and money making activities. The Spanish were particularly aggressive in this regard. The oil and gas industries of these states were particularly underdeveloped and needed Western expertise to keep them running. This also made the countries from the region dependent to some degree on EU funds and technical expertise.[13]

As far as the important issue of export routes is concerned, the latest development was the opening, on 12 November 1997, of a key oil pipeline between Baku and Novorossiysk, which will carry oil extracted by the AIOC international consortium across Russian territory via Grozny in Chechnya (WEU, 1998b).

European Union policy-making styles have been based on a mixture of strategic action (the aim to maximize preferences defined outside of the policy process externally), policy learning and shared problem-solving within the EU policy process, and, inter alia, between the EU and the states of Central Asia. This has meant that the policy process has been enhanced by the thought of rewards for Western Europe (cheap energy sources).[14] This has galvanized preference-formation structures in the member states and the main EU institutions to work together for positive-sum outcomes of cheap energy. This implies that policy preferences in the decision-making stage were relatively rational. Outcomes have been relatively positive-sum for the EU and the Central Asian and Caucasus states alike. The European Union is interested in the project, to the extent that the Caucasus region could become a zone of co-operation between East and West, thus providing European Union countries with a guaranteed supply of inexpensive oil.[15]

Clearly, completion of such a project would be of major interest to Western Europe. In 1996–97 the Commission signed partnership and technical agreements with Azerbaijan in order to offer assistance, but, also to ultimately protect Western European interests in the pipeline project (European Commission, 1996c). For the time being relatively modest quantities are involved (roughly 40 000 tonnes per month), but the opening of the pipeline is nevertheless regarded in Azerbaijan as a major step forward, since Moscow for a time severed communications with Baku and the war in Chechnya made that particular pipeline extremely vulnerable (WEU, 1998b). However, this development again reveals the difficulty of finding alternative supply lines for Azerbaijan's oil, which is primarily of interest to countries that do not want to depend exclusively on the goodwill of the Russian Federation. The available options include alternative oil supply routes from Azerbaijan to the Mediterranean. Other solutions are also being considered, involving pipelines in Kazakhstan and Azerbaijan. On 27 September 1997, China put an end to the border dispute it has had with Kazakhstan since the demise of the Soviet Union and the two countries have signed an oil agreement worth US$9.5 billion (WEU, 1998b). The settlement of the dispute was prompted by the desire to conclude oil agreements. Negotiations, which had been going on for two years, concluded with an agreement between the Kazakh President, Noursultan Nazarbaev, and former Chinese Premier Li Peng, who made a special trip to Alma-Ata, the capital of Kazakhstan in 1998 (WEU, 1998b).

Apart from energy supplies from the Uzen and Aktyubinsk sites, the concession for which has been awarded to the Chinese state oil company, the document provides for construction of two oil pipelines, to be operational by the year 2002. One, 3000 km long, will extend to the Chinese border, while the other, 250 km long, will connect with Turkmenistan. The route for two other branches in east Kazakhstan is still to be negotiated (WEU, 1998b).

Turkmenistan and Iran are currently looking at other projects for the construction of a railway and pipelines in order to exploit Turkmenistan's oil and natural gas, from which Kazakhstan could also benefit (WEU, 1998b). Thus, over the last few years, Iran and Turkmenistan have signed a number of co-operation agreements concerning oil and natural gas supply routes, including a gas pipeline construction project which would link Turkmenistan to Turkey and Europe via Iran. The former American Secretary of State, Alexander Haig, was involved in coordinating this deal (WEU, 1998b). In April 1994, Turkmenistan also concluded an agreement with Iran for the construction of an oil pipeline to supply northern Iran with Turkmen oil. There is also a project for bringing oil from Azerbaijan through Armenia and Turkey to the Mediterranean, but President Aliyev is against it, while the Americans are opposed to a pipeline passing through Iran. An alternative project for a pipeline through Georgia to Turkey is being examined but Turkey is not particularly keen on the idea. Lastly, there are even plans to build pipelines that link Turkmenistan and Pakistan to Afghanistan (WEU, 1998b).

If the present analysis has concentrated in such detail on exploitation of the Caspian Sea reserves, this is because the present authors consider that it was important to point to the complicated nature of a business deal that involves several EU member states, such as the United Kingdom, France, Germany, Italy, Greece and Belgium, as well as Turkey and Norway, which are EU/CFSP/WEU associate members (WEU, 1998b). The various projects for exploitation of the natural resources of the Caspian Sea in fact have political repercussions, as the following examples (cited in, and drawn liberally, from WEU, 1998b) serve to demonstrate.

In August 1993, in order to restrict oil supplies through the straits of the Bosporus and thus redirect them to the Mediterranean routes, Turkey requested revision, on ecological grounds, of the 1936 Convention of Montreux, which governs the status of the straits. Russia objected to this initiative, but after a collision between an oil tanker and a cargo vessel on 13 March 1994, Turkey decreed the entry into force of regulations covering maritime traffic, as from 1 July 1994 (WEU, 1998b).

The Turkish project for a 'Mediterranean route', starting from the Turkish port of Ceyhan, will enable Turkey to consolidate its links with the countries of Central Asia, take maximum advantage of its strategic position and geographic proximity to Caspian Sea oil resources, and thus considerably reduce its overheads (WEU, 1998b). According to

Turkish sources, completion of the Mediterranean route would have the following advantages: The Turkish port of Ceyhan has the necessary infrastructure for petroleum transport. The Iraqi pipeline, closed by Turkey in 1990, has its outlet here. The port can cater for ships of a tonnage four times greater than the Russian port of Novoriossiysk has capacity for. The port of Ceyhan is open 365 days a year, while the Russian port is occasionally closed on account of bad weather; transport costs towards Western Europe would be half those from the port of Novorossiysk; the fall in traffic through the straits of the Bosporus would reduce the risks of ecological disaster to the city of Istanbul (WEU, 1998b). Since 1960, the number of ships that pass through the Bosporus has increased by 150 per cent and tonnage by 400 per cent; security would be guaranteed since Turkey is a member of NATO and a leading candidate for membership of the EU (WEU, 1998b).

Russia decided to react to the Turkish decision to restrict shipping through the Bosporus in 1994, by signing a pipeline construction agreement with Greece and Bulgaria (WEU, 1998b). The pipeline would circumvent Turkey (Burgas-Alexandroupolis). The port of Burgas (in Bulgaria) has storage for 600 000 tonnes of oil, while the capacity of the port of Alexandroupolis (in Greece) is approximately 1.2 million tonnes. Tankers can be loaded in the Aegean Sea eight kilometres offshore by means of a highly sophisticated and very safe system (similar to systems that exist in Norway and Canada), which protects the environment and minimizes the risk of pollution (WEU, 1998b).

American foreign policy interests within the region: competitive co-operation with the European Union[16]

In analysing EU policy towards the Caucasus it is a useful exercise to study American foreign policy towards the region in order to: (i) highlight the global importance of the Caucasus region to world energy policy and to maintaining stability in the former Soviet Union; and (ii) highlight the international context of EU policies towards the Caucasus.

The principal concern of the United States is to avoid the Caucasus and central Asia becoming either (i) a region that is destabilized and ravaged by civil war, where nuclear proliferation or radical Islamist movements are rife; or (ii) the target for Russian ambitions (WEU, 1998b). Such instability would also be damaging to prospects for the conclusion and implementation of contracts for the exploitation of natural resources, areas in which American companies hope to play a leading role. The main competitor for these scarce and lucrative resources is the European Union, its member states and its public and private companies (European Commission, 1996a).

Officially, the United States has three major political aims within the region. (This section relies on the excellent report WEU, (1998b).) The first is to support the desire for independence and sovereignty of the countries of the region. The United States is particularly interested in the oil resources of certain countries such as Azerbaijan and Kazakhstan. These are the key to the region's future development and could also be the means of helping countries without such resources such as Armenia or Georgia, depending on the supply routes established (WEU, 1998b).

The second aim is to support US trade interests as far as regional oil production and export is concerned. US companies could hasten economic reforms and facilitate the region's entry to the world economic market. This commercial presence would strengthen US influence in the region. Furthermore, the United States hopes furthermore that oil agreements will prove profitable (WEU, 1998b).

Its third aim is to diversify its oil supplies and to reduce its dependence on the Persian Gulf. Diversification will also be necessary to keep up with an ever-increasing world demand for oil products (WEU, 1998b). The margin between supply and demand is becoming steadily narrower, owing to the fact that a number of wells are drying up. Oil from the Caspian Sea will have no impact on this trend before 2005. The United States' difficulty is to find a compromise between its commercial interests and its foreign policy which aims to contain Iraq and Iran, encourage economic and political reform in Russia, lend support for the settlement of regional conflicts (Nagorno-Karabakh, Chechnya, Georgia) and maintain good relations with Turkey (WEU, 1998b). Rapid development of oil projects is essential to these countries whose economies are still very dependent on Russia.

United States' oil policy in the region relies on four main props:

- Active diplomatic support at all levels, from embassy personnel up to the President of the United States. When they were in power President Clinton, Vice-President Gore and several members of the government actively took steps in pursuit of American aims at a number of meetings held with the oil countries. The United States has taken a special interest in the Tengizchevroil project in Kazakhstan, Azerbaijan's international petroleum consortium and in the problems relating to border demarcation on the Caspian Sea (WEU, 1998b). American representatives maintain significant levels of contact with representatives of their petroleum companies to co-ordinate strategies in order to promote their national commercial interests. It would appear that President Clinton's talks with the Azeri President, Mr Aliyev, in October 1997 made a decisive contribution to the conclusion of the agreement defining the northern and western routes for early exports (WEU, 1998b). Vice-President Gore also played a highly active part in promoting American oil policy in the region through contacts with regional leaders and talks with Mr Chernomyrdin.

- Exchanges between governments and commercial organizations. These include the Overseas Private Investment Corporation, the US Department of Trade, the Export-Import Bank and the Trade and Development Agency. These organizations are either already involved in projects or are trying to find ways of setting up projects more rapidly and efficiently (WEU, 1998b).
- Technical assistance to help these countries to develop their commercial infrastructure and legal systems and to facilitate development of their oil sectors and other export industries (WEU, 1998b).
- Support for efforts made by international financial institutions to strengthen their infrastructure policies. The United States has established several parameters to support this policy. These include the establishment of a number of short- and medium-term supply routes. The United States has encouraged this policy since 1994, because it creates trade competition and guarantees a continuous flow of energy supplies by avoiding dependence on a single route (WEU, 1998b).

Among those envisaged, the United States favours the route which would cross Turkey. This would increase total oil export capacity from the Caspian Sea while relieving current pressure on the Russian pipeline system (WEU, 1998b). The Caspian Sea countries' dependence on Russia would thus be reduced and the argument in favour of building a pipeline to the Persian Gulf through Iran would lose much of its force. The United States is also opposed to projects which would give Iran any political, material or economic advantages and has encouraged the Caspian Sea states to involve Iran as a little as possible in oil projects (WEU, 1998b). However, it would seem that US policy in this respect is not always consistent. For instance, on 25 July 1997, the White House announced that it was no longer opposed to a pipeline carrying natural gas from Turkmenistan to Turkey via Iran. Yet when Kazakhstan signed a major oil contract on 19 November 1997 in Washington with a consortium comprising four companies, President Clinton used the opportunity to strongly advise the President of Kazakhstan, Mr Nazarbaev, not to route the oil through Iran (WEU, 1998b). As far as regional security is concerned, the United States, through its Defense Department, supports the development of regional armed forces (WEU, 1998b). It hopes, by setting up military training programmes, to induce the forces of the countries in question to break with the traditions of the former Soviet army. Recent initiatives, such as the signature by then then Defense Secretary William Perry of an agreement giving Kazakhstan US$37 million worth of loans for defence industry reconversion (in particular for upgrading equipment at the Stepnogorsk chemical works), also come under this heading (WEU, 1998b). Involvement in the NATO Partnership for Peace programme will also offer these countries an alternative to Russian aid (Winn, 2000). The United States could involve itself more widely in regional development within the framework of international organizations such as the OSCE or the United Nations. It is currently involved in environmental protection programmes and programmes to combat arms proliferation, the spread of drugs and organized crime.

NATO has begun to take Russian interests into account, since destabilization of Russia would in turn destabilize Kazakhstan. From this point of view, Kazakhstan welcomed the terms of the NATO-Russia Founding Act (WEU, 1998b). Generally speaking, Kazakhstan was anxious to play a role in co-operation at international level, but also in an OSCE framework. Kazakhstan's interests were directed towards Europe – primarily towards the EU – and it saw itself as a bridge between Asia and Europe. According to anonymous Commission sources, the President of Kazakhstan was disappointed with what he considered to be insufficient efforts to strengthen the CIS, and he reportedly criticized President Yeltsin on that point. Regarding relations with the European Union, it had signed a co-operation agreement with Kazakhstan, but given the lack of a true CFSP, there was no common European policy vis-à-vis that country.[17]

Mapping implementation: the social exchange of power from the 'bottom up'

EU policy has typically been implemented on the ground in Central Asia and the Caucasus by the Commission from the bottom up. Generally, the Commission sets up implementation structures on the ground to suit any given particular case. In this sense implementation structures are not hierarchies but networks of several agencies. Individual and group interests often operate over and above organization interests. When resources have not been available for implementation, individuals and groups have created their own implementation structures via resource exchanges (for example, money for influence). Specifically, DG1A has had responsibility for energy-related policy with external relations implications. Conversely, ECHO has overall guiding responsibility for implementing humanitarian policy in the region. Policy had typically been worked out in a relatively rational manner in conditions of strained bounded rationality, and policy implementation centred around the issues of placing resources in the appropriate hands to meet policy goals. As an insider source in the Court of Auditors has pointed out, the scope for corruption of funds is great. Hence the Commission has remained close to the resources on the ground. The use of dubious unprofessional non-governmental organizations to implement policy has been greatly curtailed since 1996.[18]

The Commission and the member states are also sometimes distributing monies according to criteria other than need. Monies are distributed increasingly to open up industry to EU expertise, and, hence, potentially lucrative contracts for public and private interests in the EU. It is interesting to note that the monies allocated for humanitarian aid projects and food projects has been variable according to the country concerned. In 1997–98 ECU 853.6 million was set aside for humanitarian and technical assistance to the former Soviet Union excluding Russia (European Commission, 1997a). The monies tended to be allocated according to such factors as population size, degree of socio-economic development, malnutrition rates, daily calorie intake and level of infrastructure. Nevertheless, monies have clearly been set aside for technical assistance for oil- and gas-producing states (thereby protecting EU economic interests for the longer term). For instance, in 1997–98, Azerbaijan – the largest oil and gas producer in the region – was allocated ECU 26.9 million for TACIS help (including help for setting up gas and oil pipelines and the like), ECU 10.7 million in humanitarian aid and ECU 28 million in food security. Mongolia, a relatively small-scale producer of energy resources, was only allocated ECU 11 million from TACIS funds, despite having a multitude of domestic problems. Georgia, a large-scale producer of fossil fuels, was allocated ECU 16 million from TACIS funds, ECU 6.5 million for rehabilitation, ECU 12.2 million for humanitarian aid, and ECU 42 million for food security (WEU, 1998b).

By adopting a 'bottom-up' or 'backward-mapping' approach to implementation the member states, and the EU, have avoided costly implementation gaps, possible corruption on the ground and such like. Like in the actual policy-making *process*, therefore, the Commission's handling of policy *implementation* has actually been relatively rational in the circumstances. This is partially a product of less actors being involved in the process (hence there being less interests to take into account). However, it is also a product of the professionalism and administrative mindsets on the part of the humanitarian and external relations DGs of the Commission. This degree of rational professionalism was also achieved, to the same extent, in the actual policy process despite its inherently political nature with many more national and supranational actors in that process.

Nevertheless, as the foregoing discussion has revealed, successful policy implementation requires both 'carrots' and 'sticks'. Under the 'carrots' category we can include rewards, prestige, and resource enhancement as a result of successful implementation. In the 'stick' category we can include negative audits of the Commission initiated by the Court of Auditors, surcharging, and bad publicity generated by poor implementation.

Implementation is also affected by what we might term policy loops. This implies that the Commission receives feedback on its implementation in order to improve its techniques in the future. Policy feedback can either be taken on board, or not as the case dictates, this will also depend on the degree of rationality possessed by individual policy-makers.

STAGE 3: EVALUATION

Conclusions

Thinking empirically

Developments in Central Asia and the Caucasus over the next few decades will depend on a number of factors: First, the extent of the natural resources in the region around the Caspian Sea needs to be established with more precision compared with those of other development sites – for instance' in the Persian Gulf; at the moment there are still too many discrepancies in experts' estimates (WEU, 1998b). Second, everything possible must be done to prevent all the powers involved in the region (the EU, US Russia and China) from engaging in cut-throat competition to exploit and export those natural resources because, sooner or later, this could lead to situations of conflict liable to escalate out of control (WEU, 1998b; Herzig, 1999).

What needs to be done before anything else is to intensify the efforts being made to stabilize and consolidate the political, economic and social situation in all the countries of the region that emerged after the disintegration of the Soviet Union (Winn, 2000). Any initiatives designed to solve the ongoing regional conflicts must be stepped up and measures taken to prevent crises breaking out in zones where there is a risk of ethnic or religious confrontation. Close attention must be paid to developments in the CIS and to Russia's reactions in the event of it no longer being able to use the CIS to re-establish its influence on its southern flank, particularly in Central Asia and the Caucasus (WEU, 1998b). It is therefore important that this part of the world should become a region of economic co-operation in which all the interested countries could take part and from which they could all benefit (WEU, 1998b).

It will be necessary for the United States and Western Europe to concert their policies towards the countries concerned and put an end to a number of differences between them, notably concerning Iran, oil and gas exploitation (Europe Report, 1999). The European Union should agree on a genuine common policy towards Central Asia and the Caucasus and, with the assistance of WEU, make preparations to provide a specific peacekeeping contribution so that none of the powers of the region can pose a threat (European Commission, 1996a). It has only been a decade since the countries of central Asia and the Caucasus proclaimed their independence. We often forget this in the West where nation-states have had decades (and in some cases centuries) to grow accustomed to Western representative liberal democracy, capitalism and human rights (WEU, 1998b; European Commission, 1996a).

Thinking about preference formation

In the agenda-setting stage, the idea for the Joint Actions of 1998 dealing with human rights and the 'social' aspects of economic reconstruction in the Caucasus came from ECHO. Related EU commercial policies towards the region were authored by the General Affairs Council and the Commission in DG1A (External Political Relations) and DG1 (External Economic Relations). The GAC provided overall leadership and strategic direction from above, implying that preferences were well developed and rationally listed. The broad policies maintained quite fixed preference structures throughout the life of the policy cycle. The agenda of the Joint Actions and related commercial policies were closely specified at the agenda-setting stage in a rational way. However, as is stated above in the section on agenda-setting, the EU tended to lack an *overall conception of policies in the plural* towards the Caucasus in the agenda-setting stage of the policy process, implying that there was some degree of cross-pillar incoherence as a result of inter- and intra-institutional turf battles. Nevertheless, responsibilities were specified in a coherent planned manner as was the resourcing of the actions/policies. The end product was a relatively rational agenda-setting process according to the preference structures of the major actors during this important stage of the policy process.

For example, as is stated above, in 1996 the Commission put forward a Joint action Plan for Russia and the Caucasus region which coherently specified policy priorities according to the four main EU priorities: first, modernization of nuclear facilities; second, integration of Russia and the Caucasus to the Union's research and development programmes; third, the fight against organized crime in the former Soviet Union; and, fourth, refugee policies. Related policy objectives specified by the Commission were to secure lucrative energy contracts within the Caucasus, and to exploit the opportunities presented – which were many and varied – for Commission access to cheap energy resources in the Caucasus.

In terms of mapping preference formation in the decision-making stage of the policy process, the preferences of the main actors involved in the joint actions/economic policies of the EU towards the Caucasus largely followed those set by the GAC. The Commission and Parliament tended to fall in behind the member states in the GAC, implying a decision-making stage dominated by rational preference formation with rank ordering of choices led from above. The preferences of the main actors tended to change according to circumstances: however, the degree of change was generally rational and well planned according to standard operating procedures set by the Council. Finally, the decision-making phase was dominated by stable means–ends relations. The EU's policies were predicated on the shared understanding that Western Europe would positively gain in a collective sense from economic association with the Caucasus. Given that the various EU institutions individually and collectively perceived that their policies towards the Caucasus would produce 'win'/'win' outcomes for the Union's policies, the leading actors worked closely together to produce a virtuous outcome for all. This made the specifying of policy preferences in the decision-making stage of the policy process straightforward, thereby encouraging rationality in policy-making and related outcomes.

For example, on 12 December 1999, an agreement on 32 co-operation projects totalling ECU 122.2 million between the EU and the CIS was signed in Brussels. This money was, as is stated above, to be spent on potentially lucrative energy projects – that would hopefully lead to a pipeline supplying cheap oil and gas to Western Europe. The various EU institutions lined up behind the GAC in a rational way to ensure a positive sum outcome for the member states of the Union.

Likewise, in the policy implementation stage, the main preferences in terms of policy implementation were set by the GAC. These preferences were rational and in line with the main preferences of the member states of the EU. In this case the social exchange of resources influenced Commission implementation on the ground which was in line with the 'lead' set by the GAC. The Commission rationally exchanged resources in return for influence in the political systems of the states of Central Asia and the Caucasus. The main aim of the Commission – and the EU member states – is to have long-term political and economic influence in the region that will rival the United States and Russia.

For example, as early as 1991, the EU drew up a European Energy Charter covering the whole of Europe, and the former Soviet Union. Its purpose, as is stated above, was to establish a common code of conduct for the exploitation of energy resources and their transport, thus providing a legal guarantee for Western European investors in particular, but also to set environmental standards.

Thinking theoretically: a case of rationality

In the case of the Caucasus the main driving forces behind EU policy are: (i) democratization; (ii) technology transfer; (iii) human rights; and (iv) the opening up – most significantly in terms of EU economic policy priorities – of Caucasus energy markets in the medium to long term for Western European public and private sector companies to exploit. The latter objective is undoubtedly the main driving force behind Union politics and policy towards the Caucasus. Agenda-setting has been explicitly led by the member states (and the larger ones at that), or, when other actors have attempted to put questions on the agenda, they have done so within the known parameters of what is acceptable to the General Affairs Council. In this case, Council preferences were both dominant and autonomous: the Council was not substantially influenced by other actors in the CFSP process (unless

EU Policy towards the Caucasus, 1996–99 163

it elected by choice to be influenced for whatever reason). The Commission was used to advise the GAC on policy options and to implement policy as determined by the member states in the GAC.

For example, in 1999 the GAC set down its broad strategic priorities and objectives for EU policy towards the Caucasus region. The Commission rationally operationalized these priorities via a series of Partnership and Cooperation Agreements between the Community and various Caucasus states on 1 July 1999. EU policy was driven by the need to promote sustainable economic development, bilateral and multilateral economic co-operation with Western Europe. The GAC also strengthened the existing structured Political Dialogue between the Commission and the Caucasus states in a coherent manner with extra meetings between senior Commission officials and senior politicians and officials from the Caucasus.

In this case the priorities of EU policies in general and in particular joint actions were bargained from relatively fixed national preferences. These were formed within national bureaucracies, and, therefore, outside CFSP. Member government preferences (especially the larger member state governments) were also directly traceable to structural differences in a member state's position in the international political economy and/or strategic order, or to the need of a member government to maintain a winning coalition in electoral or partisan politics. Preferences were therefore not collegially-formed through processes of mutual justification and shared learning at the level of CFSP itself.

For example, EU policy towards the Caucasus region has been guided by the strategic importance of the region as more oil and gas fields have been discovered. The EU and its member states are keen to democratize and economically restructure the Caucasus in order to create conditions of stability in that region. It is in the best interests of the EU and its member states to exploit the economic opportunities presented by cheap energy at a time when world energy resources are subject to scarcity and escalating costs to the buyer (that is, governments) and hence to the eventual consumer. This has been actively taken up in the policy preferences set by the GAC and has been influenced critically by the French, German and British governments at the bilateral level with individual Caucasus states and through the EU: it will help to entrench Western European states' geostrategic position in the world and also keep domestic publics happier electorally speaking with the prospect of cheaper fuel bills.

The GAC dominated all stages of the decision-making cycle through to implementation in the sense that a clear agency–principal relationship was discernible, with clear instructions being laid down by the GAC. All other actors were either working to those explicit guidelines, or following the known preferences of the Council.

In the cases of Armenia and Georgia, for example, a framework GAC decision for exceptional financial support of ECU 255 million was adopted in 1997. This was achieved via a combination of grants and loans to be disbursed over a six-year period. Nevertheless, full use of this assistance is only possible if the Budgetary Authority confirms the amount to the GAC alone. A similar agreement was concluded with Tajikistan in 1998–99 along similar lines. The Commission in turn acted as the agent of the Council in implementing the details of the policy on the ground.

The policy process was characterized by a stable means–ends relationship: over the course of the most significant joint actions, and related policies, objectives only changed in response to developments that could not have been anticipated at earlier stages, and not as a result of defects in the internal decision environment.

For example, since 1997 the EU has also been implementing a programme – alongside the TACIS programme – that focuses on the rehabilitation of damaged infrastructure in the Caucasus states. In 1997–98, for instance, an amount of ECU 20.5 million was allocated to Azerbaijan, Georgia and Tajikistan. Policy, as we have stated above, was decided upon at the highest levels of EU member governments meeting within the context of the GAC, and was later implemented by ECHO and DG1A of the Commission.

As is stated above, key joint actions and related policies were underpinned by efficient means–ends relationships: a most efficient use was made of the information available at any one time to identify the means most likely to provide optimal delivery of aims within prevailing constraints and resources.

For example, in terms of humanitarian assistance, as is stated above, the most important EU-funded operation for 1998–99 was in Tajikistan. ECHO funded substantial food and medical projects worth ECU 16 million. This money was used to help the civilian victims of the civil war in that country. The decision to allocate the resources was taken by the GAC in consultation with ECHO, DG1 and DG1A. The resources were efficiently delivered on time at point of need.

Needless to say, as the evidence above points out, there existed a high level of cross- pillar coherence because the other Union bodies involved in the key joint actions – and other related policies – effectively functioned as *agents* of the GAC. For example, the current TACIS programme provides technical assistance aimed at bringing about the transition to a market economy and reinforcing democracy in the former Soviet Union. This involves a great deal of co-ordination between the GAC, the relevant DGs of the Commission, and the Parliament. Nevertheless, all major policy commitments emerge from the GAC. The other Union institutions act as agents of the GAC to ensure efficient and effective agenda-setting, decision-making and implementation.

Finally, there was very little path-dependence in the shaping of the key joint actions and related policies. Preferences were largely exogenous to the process and well specified in advance. Effective means–ends relationships were largely anticipated and reflected in a clear and stable delegation to the joint action and other related EU policies towards the Caucasus region. For example, Kazakhstan has been identified as having the largest oil and gas deposits of the countries of the former Soviet Union. The GAC and the Council have independently attempted to bring the latest Western technology to the region, in order to make it possible for Western European companies to establish themselves in the area. The strategic importance of the region to the GAC and the Commission is increasing as more oil and gas is discovered. This has encouraged stable means–ends relations in EU policies, and also encouraged the GAC to take the lead in decision-making and implementation to ensure that Western European policy is appropriately rational in order for the Commission and the EU's member states to be in a position to exploit the emerging lucrative energy markets of the Caucasus.

Notes

1 The following chapter heavily draws on Western European Union, 'Report on Central Asia and the Caucasus', Brussels, WEU, 1998b, for *factual* interpretations of Western policies, and especially specific European Union policies, towards the Caucasus. *Factual* information relating to these policies – and their historical and political contexts – is liberally drawn from the report.
2 The European Union role in the region is based upon a number of Partnership and Cooperation agreements (detailed below in this chapter). First, via political and economic assistance-related projects. Second, via a 'regional' approach to the Caucasus region emphasizing sustainable economic development, democratization, and human rights. A great deal of political conditionality influences EU assistance to the region. The main drivers behind policy have been economic in nature.

166   *EU Foreign Policy beyond the Nation-State*

3   Interview, Desk Officer, DG1A, Brussels, November 1997.
4   Interview, Desk Officer, DG1A, Brussels, January 2000.
5   Interview, Desk Officer, DG1, Brussels, January 2000.
6   Interview, Desk Officer, FCO, London, July 1998.
7   Interview, Desk Officer, DG1A, Brussels, November 1997.
8   Interview, Desk Officer, DG1A, Brussels, November 1997.
9   Interview, Desk Officer, ECHO, Brussels, November 1997.
10 Interview, Desk Officer, DG1, Brussels, November 1997.
11 Interview, Desk Officer, ECHO, Brussels, November 1997.
12 The following subsection heavily relies on WEU, (1998b, Part 1).
13 Interview, Desk Officer, ECHO, Brussels, November 1997.
14 Interview, Desk Officer, DG1A, Brussels, November 1997.
15 Interview, Desk Officer, DG1A, Brussels, November 1997.
16 The following section of the analysis heavily relies on WEU (1998b, Part 1).
17 Interview, Desk Officer, DG1A, Brussels, November 1997.
18 Interview, Official, Court of Auditors, Brussels, November 1997.

7
Conclusion

The conclusion to this book falls into three parts. The first summarizes the main findings from the case studies. The second draws out the theoretical and conceptual implications of the study. The third considers the broader implications of the study for the role of the European Union (EU) in world politics.

Conclusions of the case studies

To recapitulate, our research strategy has been to use joint actions as case studies of pillarization. We have distinguished between three stages in the 'life cycle' of a joint action: the setting of the agenda for the joint action; the decision to proceed with the joint action; and its implementation. We have also argued that there are three competing theories of policy-making that would allow us to explain how process is linked to outcome in a setting such as pillarization where foreign policy is not the product of a single bureaucracy. These are rational action, policy networks and 'garbage can' approaches. A fourth – bounded rationality – may be added as a subset of the first.

In all we have studied three joint actions: those undertaken in relation to the administration of the town of Mostar, the implementation of the Dayton Peace Accords and the development of natural resources in the Caucasus. Our own appraisal of which theories of policy-making best fits which joint action is summarized in Table 7.1.

With this in mind we further hypothesized that the full range of policy preferences articulated in the chosen EU joint actions resulted, to varying degrees, in four main policy processes and outcomes – classical rationality, patchy rationality (bounded rationality), policy

168 *EU Foreign Policy beyond the Nation-State*

Table 7.1 The relationship between the key stages of the policy process and policy outcomes

	Rationality	Patchy rationality (p.r.)	Policy network	Garbage cans
Agenda-Setting	Caucasus	Some p.r. in the Mostar and Caucasus cases	Mostar	Dayton
Decision-Making	Caucasus	Some p.r. in the Mostar and Caucasus cases	Mostar	Dayton
Policy Implementation	Caucasus	Some p.r. in the Mostar and Caucasus cases	Mostar	Dayton

networks, and garbage cans – which in turn exhaustively captured all possible preference-formation possibilities in a pillarization context.

In subsequent chapters, these research questions, research hypotheses and research variables were tested in light of three key cases of EU joint actions in a pillarization context. Table 7.1 identifies the approximate levels and qualities of preference formation, agenda-setting, decision-making and implementation according to what the cases generated in terms of results.

In the three cases that we have explored in this study, the first research hypothesis/variable – rationality – seems to be of some significance in explaining policy preferences. As is shown in Table 7.1, policy-makers in the Caucasus case typically acted in a rational manner. In that particular case EU politicians, Eurocrats and their national equivalents foresaw long-term benefits of inter-EU co-operation in the energy policy sector. Policy preferences were, therefore, calculated according to rational criteria (if according to bounded rationality principles at some junctures of the decision-making stage of the policy process). Rational choice seems to have a highly prescriptive and proscriptive explanatory power in terms of explaining policy implementation in the Caucasus case. In this case agenda-setting was explicitly led by the member states in conjunction with the GAC and the external relations DGs of the Commission. The member states and the Commission could foresee opportunities for the exploitation of resources in the Caucasus region. Preferences from the agenda-setting stage through the decision-making process to the final implementation process were fixed, but flexible enough to respond to external stimuli. In the Caucasus case there existed stable means-ends relationships: during the course of the policy cycle, objectives only changed in response to developments that were not anticipated at earlier stages. The Caucasus case was also underpinned by efficient means–ends relationships in other ways: the main actors made the most efficient use of the information available at any one time to identify those means most likely to provide optimal delivery of aims within prevailing constraints and resources. Additionally, from a pillarization context, there existed a high degree of cross-pillar coherence because other EU bodies involved in the policy process effectively functioned as agents of the GAC.

Nevertheless, we have also identified patchy (or bounded) rationality as a significant influence in shaping policy preferences and agenda-setting in the three cases to varying degrees. Elinor Ostrom (1998) has referred to 'second order' models of rational choice which recognize that policy preferences are often formed in conditions of bounded or incomplete rationality. Agenda-setting in the Mostar and Dayton cases was typically done according to semi-structured ill-conceived preferences that relied upon chance as well as some degree of semi-rational calculation on the part of policy-makers. In the Mostar case policy-making and implementation relied to a great degree on policy experts and specialists to make things happen. Likewise, policy coherence was to some degree organized around patchily rational preferences in all three cases. This implies that the pillar structure of the Union functioned relatively effectively across the pillars in joint action conditions. Decision-making styles in the Mostar and Dayton cases were also bounded by imperfect resources, time, and the limited intelligence of the policy-makers concerned. Additionally, national decision-makers, EU decision-makers and policy experts did not necessarily always coalesce and liaise in optimal decision-making relationships.

The concept of the policy network is a significant variable in explaining the dynamics of policy preference formation, agenda-setting, decision-making and implementation in the Mostar case. The policy community has utility in explaining policy coherence in the EU institutions during the Mostar Joint Action policy process. Experts and specialists in humanitarian relief, CFSP finance, democratization, and infrastructure projects each produced expert opinions in a coterminous fashion in a networked context. Politics became a nexus of nested games with specialist interests securing a central place in the policy process. Indeed, the dominant decision-making style combined aspects of strategic action, policy learning, shared problem-solving and communicative action. Nevertheless, the policy network approach also highlighted a lack of rational preference formation in the Mostar policy process: during and after the Mostar case time period, the Commission learned somewhat embarrassingly from the Court of Auditors that it had extremely lax auditing procedures for the distribution of aid on the ground. This was also pointed out by the European Parliament in a series of reports. Democratic accountability was tightened up via the granting of greater powers for the Court of Auditors in the area of CFSP finance. This worked well in both the Dayton and Central Asia/Caucasus cases. Policy networks of democracy and transparency specialists' came together to improve democratic accountability learning from the mistakes made at Mostar.

The Mostar case was characterized, as we have remarked above, by a network of specialized actors working in a web-like non-stratified policy process characterized by non-hierarchical decision-making. At no one stage of the policy cycle did one actor dominate the policy process. All the major actors were inter-linked and dependent on all the others for the delivery of resources to meet policy objectives that were agreed in the formulation of the Joint Action. Additionally, it is the case that elements of epistemic community formed between actors directly engaged in the delivery of the Joint Action. Organizational and administrative hierarchies were largely dissolved as networks of experts interacted with each other and related actors. Indeed, the Joint Action threw up the fact that there were shared normative assumptions among the actors that eased the path to agenda-setting, decision-making and implementation. Policy tended to be dominated by middle-level policy experts who contextually framed policy for the higher levels to rubber stamp.

Furthermore, in the Mostar case, communicative action dominated over strategic action. Will and preference formation was also traceable to transnational expert networks associated with CFSP. Advice from experts to national decision-makers played a leading role in shaping and influencing preference structures and hence policy itself.

In the Mostar case there also existed a good degree of cross-pillar coherence in policy-making. As is stated above, means–ends relationships were characterized by a high degree of cross-pillar coherence. Communication was generally efficient and few real problems arose as a result of poor policy co-ordination because of the employment of policy specialists. Unlike in the rational model, however, this coherence was traceable to the domination of policy by networks of experts that cross-cut the plurality of agencies involved in the Joint Action.

Conclusion 171

This coherence was also the result of shared lessons within the policy network. Indeed, the Joint Action was used as an institutionalized context for shared learning about foreign policy problems. This introduced a degree of path dependence into the Joint Action: the cost of exiting from the Joint Action would have meant that a loss of reputation for the policy-makers. Hence no major actor did this during the course of the Joint Action.

This goes against garbage can agenda-setting, decision-making and implementation with preferences being ill-defined as was the case in the instance of the Dayton Agreements. As in the policy network model, the preferences of the key actors were heavily endogenous to the policy process. Actor preferences changed frequently and unpredictably throughout the course of the Joint Action. Indeed, many of the actors did not have a well-formed list of preferences vis-à-vis the action. This was exacerbated by the fluidity of the situation on the ground and the inability of policy-makers to adjust to circumstances on the ground due to a poor rank ordering of preferences.

Poor procedures for the making and implementation of the Joint Action meant that decision outcomes were typically suboptimal. Preferences were underdeveloped and exacerbated the unstructured character of the decision-making and implementation stages of the policy processes. Confusion and disagreement reigned as to who should frame policy options and set the agenda (so-called 'internal technologies'). The GAC tried to take the lead, but was challenged by the Commission and by NATO. In terms of 'external technologies', attempts to specify means–ends relationships or resources in advance were little more than guesses that – in the end – bore little relation to the subsequent evolution of the Joint Action. This was also exacerbated by the uncertain fluidity of the situation on the ground in Bosnia.

As well as the uncertainty of the fluid situation on the ground, there were also related fluid patterns of actor participation over the course of the Joint Action. The more 'maximalist' member states of the Union relied on the CFSP to a far greater degree as an appropriate forum for expressing their preferences towards the Dayton Agreements. The infrequent and fluid 'interest' in the EU/CFSP from those member states who saw NATO as the appropriate forum for conflict resolution in Bosnia – precisely those EU member states with military capabilities – also encouraged a garbage-can-like policy process in the EU/CFSP.

In the absence of either well-specified interests (as in the rational model) or shared understandings (as in the policy network model), there existed little cross-pillar coherence in the formulation of the Joint

Action. This proved to be problematic in terms of policy-making and implementation. The end result was that the actors made up the Joint Action as they went along. Poor means–ends relations, poor policy planning, no real rank ordering of preferences and a lack of anticipation in policy-making militated against producing a rational policy process.

The degree of representation and control of policy – in terms of democracy and transparency – in all three cases was highly variable. Whilst 'patchy rationality' explains preference formation in the Caucasus case – mostly because of the professionalism of Commission decision-making practices in association with the GAC – it cannot explain preference-formation structures in the Dayton or Mostar cases. In the Mostar case democratic accountability resembled a policy community, and a garbage can in the Dayton case. In the Mostar case, for example, the Court of Auditors pointed out in a 1996 judgement that EU accountability in the Mostar Joint Action was appalling. Local elites illegally appropriated aid and trade monies supplied under the Mostar Joint Action on many occasions. The case of Dayton highlights that dismembered garbage-can-like decision-making processes militate against rationality in democratic accountability terms.

In terms of institutional developments, the three cases generate variable results in terms of the degree of rationality exhibited by the political and economic institutions involved. The Caucasus Joint Action generated patchily rational institutions that were characterized by rational choice principles. This implies that the institutions set up had been well planned and that policy preferences were largely met and implemented according to the goals set. This occurred due to a large degree of previously agreed compromises between EU officials, national politicians, and national officials engaged in institution-making. This was the most efficient way to achieve the aims and objectives of the Joint Action. Indeed, in the Caucasus case the process of the Joint Action generated an expectation of co-operation between institutions and policy-makers.

In terms of institutional developments the Mostar case revolved around policy community approaches. The pillar structure of the Union functioned effectively most of the time. Pillar one structures functioned via co-operation between policy specialists, technocrats and politicians. The policy process became relatively loosely structured. This implied some degree of rationality of policy preferences, but not in terms of the classical sense of the term. Indeed, the pillar structure of the Union functioned relatively well in difficult circumstances.

Decisions made in pillar one had spill-over consequences for pillar two decisions and so forth. Pillarization did not, therefore, greatly affect the ability of the Union either to make policy in a professional manner or to implement policy relatively efficiently in the Mostar case. In terms of representation and control the Dayton case highlighted garbage can decision-making. Democratic control of resources on the ground was extremely poor in both the policy-making and implementation phases of the policy process. In its report to the Council, Parliament and Commission of 1996 the Court of Auditors remarked on the lack of forward planning, the lack of an effective EU strategy in resource allocation and widespread abuses of funds in Bosnia and Herzegovina. Through policy learning, however, similar mistakes have not been made after 1996.

Garbage-can-like policy implementation was evidenced in the Dayton case, as highlighted immediately above. A list of well-defined policy preferences was not fully worked out by EU officials. The impact of exogenous policy shocks (on the ground in Bosnia) confused EU policy-makers and clouded their judgement at critical junctures of the evolving Joint Action. The result was that endogenous policy preferences reacted to exogenous shocks, thereby altering the structure of policy-making preferences in the EU. Quite often the restructuring of preferences was a reaction to the fluidity of events and this meant that decision-making consistency was not always rational. The end result was implementation gaps and strained policy-making.

Pillarization, theoretical and conceptual implications of the study

So what are the implications of our analysis for pillarization? As was stated in chapter 1, pillarization is nothing less than the central organizing principle of the contemporary EU. Pillarization, as we have previously also stated, is best understood by contrasting it with its two logical alternatives. The first alternative to pillarization is that differences between 'high' and 'low' politics should be accommodated outside the Union's Treaties. The second alternative is that all policies should be subject to a uniform institutional and constitutional process. At the end of the day, as we also stated in the opening chapters, it was the temple of many pillars, and not the tree with a single institutional trunk, that was adopted in the Treaty on European Union (TEU). The Amsterdam Treaty of 1997 adjusted the content and some of the procedures of pillarization, without abandoning the principle of institutional differentiation. Indeed, the pillar structure of the Union was re-emphasized at Amsterdam with the need to gain the unanimous approval of member states for Treaty changes.

The central concern of this book has been to use joint actions – the main policy instrument established under CFSP – in order to illustrate the operation of pillarization in its original form between 1993–98; that is to say, prior to the TEU being amended by the Amsterdam Treaty. In the foregoing analysis we sought to answer the following questions in some detail:

- *How different are the pillars in practice?* Our cases have indicated that the European Commission does, indeed, have scope to act as a policy entrepreneur in relation to pillars two and three. The character of that policy entrepreneurship can, however, be expected to vary as a direct consequence of our further finding that there is no uniformity in the type of foreign policy problem – as measured by patterns of preference formation and completeness of information – that is remitted to CFSP to manage by joint action: where, at one extreme, actors have well-formed preferences and relatively full information (rational actor models) the Commission will develop initiatives as an agent of the Council; where, at the other extreme, preferences are ill-defined, and decisions are taken under conditions of extreme uncertainty (garbage can approaches), the Commission will have greater scope for political leadership.
- *How separate are the pillars in practice?* Although each pillar has its own distinctive decision-making procedures and rules, there are limits to how far the pillars can function alone. Regardless of the type of foreign policy problem, a common finding of our case studies has been that joint actions established under pillar two are heavily dependent on pillar one resources and policy instruments.
- *How are the pillars co-ordinated?* Our case studies have confirmed the need for co-ordination by demonstrating the extent of pillar two dependence on pillar one. However, they also indicate that three theoretically different solutions to co-ordination problems have all featured in practice. Co-ordination via a well-defined principal–agent relationship between the Council and the Commission was evident in the Caucasus Joint Action. The Mostar Joint Action illustrated the role that a network of middle-ranking policy experts can play in delivering the collaboration of multiple institutions. A further possibility was, however, demonstrated by the Dayton Joint

Action: co-ordination problems may not be solved at all, or only spasmodically according to shifting patterns of policy leadership.
- *Does pillarization work?* While confirming that pillarization does indeed produce co-ordination problems, the case studies also demonstrate that there is a range of possible solutions as set out in the previous paragraph. Yet the cases also confirm a series of hypotheses about the limited nature of joint actions: they are only likely to emerge where they involve limited expenditure of resources and high levels of consensus between the member states, or if they are accessory to other foreign policy initiatives. The implication is plain: joint actions continue to operate towards the middle and lower ends of foreign policy-making. The capacity of pillarization to go beyond 'lowest common denominator' decision-making, therefore, remains untested, though the formalization of constructive abstention by the Amsterdam Treaty opens up a whole new dimension to co-ordination between the first and second pillars: it may be possible to gain consensus between limited groups of member states for foreign policy interventions that involve hard choices, but how far are such agreements likely to be underpinned by first-pillar resources and instruments that 'belong' to the Union as a whole?

The case studies and theoretical arguments presented here have implications with respect to theories of policy preference formation, especially to theories of European-level agenda-setting. The cases and theoretical arguments also tell us much about how the pillar structure of the Union functions in policy-making terms (the problematique of 'pillarization'). The cases studied and the theoretical arguments presented also have ramifications for our understanding of policy coherence, decision-making styles, representation and control of policy, and policy implementation. In addition, the findings in this study are also relevant to the study of power relations in international organizations, alliances and theories of decision-making in general. More significantly, the study has demonstrated that the EU is most appropriately studied by comparative politics, public administration and international relations approaches: neither traditional foreign policy analysis *nor* public administration models are sufficient *in themselves* for understanding foreign policy-making and implementation in the EU.

First, this study has significant implications for the study of agenda-setting theory and policy, especially relating to preference formation. The conclusion of the study must be that classical rational choice does not – and cannot – explain all decision-making scenarios. The study highlights the importance of neglected elements in preference formation: patchy rationality, policy networks, and garbage cans. In all these cases policy-makers displayed behaviour that was to some extent non-rational at various stages of the agenda-setting, decision-making and implementation process in the cases. It is quite clear from the case studies that policy-makers were typically behaving towards policy in a non-rational fashion. It is also necessary to make the methodological point that policy-makers were also capable of behaving in ways which were more in line with policy network and garbage can agendas. To suggest that rational choice represents the *only* possible model for studying agenda-setting and preference formation is myopic and partial, even if the dominant form of decisional intercourse was dominated by rational policy preferences in some instances. A 'one size fits all' approach will simply not do.

Second, this study has significant implications for how European foreign policy is studied. The traditional approach of foreign policy analysis (FPA) has much to applaud it. However, it alone cannot explain European-level decision-making. The study of European foreign policy, in this particular study, has greatly benefited from comparative politics and public administration models of decision-making. These models allow the theorist to look at insights into preference formation, agenda-setting, national foreign policy inputs, policy learning, strategic action, and backward-mapping implementation in another, and perhaps richer, light. This is significant and alludes to the 'international', 'comparative' and 'administrative' nature of the EU's policy process: the EU is a multi-arena actor operating on a number of levels and therefore requires a number of theoretical tools to understand its multilayered complexity.

Third, the study also points to the contradictory nature of the EU's pillar structure. The main resources for policy-making and implementation are contained in pillar one, whilst the important decisions are often taken in pillar two. The different political, legal and administrative rules of the game in pillars one and two respectively, however, do not necessarily produce a non-rational decision-making policy process and related policy outcomes. On the contrary, evidence exists to point out that the policy actors often try harder to produce rational outcomes and thus orient their policy preferences in a rational manner to varying degrees. This is an interesting conclusion relating to the increasing role of experts in the EU/CFSP Joint Actions policy process. Pillarization in the EU formed a major research focus in this study. In chapter 1 we outlined a framework for analysis that emphasized the dual nature of the European foreign affairs system. Political and economic policies exist alongside each other and operate within a pillar structure with differing rules, procedures and legal obligations. We moved on to highlight the fact that the pillar structure of the Union influences the array of policy choices presented to policy-makers. It was also the case that these policy choices affected how policy-makers *perceived* the agenda-setting, decision-making and implementation phases of the policy process. This in turn influenced (and in some instances *structured*) policy inputs and in turn affected policy outputs in terms of the actual policies implemented. The pillar structure of the EU can therefore deeply influence (and even partially structure) the policy process as a whole.

Fourth, in chapter 2 of the study we made a distinction between European Foreign Policy and European Union Foreign Policy. The latter approach has historically tended to narrowly focus on the institutions, procedures, and outcomes of the CFSP (Tonra, 2000). The former approach emphasizes a broader, indeed, more sophisticated, approach to the study of European foreign and defence policy-making. In the present study we have highlighted the importance of economic, ideological, normative and domestic-level inputs into the broader foreign policy process. We believe that this is an advance in the study of foreign policy at the European level. Indeed, the inclusion of theoretical models drawn from political science, public administration and sociology that emphasize economic, ideological, normative and domestic-level inputs into foreign policy-making at the European level has in some ways extended the scope of traditional FPA. This has implications for developing new and more sophisticated models that methodologically incorporate all levels and types of European decision-making. In the present analysis this broad methodology has allowed us to treat the EU foreign affairs system as a complex web of nodal interconnections akin to the model suggested by Tonra (2000) as outlined in chapter 1. In other words, this research project has hopefully highlighted that the EU system of governance is multi-level, multi-nodal, non-hierarchical, knowledge-based, and in some ways polity-like.

Fifth, and finally, in a more substantive sense the study has also highlighted that Joint Actions are the *most* concrete form of European Foreign Policy *in practice*. The Joint Action adds actuality to foreign policy actions decided in the confines of national foreign ministries, the EU Commission, the European Parliament and in the offices of national leaders. At present time the Joint Action is the most advanced expression of the CFSP. As such it forms a major component part of what we might term European Foreign Policy.

Broader implications of the study

This study has highlighted the fact that the EU still has to decide whether it wants to take on the trappings of civilian and military power in world politics. Europe is now once again reinventing itself, but within the context of old Cold War institutions. Europe is attempting to come to terms with its varied past, its foreign policy identity and aspirations. It is also slowly developing a sense of shared responsibility outside its own geographical borders.

Following Hill (1993), we maintain that the EU's growing presence in world politics is of growing salience to the practice of international relations in the post-Cold War world. Since 1993, the Joint Action has been the most significant and concrete instrument of the CFSP. Via the Joint Action the EU and its member states have increasingly developed a mature role in peacekeeping, peace enforcement, and crisis management. Following on from Hill we can conceptualize the Union's world role in the following terms:

- *Presence*. In this study we have conceptualized the relationship between internal developments of the EU/CFSP and external expectations. We have highlighted that the Union has developed new responsibilities since 1989 and that its presence in the world has correspondingly changed. The EU has developed the Joint Action to provide concrete reality to its foreign policy objectives. We have also concluded that the Union's foreign policy process is increasingly predicated on the formulation of networks of interested actors each seeking to influence the policy process.
- *Opportunity and actorness*. In this study we have analysed several different external environments which enable and/or constrain the EU's 'actorness' in world politics (the ability of the Union to act in a coherent fashion meeting its foreign policy objectives). We have highlighted that the EU's pillar structure affects its ability to fashion appropriate responses to external policy stimuli. The EU's supranational institutions periodically act as policy entrepreneurs in the wider decision-making process, thereby cutting across the Union's pillar structure.
- *Capability*. In this study we have also analysed the capacity of the EU to respond appropriately to external expectations and opportu-

nities generated by exogenous factors. The study has made it clear that the pillar structure of the EU indirectly influences Union capabilities in foreign affairs.

The upshot of all this is as follows. Europe's future lies in the ability of its member states and supranational institutions to adapt to new patterns of domestic and foreign policy configurations in the wider world. As we have seen from the above cases, the EU itself is taking on a broader conception of its external political and economic policies than ever before. (This is reflected in the division of responsibilities between its three main pillars.) Indeed, resulting internal institutional reforms have been made to the Brussels bureaucracy accordingly. There are actually occasions where pillarization has led to enhanced decision-making.

In international relations more generally, Europe is operating in an international system that is characterized by forces which militate against the use of violence as a means for solving the world's problems. Europe must therefore develop new and broader approaches to European and wider global security. The EU is a particularly well-qualified and an increasingly broadly-based institution that is continually redefining its conception(s) of security in the plural.

As the cases above have demonstrated, there is an increasing enmeshing of states, international organizations, non-governmental organizations and other non-state actors through pragmatic functional responses to common problems. This has meant a greater use of experts in policy-making and implementation in European diplomacy. Those with knowledge are increasingly being intertwined into previously 'political' decision-making circles. The nature of European foreign policy-making and implementation is increasingly non-hierarchical, multi-actor and multi-level in orientation, and multifunctional. An increasing enmeshing of international actors through pragmatic responses to common foreign policy problems is the *leitmotif* of contemporary European foreign policy actions. It might also augur for a more democratic and inclusive foreign policy for Europe in the decades to come.

Bibliography

Algieri, F., Janning, J. and Rumberg, D. (eds) (1996) *Managing Security in Europe: the European Union and the Challenge of Enlargement*. Gütersloh, Bertelsmann.
Allen, D. Rummel, R. and Wessels, W. (eds) (1982) *European Political Co-operation: Toward a Foreign Policy for Western Europe*. London, Butterworths.
Allison, G. (1971) *Essence of Decision: Explaining the Cuban Missile Crisis*. Boston, Little Brown and Company.
Arrow, K. (1951) *Social Choice and Individual Values*. New York, Wiley.
Bass, W. (1998) 'The Triangle of Dayton', *Foreign Affairs*, vol. 77, no. 5, September/October, pp. 95–107.
Bieber, R. and Monar, J. (1995) *Justice and Home Affairs in the European Union: the Development of the Third Pillar*, Bruges, College of Europe Press.
Bildt, C. (2000) 'Force and Diplomacy', *Survival*, vol. 42, no. 1, Spring, pp. 141–48.
Borden, A. and Kaplan, R. (1997) 'The Former Yugoslavia: the War and the Peace Process', *SIPRI Yearbook 1996*. Stockholm, SIPRI Publications.
Bretherton, C. and Vogler, J. (1999) *The European Union as a Global Actor*. London, Routledge.
Bulletin of the European Union, various issues.
Calic, M.-J. (1995) *Der Krieg in Bosnien-Hercegovina*. Frankfurt/Main, Luger.
Cameron, F. (1996) in F. Algieri, J. Janning and D. Rumberg (eds), *Managing Security in Europe: The European Union and the Challenge of Enlargement*. Gütersloh, Bertelsmann.
Cameron, F. (2000) *The Common Foreign and Security Policy*. Sheffield, Sheffield Academic Press.
Chandler, D. (1999) *Bosnia: Faking Democracy after Dayton*. London, Verso.
Christansen, T., Jorgensen, K.E. and Wiener, A. (1999) 'Constructivist Approaches to the European Union', *Journal of European Public Policy*, Special Edition.
Cohen, M., March, J. and Olsen, J. (1972) 'A Garbage Can Model of Institutional Choice', *Administrative Science Quarterly*, vol. 17, pp. 1–25.
Cohen, R. (1998) 'After the Vultures: Holbrooke's Bosnia Peace Came Too Late', *Foreign Affairs*, vol. 77, no. 3, May/June, pp. 106–11.
Court of Auditors (1995) 'Strategy for EU Administration of Mostar', 13 May 1995, No. 8.
Court of Auditors (1996) 'Observations by the Court of Auditors Concerning the European Union Administration of Mostar (EUAM)'. *Official Journal of European Communities*, C287, vol. 39, 30 September 1996.
Crawford, C. (1998–99) 'The Balkan Chill', *Harvard International Review*, vol. 21, no. 1, Winter, pp. 84–5.
Daadler, I.H. and Froman, M.G.B. (1999) 'Dayton's Incomplete Peace', *Foreign Affairs*, vol. 78, no. 6, November/December.
Dehousse, R. and Weiler, J. (1991) 'EPC and the Single Act: From Soft Law to Hard Law?', in M. Holland (ed.), *The Future of European Political Co-operation: Essays on Theory and Practice*. London, Macmillan.

De La Serre, F. (1996) 'France, the Impact of François Mitterrand', in C. Hill (ed.), *The Actors in Europe's Foreign Policy*. London, Routledge.
Delcourt, B. and Remacle, R. (1997) 'Bosnie-Herzegovine: La Paix Imposée', *L'Europe et la Securite Internationale, 1997*. Brussels, Publications du Grip, pp. 74–87.
Deprez, P. (2000) 'A Mostar, la Croatie semble bien loin: La ville historique reste divisée entre communautés croate et musulmane'. *Le Soir*, 7 February.
Devuyst, Y. (1999) 'The Community Method after Amsterdam', *Journal of Common Market Studies*, vol. 37, no. 1, pp. 109–20.
de Schoutheete, P. (1986) *La Coopération Politique Européenne*. Brussels, Labor.
de Schoutheete, P. (1997) 'The Creation of the CFSP: The Reform Debate During the IGC on Political Union', in E. Regelsberger, P. de Schoutheete and W. Wessels (eds), *Foreign Policy of the European Union: From EPC to CFSP*. Boulder, CO, Lynne Rienner.
Duchêne, F. (1971) 'Civilian Power', in R. Mayne (ed.), *Europe Tomorrow*. London, Oxford University Press/Royal Institute of International Affairs.
Duke, S. (2000) *The Elusive Quest for European Security: From EDC to CFSP*. London, Macmillan.
Easton, D. (1957) *A Framework for Political Analysis*. New York, Basic Books.
Economist, The, various issues.
Eliassen, K.A. (ed.) (1998) *Foreign and Security Policy in the European Union*. London, Sage.
Europe Documents: Agence Europe (various issues).
European Commission (1986) *Treaties Revising the Treaties Establishing the European Communities and Acts Relating to the Communities (The Single European Act)*. Brussels, European Commission.
European Commission (1992) *The Treaty of European Union (The Maastricht Treaty)*. Brussels, European Commission.
European Commission (1996a) 'Joint Action Plan for Russia and the Caucasus', DG1A of the Commission of the European Union, Brussels.
European Commission (1996b) 'Trade Partnership and Technical Assistance Agreement with Kazakhstan', Bulletin EU, 5–1996, 1.4.71.
European Commission (1996c) 'Partnership Agreement with Azerbaijan', Bulletin EU, 4–1996, 1.7.72.
European Commission (1996d) 'Partnership Agreement with Georgia', Bulletin EU, 4–1996, 1.4.72.
European Commission (1996e) 'Trade and Technical Agreement with Uzbekistan', Bulletin EU, 11–1996, 1.4.91.
European Commission (1996f) 'Tacis: Indicative Programme for Turmenistan', DG1A of the Commission of the European Union.
European Commission (1996g) 'Partnership Agreement with Armenia', Bulletin EU, 4–1996, 1.4.72.
European Commission (1997a) 'The Russian Crisis and its Impact on the Newly Independent States and Mongolia', Communication to the Council and the European Parliament, Brussels, DG1A of the Commission of the European Union, Annex 2.
European Commission (1997b) 'Human Rights and Democratization Priorities in Bosnia and Herzegovina', Joint Statement Released in Conjunction with the US–EU Summit in Washington, DC, 5 December.

182 Bibliography

European Commission (1997c) *The European Union Administration of Mostar* (report by S. Reichel). Brussels, DG1-A of the Commission of the European Union.

European Council (1992) 'Report to the European Council in Lisbon on the Likely Development of the Common Foreign and Security Policy with a view to Identifying Areas open to Joint Action *vis à vis* Particular Countries or Groups of Countries' (The Lisbon Report).

European Council (1994) 'Report of the Council on the Functioning of the Treaty on European Union', Office for Official Publications of the European Union, Brussels and Luxembourg.

European Council (1995) 'Report on the Functioning of the Treaty on European Union', Brussels, Council of the European Union.

European Parliament (1995) *Report on the Establishment of a European Analysis Centre for Active Crisis Prevention (The Rocard Report)*, PE 211.027. Brussels, European Parliament.

European Parliament, (1996) *Report on the Conference and Security and Cooperation in Europe, (The Balfe Report)*, PE 207.636. Brussels, European Parliament.

European Parliament (1997a) *Report on Improving the Impact of Joint Actions (The Baron–Crespo Report)*, PE217.053. Brussels, European Parliament.

European Parliament (1997b) *Report on the Formulation of Perspectives for the CFSP of the EU (The Tindemans Report)*, PE217.532. Brussels, European Parliament.

European Parliament (1997c) *Report on Progress in Implementing the CFSP (The Fernandez-Albor Report)*, PE216.369. Brussels, European Parliament.

European Parliament (1997d) *Report on Progress in Implementing the Common Foreign and Security Policy (The Matutes Report)*, PE 211.241. Brussels, European Parliament.

European Parliament (1998) *Report on the Role of the Union in the World. Implementation of the Common Foreign and Security Policy for 1997*. Brussels, European Parliament.

European Report (1999) 'EU-Caucasus: EU Gives Conditional Support to the Region', *European Report*, Europe Information Service, Brussels, 23 June 1999, 2pp.

Fonseca-Wollheim, H. (1981) *Ten Years of European Political Co-operation*. Brussels, Commission of the European Communities.

Forster, A. (1999) *Britain and the Maastricht Negotiations*. London, Macmillan/ St Antony's now Palgrave.

Forster, A. and Wallace, W. (1996) 'Common Foreign and Security Policy', in H. Wallace and W. Wallace (eds), *Policy Making in the European Union*. Oxford, Oxford University Press, pp. 411–39.

Fursdon, E. (1980) *The European Defence Community: a History*. London, Macmillan.

Garrett, G. and Weingast, B. (1993) 'Ideas, Interests and Institutions: Constructing the European Community's Internal Market', in J. Goldstein and R. Keohane (eds), *Ideas and Foreign Policy*. Ithaca, NY, Cornell University Press.

Ginsberg, R. (1989) *Foreign Policy Actions of the European Community: the Politics of Scale*. London, Adamantine.

Ginsberg, R. (1997) 'The EU's CFSP: the Politics of Procedure', in M. Holland (ed.), *Common Foreign and Security Policy: the Record and Reforms*. London, Cassell.

Ginsberg, R. (1999) 'Conceptualizing the EU as an International Actor: Narrowing the Theoretical-Expectations Gap', *Journal of Common Market Studies*, vol. 37, no. 3, pp. 429–54.

Glitman, M. (1997–98) 'US Policy in Bosnia: Rethinking a Flawed Approach', *Survival*, vol. 39, no. 4, Winter, pp. 5–18.

Haas, P. (1992) 'Introduction: Epistemic Communities and the Dynamics of International Environmental Co-operation', *International Organisation*, vol. 46, pp. 1–35.

Hayes-Renshaw, F. and Wallace, H. (1997) *The Council of Ministers*. London, Macmillan.

Héritier, A. (1997) 'Policy-Making by Subterfuge: Interest Accommodation, Innovation and Substitute Democratic Legitimation in Europe – Perspectives from Distinct Policy Areas', *Journal of European Public Policy*, vol. 4, no. 2, pp. 171–89.

Herzig, E. (1999) *The New Caucasus: Armenia, Azerbaijan and Georgia*. London, Cassell/RIIA.

Higley, J. et al. (1993) 'Elite Integration in Stable Democracies', in M. Olsen and M. Marger (eds), *Power in Modern Societies*. Boulder, CO, Westview Press.

Hill, C. (1993) 'The Capability–Expectations Gap, or Conceptualising Europe's International Role', *Journal of Common Market Studies*, vol. 31, no. 3, pp. 305–28.

Hill, C. (ed.) (1996) *The Actors in Europe's Foreign Policy*. London, Routledge.

Hill, C. and Wallace, W. (1996) 'Introduction', in C. Hill (ed.), *The Actors in Europe's Foreign Policy*. London, Routledge.

Hix, S. (1999) *The Political System of the European Union*. Basingstoke, Macmillan – now Palgrave.

Hix, S. and Lord, C. (1997) *Political Parties in the European Union*. London, Macmillan – now Palgrave.

Hoffmann, S. (1966) 'Obstinate or Obsolete? The Fate of the Nation-State in Western Europe Today', *Daedalus*, Spring.

Hoffmann, S. and Keohane, R. (1991) *The New European Community: Decision-Making and Institutional Change*. Boulder, CO, Westview Press.

Holbrooke, R. (1995) 'America: a European Power', *Foreign Affairs*, vol 1. 74, no. 4.

Holbrooke, R. (1998) *The End of a War: From Sarajevo to Dayton and Beyond*. New York, Random House.

Holland, M. (1995) *European Union Common Foreign Policy: from EPC to CFSP Joint Action on South Africa*. London, Macmillan.

Holland, M. (ed.) (1991) *The Future of European Political Co-operation: Essays on Theory and Practice*. London, Macmillan.

Holland, M. (ed.) (1997) *Common Foreign and Security Policy: the Record and Reforms*. London, Cassell.

Honig, J.W. and Both, N. (1997) *Srebrenica: Record of a War Crime*. London, Penguin.

Hurd, D. (1981) 'Political Co-operation', *International Affairs*, vol. 57, pp. 383–97.

Hurwitz, L. (1976) 'The EEC and Decolonisation: the Voting Behaviour of the Nine in the UN General Assembly', *Political Studies*, vol. 24, pp. 435–47.

Ifestos, P. (1987) *European Political Co-operation*. Aldershot, Avebury.

Janning, J. (1996) 'Europe's Common Foreign and Security Policy', in F. Algieri, J. Janning and D. Rumberg (eds), *Managing Security in Europe: the European Union and the Challenge of Enlargement*. Gütersloh, Bertelsmann.

Janis, I. (1982) *Groupthink: Psychological Studies of Policy Decisions and Fiascoes*. Boston, Houghton Mifflin.

Jervis, R. (1976) *Perception and Misperception in World Politics*. Princeton, Princeton University Press.

Joerges, C. and Neyer, J. (1997) 'Transforming Strategic Interaction into Deliberative Problem-Solving: European Comitology in the Foodstuffs Sector', *Journal of European Public Policy*, vol. 4, no. 4, pp. 609–25.

Jorgensen, K.E. (ed.) (1997) *European Approaches to Crisis Management*. The Hague, Kluwer Law International.

Jorgensen, K.E. (1997) 'Petersberg Tasks', in K.E. Jorgensen (ed.), *European Approaches to Crisis Management*. The Hague, Kluwer Law International.

Kahnemann, D. and Tversky, A. (1979) 'Prospect Theory: an Analysis of Decision-Making under Risk', *Econometrica*, vol. 47, pp. 263–91.

Keukeleire, S. (1994) 'The European Community and Conflict Management', in W. Bauwens and K. Reychler (ed.), *The Art of Conflict Prevention*. London, Brassey's.

Kiewiet, D. and McCubbins, M. (1991) *The Logic of Delegation: Congressional Parties and the Appropriation Process*. Chicago, Chicago University Press.

Kingdon, J. (1984) *Agendas, Alternatives and Public Policies*, 1st edition. Boston, Little Brown.

Kingdon, J. (1995) *Agendas, Alternatives and Public Policies*, 2nd edition. Boston, Little Brown.

Kintnis, A. (1997) 'The EU's Foreign Policy and the War in Former Yugoslavia', in M. Holland (ed.), *Common Foreign and Security Policy: the Record and Reforms*. London, Pinter.

Kirchner, E. (1992) *Decision-making in the European Community: the Council Presidency and European Integration*. Manchester, Manchester University Press.

Kiser, L.L and Ostrom, E. (1982) 'The Three Worlds of Action: a Metatheoretical Synthesis of Institutional Approaches', in E. Ostrom, *State of Political Enquiry*. Beverly Hills, Sage, pp. 179–222.

Laignel-Lavastine, A. (1998) 'L'Europe Central et Occidentale', *L'Année Strategique, 1998*. Brussels, Editions Complexe/Iris.

Lak, M. (1989) 'Interaction between European Political Co-operation and the European Community (External) – Existing Rules and Challenges', *Common Market Law Review*, vol. 26, pp. 281–99.

Laursen, F. and Van Hoonacker, S. (eds) (1992) *The Intergovernmental Conference on Political Union*. Maastricht, European Institute of Public Administration.

Lebessis, N. and Paterson, J. (1997) *Evolutions in Governance. What Lessons for the Commission? A First Assessment*. Forward Studies Unit Working Paper. Brussels, European Commission.

Lindemann, B. (1982) 'European Political Co-operation at the UN: a Challenge for the Nine', in D. Allen, R. Rummel and W. Wessels (eds), *European Political Co- operation: Toward a Foreign Policy for Western Europe*. London, Butterworths.

Lucarelli, S. (1997) 'The Yugoslav Imbroglio', in K.E. Jorgensen (ed.), *European Approaches to Crisis Management*. The Hague, Kluwer Law International.

Luif, P. (1993) *Abstimmungsverhalten der EG Staaten und anderer ausgewählter Staaten in der UN-Generalversammlung*. Laxenburg, Österreichisches Institut für Internationale Politik.

Malcolm, N. (1994) *Bosnia: a Short History*. London, Macmillan.

March, J. and Olsen, J. (1984) 'The New Institutionalism: Organisational Factors in Political Life', *American Political Science Review*, vol. 78, pp. 738–49.

March, J. and Simon, H. (1957) *Organisations*. New York, Wiley.

McCubbins, M., Noll, R. and Weingast, B. (1987) 'Administrative Procedures as Instruments of Public Control', *Journal of Law, Economics and Organisation*, vol. 3, pp. 243–77.

McKelvey, R. (1976) 'Intransitivities in Multidimensional Voting Models', *Journal of Economic Theory*, no. 12, pp. 472–82.

Monar, J. (1996) 'Financing the Common Foreign and Security Policy', mimeo, University of Leicester.

Monar, J. (1997) 'The Finances of the Union's Intergovernmental Pillars: Tortuous Experiments with the Community Budget', *Journal of Common Market Studies*, vol. 35, no. 1, pp. 57–78.

Moravcsik, A. (1991) 'Negotiating the Single European Act: National Interests and Conventional Statecraft in the European Community', *International Organisation*, vol. 45, no. 1, pp. 19–56.

Moravcsik, A. (1993) 'Preferences and Power in the European Community: a Liberal Intergovernmentalist Approach', *Journal of Common Market Studies*, vol. 31, no. 4, pp. 473–524.

Moravcsik, A. (1998) *The Choice for Europe: Social Purpose and State Power from Messina to Maastricht*. Ithaca, Cornell University Press.

Moravcsik, A. and Nicolaïdes, K. (1998) 'Keynote Article: Federal Ideals and Constitutional Realities in the Treaty of Amsterdam', *Journal of Common Market Studies: Annual Review*, vol. 36, pp. 13–38.

Nisbett, R. and Ross, L. (1980) *Human Inference: Strategies and Shortcomings of Human Judgment*. New York, Appleton-Century-Crofts.

North Atlantic Treaty Organization (1995) 'Dayton Agreements on Bosnia-Herzegovina'. Signed in Paris, 14 December 1995. The full text can be viewed on the www page of NATO: http://www.nato.org

Nuttall, S. (1992) *European Political Co-operation*. Oxford, Clarendon Press.

Nuttall, S. (2000) *European Foreign Policy*. Oxford, Oxford University Press.

O'Hanlan, M. (1998) 'Turning the Bosnia Ceasefire into Peace', *The Brookings Review*, vol. 16, no. 1, Winter, pp. 41–4.

Ostrom, E. (1986) 'An Agenda for the Study of Institutions', *Public Choice*, vol. 48, pp. 3–25.

Ostrom, E. (1998) 'A Behavioral Approach to the Rational Choice Theory of Collective Action: Presidential Address, APSA, 1997', *American Political Science Review*, vol. 92, no. 1, pp. 69–93.

Peters, B. (1994) 'Agenda-Setting in the European Community', *Journal of European Public Policy*, vol. 1, no. 1, pp. 9–26.

Peters, B. (1999) *Institutional Theory in Political Science: the 'New Institutionalism'*. London, Pinter.

Peterson, J. (1995) 'Decision-Making in the European Union: towards a Framework for Analysis', *Journal of European Public Policy*, vol. 1, no. 2, pp. 69–93.

Peterson, J. and Begg, I. (1998) 'Editorial', *Journal of Common Market Studies*, vol. 36, no. 1.
Peterson, J. and Bomberg, E. (1999) *Decision-Making in the European Union*. London, Macmillan – now Palgrave.
Peterson, J. and Sjursen, H. (eds) (1998) *A Common Foreign and Security Policy for Europe? Competing Visions of the CFSP*. London, Routledge.
Piening, C. (1997) *Global Europe: the European Union in World Affairs*. Boulder, CO, Lynne Rienner.
Pierson, P. (1998) 'The Path to European Integration: a Historical-Institutional Analysis' in W. Sandholtz and A. Stone Sweet (eds), *European Integration and Supranational Governance*, Oxford, Oxford University Press.
Pierson, P. (2000) 'Increasing Returns, Path Dependence, and the Study of Politics', *American Political Science Review*, vol. 94, no. 2, pp. 251–67.
Pollack, M. (1997) 'Delegation, Agency and Agenda-Setting in the European Community', *International Organisation*, vol. 51, no. 1, pp. 99–134.
Popper, K. (1957) *The Logic of Scientific Discovery*. London, Macmillan.
Quermonne, J.-L. (1994) *La Système Politique de l'Union Européenne*. Paris, Montchrétien.
Radha, K. (1997) 'The Troubled History of Partition', *Foreign Affairs*, vol. 75, no. 1, January/February, pp. 22–34.
Regelsberger, E. (ed.) (1994) *Die Gemeinsame Außen und Sicherheitspolitik der Europäischen Union, Profilsuche mit Hindernissen*. Bonn, Europa Union Verlag.
Rhodes, R. (1996) 'The New Governance: Governing without Government', *Political Studies*, no. 4, vol. 44, pp. 652–68.
Richardson, J. (1996) 'Eroding EU Politics: Implementation Gaps, Cheating and Re-Steering', in J. Richardson (ed.), *European Union: Power and Policy-Making*. London, Routledge, 1996, pp. 280–5.
Rose, General Sir M. (1998) *Fighting for Peace: Bosnia 1994*. London, Harvill Press.
Sartori, G. (1987) *The Theory of Democracy Revisited I: The Contemporary Debate*. Chatham, NJ, Chatham House Publishers.
Shepsle, K. (1989) 'Studying Institutions: Some Lessons from the Rational Choice Approach', *Journal of Theoretical Politics*, vol. 1 pp. 131–47.
Shepsle, K. and Bonchek, M. (1997) *Analyzing Politics: Rationality, Behaviour and Institutions*. New York, W.W. Norton.
Simon, H. (1957) *Administrative Behaviour*, 2nd edition. New York, Macmillan.
Smith, K.E. (1998) *The Making of EU Foreign Policy*. London, Macmillan.
Smith, M. (1996) 'The EU as an International Actor', in J. Richardson (ed.), *European Union: Power and Policy-Making*. London, Routledge, pp. 247–62.
Smith, M.E. (1998) 'Rules, Transgovernmentalism and the Expansion of European Political Co-operation', in W. Sandholtz and A. Stone Sweet (eds), *European Integration and Supranational Governance*. Oxford, Oxford University Press.
Steinbrunner, R. (1974) *The Cybernetic Theory of Decision*. Princeton, NJ, Princeton University Press.
Timmermans, C. (1996) 'The Uneasy Relationship between the Communities and the Second Union Pillar: Back to the "Plan Fouchet"?', *Legal Issues of European Integration*, no. 1, pp. 64–5.

Tonra, B. (2000) 'Mapping EU Foreign Policy Studies', *Journal of European Public Policy*, vol. 7, no. 1, pp. 163–9.

Touval, S. (1996) 'Coercive Mediation on the Road to Dayton', *International Negotiation*, vol. 1, no. 3, pp. 547–70.

Tsebelis, G. (1990) *Nested Games: Rational Choice in Comparative Politics*. Berkeley, CA, University of California Press.

United Nations (1993) 'Agreement Relating to Bosnia and Herzegovina', 20 September, Appendix II, Part 2, B2.

United Nations (1994a) 'Bosnia and Herzegovina-Croatia: Preliminary Agreement Concerning the Establishment of a Confederation', Introductory Note, 18 March 1994, in in *International Legal Materials*, vol. 33, no. 3, May 1994, p. 605.

United Nations (1994b) 'Bosnia and Herzegovina: Constitution of the Federation', 18 March 1994, in *International Legal Materials*, vol. 33, no. 3, May 1994, p. 744.

United Nations (1994c) 'Constitution of the Federation of Bosnia-Herzegovina. Section 11: Human Rights and Fundamental Freedoms'.

United Nations (1995) 'Memorandum of Agreement on the European Union Administration of Mostar'.

United Nations (1999) 'Report of the Secretary-General Pursuant to General Assembly Resolution 53/35 (1998) – The Fall of Srebrenica.'

von Hippel, K. (2000) *Democracy by Force: US Military Intervention in the Post-Cold War World*. Cambridge, Cambridge University Press.

von Jagow, P. (1993) 'Das Krisenmanagement der EG/EPZ in Jugoslawienkrieg – eine gemischte Bilanz', in E. Regelsberger (ed.), *Die Gemeinsame Außen und Sicherheitspolitik der Europäischen Union, Profilsuche mit Hindernissen*. Bonn, Europa Union Verlag.

Wallace, W. (1983) 'Political Co-operation: Procedure as a Substitute for Policy', in H. Wallace, W. Wallace and C. Webb (eds), *Policy Making in the EC*. Chichester, John Wiley, pp. 227–48.

Waltz, K. (1979) *Theory of International Politics*. New York, McGraw-Hill.

Wendt, A. (1999) *Social Theory of International Politics*. Cambridge, Cambridge University Press.

Wessels, W. (1992) 'Staat und (west-europäische integration) Integration, Die Fusionthese', in M. Kreile (ed.), *Die Integration Europas*. PVS Sonderheft, no. 23, pp. 36–61.

Wessels, W. (1997) 'The Growth and Differentiation of Multi-Level Networks: a Corporatist Mega-Bureaucracy or Open City', in H. Wallace and A. Young (eds), *Participation and Policy-Making in the European Union*. Oxford, Clarendon Press.

Western European Union (1995) 'History, Structure and Prospects', Brussels, WEU.

Western European Union (1998a) 'Security: A Joint Perspective', Brussels, WEU.

Western European Union (1998b) 'Report on Central Asia and the Caucasus', Brussels, WEU.

Western European Union (1998c) 'European Security in Stages: Report on the Former Yugoslavia and the Implementation of the Dayton Agreements', Brussels, WEU.

White, B. (1999) 'The European Challenge to Foreign Policy Analysis', *European Journal of International Relations*, vol. 5, no. 1, pp. 37–66.
White, B. (2001) *Understanding European Foreign Policy*. Basingstoke, Palgrave.
Wiberg, H. (1996) 'Third Party Intervention in Yugoslavia: Problems and Lessons', in J. de Wilde and H. Wiberg (eds), *Organised Anarchy in Europe: the Role of Intergovernmental Organisations*. London, Tauris Academic Studies.
Williamson, O. (1985) *The Economic Institutions of Capitalism*. New York, Free Press.
Williamson, O. (1996) *The Mechanics of Governance*. Oxford, Oxford University Press.
Winn, N. (1997) 'The Proof of the Pudding is in the Eating: the European Union "Joint Action" as an Effecitve Foreign Policy Instrument', *International Relations*, vol. XIII, no. 6, pp. 19–32.
Winn, N. (2000) 'European: Old Institutions, New Realities', in C. Jones and C. Kennedy-Pipe (eds), *International Security*. London, Frank Cass.
Woodward, S. (1997) 'Bosnia after Dayton: Year Two', *Current History*, vol. 96, no. 608, March.
Young, O. (1989) *International Cooperation: Building Regimes for Natural Resources and the Environment*. Ithaca, NY, Cornell University Press.
Zielonka, J. (1998a) *Explaining Euro-Paralysis: Why Europe is Unable to Act in International Politics*. London, Macmillan.
Zielonka, J. (ed.) (1998b) *Paradoxes of European Foreign Policy*. The Hague, Kluwer Law International Press.

Index

Acquis politique, 28, 29, 51
Agency loss, 57
Agenda-setting, 47, 80, 82, 112, 116, 143, 145
Albania, 80
Albright, M., Former US Secretary of State, 130
Allison, G., 53
Amsterdam Treaty, 5, 7, 11, 45, 46
Atlanticism, 42
Austria, 87

Belgium, 153
Berger, Sandy, Former US National Security Adviser, 131
Bildt, C., Former EU High Representative to Bosnia-Herzegovina, 81, 83, 95, 96, 100, 101
Bosnia-Herzegovina, 74, 75, 106, 117, 125, 129
Bosnian Croats, 74, 76, 79, 84, 91, 95, 118
Bosnian Muslims, 74, 76, 79, 81, 84, 91, 95, 116, 118
Bosnian Serbs, 74, 76, 79, 95, 106, 111, 116
Bosnian Serb Army (BSA), 83, 84
British Government, 3, 11

Capability–Expectations Gap, 27, 179
Caspian Sea, 159
Caucasus case, 140, 142, 168
Central America, 24
Chechnya, 141, 145, 150, 151, 152
Clark, W., General, Former NATO SACEUR, 121, 127, 129
Clinton, B., President, Former US President, 129, 131
Cognitive framing of decisions, 47
Common Foreign and Security Policy (CFSP), 1, 39, 54, 58, 61

Committee of Permanent Representatives (COREPER), 7, 9, 61, 64
Commonwealth of Independent States (CIS), 140, 143
Conference on Security and Co-operation in Europe (CSCE), 24
Cook, R., UK Foreign Secretary, 115
Co-ordination reflex of EPC/CFSP, 27
Copenhagen Report (1973), 27
Correspondance Européenne (COREU), 24, 30, 60
Council of Ministers (EU), 1, 32, 33, 132
Court of Auditors (EU), 88, 94, 159, 173
Croatia, 80, 126
Crouch, W. General, Former NATO AFCENT Commander, 126

Danish Maastricht Referendum (1992), 35
Dayton Accords, 107, 119, 120, 124, 128, 171
Dayton case, 106, 168
Decision-making, 80, 85, 112, 126, 143, 147
Delors, J., President, Former President of the European Commission, 31, 36
Delors Commission, 31
Democratization, 14, 162
Directorate General 1 for External Economic Relations (EU Commission), 160, 164
Directorate General 1A for External Political Relations (EU Commission), 51, 89, 96, 113, 124, 158, 160, 164

Easton, D., 8
Embassy co-ordination (EU), 25
Energy markets, 162

European Bank for Reconstruction and Development (EBRD), 142
European Commission, 7, 32, 33, 132, 133, 144, 161
European Community (EC), 10, 21
European Community Humanitarian Office (ECHO), 87, 97, 118, 132, 145, 150, 158, 164
European Council, 1, 7, 32, 33, 132, 133, 144, 163
European Court of Justice (ECJ), 1, 8, 12
European Defence Community (EDC), 20
European Monetary Union (EMU), 4
European Parliament (EP), 1, 11, 41, 86, 115, 133
European Political Co-operation (EPC), 2, 23, 26, 29, 34, 39
European Union (EU), 1
European Union Administration of Mostar (EUAM), 74, 75, 85, 86, 94, 95, 98

Falklands crisis (1982), 37
Finance of EPC/CFSP, 31, 66
Foreign Policy Analysis (FPA), 15, 53, 176, 177
Fouchet Plan (1961–63), 20
Franco-German axis (EU), 41, 42
France, 3, 11, 136, 153, 163
Frowick, R., Former Head of OSCE Electoral Commission in Bosnia, 126, 130

Gas in the Caucasus, 160
General Secretariat of the Council (EU), 7
Group of Seven Leading Industrial Nations Summits (plus Russia) (G7/G8 Summits), 12, 33
'Garbage can' model, 61, 71, 133, 168
German recognition of Croatia and Slovenia (1992), 38
Germany, 136, 153, 163
Ginsberg, R., 61

Gonzales, F., Prime Minister, Former Prime Minister of Spain, 113
Greece, 153, 154
Gulf Crisis (1990–91), 38

Haas, E., 11, 55, 60
Hague Conference (December 1969), 22
Helvig-Peterson, N., Former Danish Foreign Minister, 114
Héretier, A., 59
High politics, 3, 21, 138
Hill, C., 11, 178
Holbrooke, Richard, Former US Assistant Secretary of State, 111, 130
Human rights, 14, 160, 162
Hypothesis testing, 72

Implementation (of policy), 89, 127, 157
Intergovernmentalism, 48
International Implementation Force for Bosnia-Herzegovina (IFOR), 107, 126
International Criminal Court on the Former Yugoslavia (ICTY), 118, 119, 121, 122, 127, 135
International Monetary Fund (IMF), 33, 126
Invincible Peace Talks, 76
Iraq, 154
Ireland, 37
Italy, 37
Izetbegovic, A., Former President of the Bosnian-Muslim Federation, 91

Joint Actions (generally), 12, 13, 47, 66, 67, 74, 106, 108
Joint Action on the Korean Peninsula, 67
Joint Action on Non-Proliferation of WMD, 67
Joint Action on Palestinian Police Force, 66

Joint Action on South African Elections, 66
Justice and Home Affairs (JHA), 1, 5

Karadzic, R., Former Premier of the Bosnian Serb Republic, 111, 113, 115, 120, 122
Kingdon, J.W., 61
Kinkel, K., Former German Foreign Minister, 114
Koschnick, H., Former EU Representative to Mostar (EUAM), 81

Lamoureux, F., Former Deputy Director-General of DG1A, 113
Local elections in Bosnia-Herzegovina, 122, 123, 124
London Report (1981), 25
Luxembourg Report (1971), 24

Macedonia (FYROM), 80
Malcolm, N., 122
Mandela, N., Former President of South Africa, 37
Memorandum of Understanding (MoU), 82, 84, 90, 98
Methodology, 68
Middle East, 24
Middle East Peace Process, 36
Milosevic, S., Former President of Serbia, 107, 113, 123
Missing persons, 118
Mladic, R. General, Former Chief of Staff Bosnian Serb Army, 106
Moravcsik, A., 54, 55
Mostar case, 66, 74, 168

New Scotland Yard (London), 100
New York Police Department (NYPD), 100
Non-governmental organizations (NGOs), 99, 103
North Atlantic Treaty Organization (NATO), 21, 33, 41, 91, 106, 121, 127, 141, 171

Operation Joint Guard, 128, 129, 137
Opportunity and actorness, 178
Organization for Security and Co-operation in Europe (OSCE), 122, 123, 124, 141
Ostrom, E., 50, 51, 52, 169
Owen, D. Lord Dr., Former UK Foreign Secretary and EU Representative to Vance/Owen, 76, 77

Pack, Doris, Former Chair of the European Parliament Committee on Eastern Europe, 81, 115
Pareto condition, 57
Path-dependence theory, 16, 42
PHARE (European Union assistance programme for Eastern Europe), 113
Peace Implementation Council (PIC), 110, 117
Peng, L., Former Prime Minister of China, 152
Persian Gulf, 159
Pierson, P., 42, 43
Pillar I (EU), 9, 10, 172 see also EC
Pillar II (EU), 1, 9, 10, 138 see also CFSP
Pillar III (EU), 1 see also JHA
Pillarization, 1,6, 20, 42, 47, 173
Plavsic, I., Former President of the Bosnian Serb Republic, 122, 123
Policy evaluation, 93, 129, 159
Policy networks model, 58, 69, 98, 170
Political Directors (CFSP), 30, 41
Popper, K., 72
Presence, 178
Presidency of the EU, 56, 57, 87, 97
Primakov, Y. Former Russian Foreign Minister, 121

Rational choice model, 54, 69, 162, 168
Refugees and misplaced persons, 116, 117, 118, 132

Index

Richardson, J., 89
Red Cross, 118
Relationship between the EC and CFSP, 40, 41
Rome Summit (1996), 81
Royaumont Process, 145
Russia, 141, 142, 151, 161

Sarajevo, 117, 118
Single European Act (SEA), 11, 30
Smith, M., 85
Solana, J., Former Secretary-General of NATO, 112, 114, 122, 123
Srebrenica, 106, 107, 123
Stabilisation Force for Bosnia-Herzegovina (SFOR), 107, 110, 116, 120, 121, 126, 127, 131
Soviet Union (USSR), 39, 40
Steinbrunner, R., 62
Supranational intergovernmentalism, 10, 33
Supranationalism, 49
Sweden, 87
Switzerland, 86

TACIS (European Union Technical Assistance Programme for the former Soviet Union), 146, 144, 150, 158, 164
Tadic, D., 121
Technology transfer, 162
Transgovernmentalism, 48
Treaty on the European Union (TEU), 1, 3, 7, 9, 39, 40, 64, 79, 86, 86, 90
Treaty of Rome (TOR), 21
Troika (CFSP), 46
Tsebelis, G., 54, 56

Tudjman, F. Former President of Croatia, 112
Turkey, 153, 154

United Kingdom (UK), 136, 141, 153, 163
United Nations (UN), 24, 78, 141
United States of America (USA), 124, 136, 154, 155, 156, 157, 159
UNPROFOR (United Nations Protection Force for Bosnia-Herzegovina), 75, 83
United Police Force of Mostar (UPFM), 84, 90, 92

Van den Broek, H. Former European Commissioner for External Political Relations, 80, 81, 112, 114, 125
Vance, C., Former US Secretary of State and American Representative to Vance–Owen, 76, 77
Vukovar, 120

War criminals, 119, 120, 121, 122
Washington Peace Agreement, 74
Wessels, W., 59
Westendorp, C., Former EU High Representative to Bosnia-Herzegovina, 115, 129
Western European Union (WEU), 82, 85, 87, 120, 141
Working Groups (CFSP), 30
World Bank, 126, 142

Yeltsin, B. Former President of Russia, 144, 157
Yugoslavia, 111, 144, 157